College Korean

대학 한국어

College Korean

대학 한국어

Michael C. Rogers, Clare You,
and Kyungnyun K. Richards

University of California Press / *Berkeley, Los Angeles, London*

University of California Press, Ltd.
London, England

University of California Press, Ltd.
London, England

©1992 by
The Regents of the University of California

Library of Congress Cataloging-in-Publication Data

Rogers, Michael C., 1923–
   College Korean = [Taehak Han'gugŏ] / Michael C. Rogers,
Clare You, and Kyungnyun K. Richards.
     p. cm.
   English and Korean.
   Parallel title in Korean characters.
   Includes indexes.
   ISBN 0-520-06994-3 (alk. paper)
   1. Korean language—Textbooks for foreign speakers—
English.   I. You, Clare.   II. Richards, Kyungnyun K.   III.
Title.   IV. Title: Taehak Han'gugŏ.
PL913.R64 1992
495.7'82421 dc20   90-11282
                                                   CIP

Printed in the United States of America
   2   3   4   5   6   7   8   9

Contents

Preface

This text is intended to be the main textbook for beginning college students of Korean. It teaches the basics of the Korean language through speaking, reading, and writing. Although many educators believe that students learn languages best by imitating spoken patterns, just as children first learn to speak their native tongue, it has been our experience that the intellectual curiosity of college students and other adults cannot be satisfied unless speaking is enhanced by reading and writing.

We introduce *hangŭl*, the Korean writing system, from the beginning of the course. Invented in the fifteenth century to teach common citizens how to read and write, *hangŭl*, is one of the easiest writing systems to learn. It is neither a syllabary as in Japanese nor a set of meaning-based symbols as in Chinese but an alphabet composed of vowels and consonants. Thus it is especially easy for speakers of languages using alphabets. To help students learn to identify unique Korean sounds with the *hangŭl* letters directly rather than relying on romanization, we use *hangŭl* from the first page of the text. Only in Lesson 1 do we use both *hangŭl* and romanization to help those who would not yet be comfortable in *hangŭl* alone.

This text contains twenty-six lessons preceded by introductory material on sounds and the Korean writing system. The lessons are based on material closely associated with college students and their daily activities, though the text is also suitable for adolescents and adults. Most of the largely factual content of the text is presented in the dialect generally regarded as standard, that is, the dialect spoken around Seoul and in Kyunggi province. We also stay with full and standard forms of Korean rather than contracted or colloquial forms on the assumption that going from full forms to contracted forms is easier than the reverse process. For similar reasons we introduce the more complex polite-formal style of speech before the less complex polite-informal style.

Each lesson has three parts: dialogues, grammar and notes, and exercises. Dialogues, sentence patterns, and vocabulary comprise the first part of the lesson, where the new material is introduced. The patterns and substitutions are usually short to highlight and reinforce features introduced in the dialogues or readings. Students should practice the dialogues and patterns until they can do them automatically, for these materials provide the foundation on which the following lessons build.

The second part of each lesson, grammar and notes, provides basic grammatical explanations for beginners, especially where Korean differs from English either grammatically or idiomatically. We have tried to keep grammatical terminology to a minimum. Beginning with Lesson 7, 6 to 10 Sino-Korean characters, *hanja*, are introduced in each lesson, for a total of 142 *hanja* for the course. Instructors may choose to omit this part of the course, depending on the needs of the students. For students who are studying Chinese or Japanese or who have a background in one of these languages, learning *hanja* along with Korean is very helpful.

The third part of each lesson, the exercises, reviews the new material and gives students the chance to use it. The exercises in this text are more selective than exhaustive; a workbook to accompany the text will have many more exercises for each feature introduced in the lessons. Whenever possible, we designed the exercises to be used for either oral or written practice.

An index of grammatical features, lists of *hanja*, and a complete glossary follow the lessons and will help students make best use of the text.

This textbook is the fruit of many years of language teaching experience by the three authors. From our early years of teaching, we have sought fresh material suitable for a new generation of students interested in learning Korean. Lesson by lesson we began to write and to introduce it to our students. The results have been uniformly good, and for the last three years our material has been the official text for the beginning Korean course at the University of California at Berkeley.

We wish to thank Professor Jae-Kee Shim of Seoul National University for reading the first draft, Professor George DeVos of the University of California at Berkeley for his encouragement and support, Betsey Scheiner of the University of California Press for making this publication possible, and Amy Klatzkin of the Press for editing the manuscript. Our thanks are also due to the instructors Eun-Young Kim, Jeong-Woon Park, and Sung-Taek Cho of the University of California at Berkeley for their valuable comments.

Using the Text

A few points may be helpful for instructors and students unfamiliar with our text.

1. *Pace of study.* We planned the twenty-six lessons to occupy students for about one week each, with thirteen lessons per fifteen-week semester. The first two weeks of the first semester are taken up with our introductory materials on Korean sounds and the writing system. In the second semester, we have found that Lessons 22, 23, and 24 require more than a week each and that thirteen lessons easily take up the fifteen weeks. Instructors can readily adapt the pace to a quarter system.

2. *Introducing each lesson.* Each lesson begins with one to three short dialogues or readings followed by pattern practice, a list of vocabulary, grammar and notes, Sino-Korean characters, and exercises. Instructors can proceed in the order of presentation or can introduce the new grammatical points from the grammar and notes before the dialogues and patterns, whichever order is more helpful to the students. Another effective approach is to introduce dialogues and readings orally without explaining grammar in English. Visual aids and real objects are useful for this method. In this approach the whole class period can be conducted entirely in Korean, centering around the topic and the patterns introduced in each chapter. Students should use the grammar and notes as a reference.

3. *Oral practice and memorization.* Students should memorize the short sentences in the dialogues and readings to acquire new

patterns and vocabulary. Classroom performances of the dialogues allow students to practice using the sentences. Students who make up their own sentences by substituting new words, different tenses, or different styles become creative in using the language.

4. *Copying exercise and dictation.* Because *hangŭl* copying exercises and dictations are essential for learning the writing system, students' daily assignments should include copying the dialogues and patterns of lessons and short daily dictations of words and sentences until they can read and write easily. Several weeks of special practice in the beginning of the course usually suffice.

5. *Sino-Korean characters.* If Sino-Korean characters are a part of the curriculum, we recommend that in addition to classroom instruction on writing *hanja*, students follow the instructions in the workbook *A Beginner's Guide to Hanja*, by C. You and K. Richards, which illustrates the stroke-by-stroke process of writing Sino-Korean characters and gives their meaning and usage. (The workbook is available from the authors upon request.)

6. *Review and quizzes.* A weekly quiz on the fifth day of each lesson works nicely to reinforce and check students' progress. Also a review quiz every fifth week recaps what has been learned in the preceding five lessons.

We offer these points as guides for those using this text but have left ample room for instructors to alter, improve, and be creative with the lessons.

7. *Audio tapes and CD ROM.* The audio tapes accompanying *College Korean* are available from the language laboratory at the University of California, Berkeley. The CD ROM (Mac version) is also available from the authors.

Abbreviations and Symbols

ADJ.	adjective
ADV.	adverb
A.V.	action verb
AUX.	auxiliary
COMP.	complement
CON.	connective
CONJ.	conjunction
D.V.	descriptive verb
DIR. OBJ.	direct object
HON.	honorific
INDIR. OBJ.	indirect object
N.	noun
N.P.	noun phrase
NEG.	negative
OBJ.	object
POST.	postposition
PRON.	pronoun
SUBJ.	subject
V.	verb
V. MOD.	verbal modifier

1. Superscript numbers that appear in the dialogues and texts refer to the grammar and notes of each lesson.

2. In vocabulary (낱말) sections, words in parentheses that follow the text form are the dictionary forms.

3. "L3, GN6" refers to Lesson 3, grammar and notes number 6.

4. In translation exercises, words in italics refer to the pattern and vocabulary introduced in the lesson. These new expressions are expected to be used for the translation.

5. In grammar and notes, (   ) means either optional or phonologically alternating features such as -(으)나, -(으)면, and -(으)로.

6. "+" means "when combined with."

7. "/ " means "or."

8. ". . ." indicates an unfinished sentence.

9. "→" means "changes to" or "becomes."

10. "-" identifies suffixes, dependent nouns, and other bound forms.

11. "*" refers to additional notes or remarks at the end of a section.

12. "=" means "same as" or "equal to."

Korean Sounds and *Hangŭl* Letters

VOWELS

Hangŭl letter	Romanization*	Approx. sound	Name of letter
ㅏ	a (aa)	f<u>a</u>ther	아
ㅑ	ya	<u>ya</u>rd	야
ㅓ	ŏ(eo)	c<u>au</u>ght	어
ㅕ	yŏ	<u>you</u>ng	여
ㅗ	o	<u>o</u>rbit	오
ㅛ	yo	<u>yo</u>ke, <u>yo-yo</u>	요
ㅜ	u (oo)	m<u>oo</u>n	우
ㅠ	yu (yoo)	<u>you</u>	유
ㅡ	ŭ	l<u>oo</u>k	으
ㅣ	i (ee)	f<u>ee</u>l, p<u>ee</u>l	이
ㅐ	ae	c<u>a</u>t	애
ㅒ	yae	<u>ya</u>m	애
ㅔ	e	b<u>e</u>t, p<u>e</u>n	에
ㅖ	ye	<u>ye</u>s	예
ㅘ	wa	<u>wi</u>ne	와
ㅙ	wae	q<u>ua</u>ck	왜
ㅚ	we (ö)	<u>wh</u>en	외
ㅝ	wŏ	<u>wo</u>nder	워
ㅞ	we	<u>wh</u>en	웨
ㅟ	wi	<u>we</u>	위
ㅢ	ŭi	—	의

* Modified McCune-Reischauer system.

CONSONANTS

Hangŭl letter	*Romanization**	*Name of letter*	
ㄱ	k/g	기역	kiyŏk
ㄴ	n	니은	niŭn
ㄷ	t/d	디귿	tigŭt
ㄹ	r/l	리을	riŭl
ㅁ	m	미음	miŭm
ㅂ	p/b	비읍	piŭp
ㅅ	s/sh	시옷	siot
ㅇ	ø/-ng	이응	iŭng
ㅈ	č/j	지읒	čiŭt
ㅊ	čh	치읓	čhiŭt
ㅋ	kh	키읔	khiŭk
ㅌ	th	티읕	thiŭt
ㅍ	ph	피읖	phiŭp
ㅎ	h	히읗	hiŭt
ㄲ	kk	쌍기역	ssang kiyŏk
ㄸ	tt	쌍디귿	ssang tigŭt
ㅃ	pp	쌍비읍	ssang piŭp
ㅆ	ss	쌍시옷	ssang siot
ㅉ	čč	쌍지읒	ssang čiŭt

* Modified McCune-Reischauer system.

CONSONANT AND VOWEL COMBINATIONS

Vowels Cons.	ㅏ a	ㅑ ya	ㅓ ŏ	ㅕ yŏ	ㅗ o	ㅛ yo	ㅜ u	ㅠ yu	ㅡ ŭ	ㅣ i
ㄱ k	가	갸	거	겨	고	교	구	규	그	기
ㄴ n	나	냐	너	녀	노	뇨	누	뉴	느	니
ㄷ t	다	댜	더	뎌	도	됴	두	듀	드	디
ㄹ r	라	랴	러	려	로	료	루	류	르	리
ㅁ m	마	먀	머	며	모	묘	무	뮤	므	미
ㅂ p	바	뱌	버	벼	보	뵤	부	뷰	브	비
ㅅ s	사	샤	서	셔	소	쇼	수	슈	스	시
ㅇ ø/ng	아	야	어	여	오	요	우	유	으	이
ㅈ č	자	쟈	저	져	조	죠	주	쥬	즈	지
ㅊ čh	차	챠	처	쳐	초	쵸	추	츄	츠	치
ㅋ kh	카	캬	커	켜	코	쿄	쿠	큐	크	키
ㅌ th	타	탸	터	텨	토	툐	투	튜	트	티
ㅍ ph	파	퍄	퍼	펴	포	표	푸	퓨	프	피
ㅎ h	하	햐	허	혀	호	효	후	휴	흐	히
ㄲ kk	까	꺄	꺼	껴	꼬	꾜	꾸	뀨	끄	끼
ㄸ tt	따	땨	떠	뗘	또	뚀	뚜	뜌	뜨	띠
ㅃ pp	빠	뺘	뻐	뻐	뽀	뾰	뿌	쀼	쁘	삐
ㅆ ss	싸	쌰	써	쎠	쏘	쑈	쑤	쓔	쓰	씨
ㅉ čč	짜	쨔	쩌	쪄	쪼	쬬	쭈	쮸	쯔	찌

Vowels Cons.	ㅐ ae	ㅒ yae	ㅔ e	ㅖ ye	ㅘ wa	ㅙ wae	ㅚ we	ㅝ wŏ	ㅞ we	ㅟ wi	ㅢ ŭi
ㄱ k	개	걔	게	계	과	괘	괴	궈	궤	귀	긔
ㄴ n	내	냬	네	녜	놔	놰	뇌	눠	눼	뉘	늬
ㄷ t	대	댸	데	뎨	돠	돼	되	둬	뒈	뒤	듸
ㄹ r	래	럐	레	례	롸	뢔	뢰	뤄	뤠	뤼	릐
ㅁ m	매	먜	메	몌	뫄	뫠	뫼	뭐	뭬	뮈	믜
ㅂ p	배	뱨	베	볘	봐	봬	뵈	붜	붸	뷔	븨
ㅅ s	새	섀	세	셰	솨	쇄	쇠	숴	쉐	쉬	싀
ㅇ ø/ng	애	얘	에	예	와	왜	외	워	웨	위	의
ㅈ č	재	쟤	제	졔	좌	좨	죄	줘	줴	쥐	즤
ㅊ čh	채	챼	체	쳬	촤	쵀	최	춰	췌	취	츼
ㅋ kh	캐	컈	케	켸	콰	쾌	쾨	쿼	퀘	퀴	킈
ㅌ th	태	턔	테	톄	톼	퇘	퇴	퉈	퉤	튀	틔
ㅍ ph	패	퍠	페	폐	퐈	퐤	푀	풔	풰	퓌	픠
ㅎ h	해	햬	헤	혜	화	홰	회	훠	훼	휘	희
ㄲ kk	깨	꺠	께	꼐	꽈	꽤	꾀	꿔	꿰	뀌	끠
ㄸ tt	때	떄	떼	뗴	똬	뙈	뙤	뚸	뛔	뛰	띄
ㅃ pp	빼	뺴	뻬	뼤	뽜	뽸	뾔	뿨	뿰	쀠	쁴
ㅆ ss	쌔	썌	쎄	쎼	쏴	쐐	쐬	쒀	쒜	쒸	씌
ㅉ čč	째	쨰	쩨	쪠	쫘	쫴	쬐	쭤	쭸	쮜	찌

HANGŬL CALLIGRAPHY

가	갸	거	겨	고	교	구	규	그	기
나	냐	너	녀	노	뇨	누	뉴	느	니
다	댜	더	뎌	도	됴	두	듀	드	디
라	랴	러	려	로	료	루	류	르	리
마	먀	머	며	모	묘	무	뮤	므	미
바	뱌	버	벼	보	뵤	부	뷰	브	비
사	샤	서	셔	소	쇼	수	슈	스	시
아	야	어	여	오	요	우	유	으	이
자	쟈	저	져	조	죠	주	쥬	즈	지
차	챠	처	쳐	초	쵸	추	츄	츠	치
카	캬	커	켜	코	쿄	쿠	큐	크	키
타	탸	터	텨	토	툐	투	튜	트	티
파	퍄	퍼	펴	포	표	푸	퓨	프	피
하	햐	허	혀	호	효	후	휴	흐	히

SOUND VALUES OF CONSONANTS

ㄱ	initial [k]	가을 [kaŭl]	autumn
	medial [g]	가게 [kage]	store
	final [k̚]	속 [sok̚]	inside
ㄴ	initial [n]	나 [na]	I
	medial [n]	어느 [ŏnŭ]	which
	final [n]	문 [mun]	door
ㄷ	initial [t]	달 [tal]	moon
	medial [d]	어디 [ŏdi]	where
	final [t̚]	곧 [kot̚]	soon
ㄹ	initial [r]	라디오 [radio]	radio
	medial [r]	다리 [tari]	leg, bridge
	final [l]	달 [tal]	moon
ㅁ	initial [m]	마음 [maŭm]	mind
	medial [m]	나무 [namu]	tree
	final [m]	이름 [irŭm]	name
ㅂ	initial [p]	비 [pi]	rain
	medial [b]	나비 [nabi]	butterfly
	final [p̚]	밥 [pap̚]	rice
ㅅ	initial [s]	새 [sae]	bird
	medial [s]	미소 [miso]	smile
	final [t̚]	옷 [ot̚]	clothing
ㅇ	initial [ø]*	애기 [aegi]	baby
	medial [ø]	예의 [yeŭi]	etiquette
	final [ng]	강 [kang]	river
ㅈ	initial [č]	자유 [čayu]	liberty
	medial [j]	아주 [aju]	very
	final [t̚]	낮 [nat̚]	daytime
ㅊ	initial [čh]	차 [čha]	tea, car
	medial [čh]	아침 [ačhim]	morning
	final [t̚]	빛 [pit̚]	light

* ø means silent.

ㅋ initial [kh]   키 [khi]   height
    medial [kh]   바퀴 [pakhwi]   wheel
    final [kʾ]   부엌 [puŏkʾ]   kitchen

ㅌ initial [th]   탈 [thal]   mask
    medial [th]   이틀 [ithŭl]   two days
    final [tʾ]   밭 [patʾ]   growing field

ㅍ initial [ph]   파 [pha]   green onion
    medial [ph]   소풍 [sophung]   picnic
    final [pʾ]   앞 [apʾ]   front

ㅎ initial [h]   하나 [hana]   one
    medial [h]   아홉 [ahopʾ]   nine
    final [h]   좋다 [čotha]   to be good

ㄲ initial [kk]   까치 [kkačhi]   magpie
    medial [kk]   토끼 [thokki]   rabbit
    final [kʾ]   밖 [pakʾ]   outside

ㄸ initial [tt]   딸 [ttal]   daughter
    medial [tt]   메뚜기 [mettugi]   grasshopper

ㅃ initial [pp]   뿔 [ppul]   horn
    medial [pp]   기쁨 [kippŭm]   joy

ㅆ initial [ss]   싸움 [ssaum]   fight
    medial [ss]   아저씨 [ajŏssi]   uncle
    final [tʾ]   있다 [itta]   to exist

ㅉ initial [čč]   짜다 [ččada]   to be salty
    medial [čč]   세째 [seččae]   the third

VOWEL CONTRASTS

어	거리	street	커	is big		더	more
[ŏ]	[kŏri]		[khŏ]			[tŏ]	
오	고리	handle	코	nose		도	degree
[o]	[kori]		[kho]			[to]	
어	어디	where	머리	head		서울	Seoul
[ŏ]	[ŏdi]		[mŏri]			[sŏul]	
우	우리	we	무리	herd		수원	Suwon
[u]	[uri]		[muri]			[suwon]	
어	거리	street	언	frozen		썬	sliced
[ŏ]	[kŏri]		[ŏn]			[ssŏn]	
으	그리	there	은	silver		쓴	bitter
[ŭ]	[kŭri]		[ŭn]			[ssŭn]	
에	게	crab	세	rent		네	yes
[e]	[ke]		[se]			[ne]	
애	개	dog	새	bird		내	my
[ae]	[kae]		[sae]			[nae]	
외	쇠	iron	꾀	wit, trick			
[we]	[swe]		[kkwe]				
왜	쒜기	wedge	꽤	fairly, quite			
[wae]	[sswaegi]		[kkwae]				
와	관	coffin	완전	complete			
[wa]	[kwan]		[wanjŏn]				
워	권	tome	원본	original text			
[wŏ]	[kwŏn]		[wŏnbon]				

CONSONANT CONTRASTS

ㄱ	공	ball	근	pound	글	writing
[k]	[kong]		[kŭn]		[kŭl]	
ㄲ	꿩	pheasant	끈	rope	끌	chisel
[kk]	[kkwŏng]		[kkŭn]		[kkŭl]	
ㅋ	콩	bean	큰	large	클	will be large
[kh]	[khong]		[khŭn]		[khŭl]	
ㄷ	달	moon	남	wall	들	field
[t]	[tal]		[tam]		[tŭl]	
ㄸ	딸	daughter	땀	sweat	뜰	yard
[tt]	[ttal]		[ttam]		[ttŭl]	
ㅌ	탈	mask	탐	envy	틀	frame
[th]	[thal]		[tham]		[thŭl]	
ㅂ	불	fire	벼	rice plant	비	rain
[p]	[pul]		[pyŏ]		[pi]	
ㅃ	뿔	horn	뼈	bone	삐다	to sprain
[pp]	[ppul]		[ppyŏ]		[ppida]	
ㅍ	풀	grass	펴다	to spread	피	blood
[ph]	[phul]		[phyŏda]		[phi]	
ㅈ	자다	to sleep	잠	sleep	짐	load
[č]	[čada]		[čam]		[čim]	
ㅉ	짜다	to be salty	짬	leisure	찜	steamed dish
[čč]	[ččada]		[ččam]		[ččim]	
ㅊ	차다	to be cold	참	true	침	saliva
[čh]	[čhada]		[čham]		[čhim]	
ㅅ	살	flesh	사다	to buy	시	poem
[s]	[sal]		[sada]		[si]	
ㅆ	쌀	rice	싸다	to wrap	씨	seed
[ss]	[ssal]		[ssada]		[ssi]	
ㅁ	밤	night	감	persimmon	솜	cotton
[m]	[pam]		[kam]		[som]	
ㄴ	반	half	간	liver	손	hand
[n]	[pan]		[kan]		[son]	
ㅇ	방	room	강	river	송이	cluster
[ng]	[pang]		[kang]		[song i]	

Pronunciation Rules

1. ㄱ, ㄴ, ㅂ, and ㅈ are pronounced as voiced [g, d, b, j] when they:

   a. fall between two vowels

아기 [agi]	baby	아버지 [abŏji]	father
어디 [ŏdi]	where	아저씨 [ajŏssi]	uncle

   b. fall after ㄴ, ㅁ, ㅇ, or ㄹ and are followed by a vowel

안개 [angae]	fog	인도 [indo]	India
감기 [kamgi]	cold	삼단 [samdan]	third degree
상가 [sangga]	shopping strip	장단 [čangdan]	rhythm
일기 [ilgi]	journal	살다 [salda]	to live
신분 [shinbun]	identity	편지 [phyŏnji]	letter
냄비 [naembi]	saucepan	심장 [simjang]	heart
장비 [čangbi]	equipment	용지 [yongji]	form paper
일반 [ilban]	general	실제 [silje]	reality

2. Single consonants ㄷ, ㅌ, ㅈ, ㅊ, ㅅ, and ㅆ at the end of a syllable in isolation (받침) or followed by another consonant are pronounced [t⁷] (unreleased [t⁷]):

맏 [mat⁷]	the first born	빛	[pit⁷]	light
볕 [pyŏt⁷]	sunlight	빗	[pit⁷]	comb
낮 [nat⁷]	daytime	낯	[nat⁷]	face
		있다	[it⁷ta]	to exist

   When another vowel follows, in suffixes, the original consonant is pronounced as in a regular syllabic medial position.

끝 + 에 → [끄테] at the end	빛 + 이 → [비치] light (subj.)
[kkŭth + e → kkŭthe]	[pič + i → pičhi]
낮 + 에 → [나제] in the daytime	빗 + 이 → [비시] comb (subj.)
[nač + e → naje]	[pis + i → pisi]

3. As we have seen in the sound charts on pages 6-7, ㄱ, ㅋ, and ㄲ are pronounced as [k˺] at the end of a syllable in isolation:

속	[sok˺]	inside
부엌	[puŏk˺]	kitchen
밖	[pak˺]	outside

Compare with the sounds in the nonfinal position:

속에	[soge]	on the inside
부엌에	[puŏkhe]	in the kitchen
밖에	[pakke]	on the outside

4. ㅂ and ㅍ are pronounced as unreleased [p˺] in the word final position:

삽	[sap˺]	spade
답	[tap˺]	answer
앞	[ap˺]	front
옆	[yŏp˺]	side

But:

삽으로	[sabŭro]	with a spade
답을	[tabŭl]	answer (dir. obj.)
앞에	[aphe]	in front
옆이	[yŏphi]	side (subj.)

5. ㅎ at the end of a syllable brings the following changes in pronunciation (see rule 8a below):

   a. ㅎ becomes silent before a vowel.

좋아!	[čowa]*	Good!
좋으면	[čoŭmyŏn]	if you like
좋을때	[čoŭlttae]	when you like

*The vowel sequence [o] and [a] becomes [owa] in spoken language. See rule 10 below.

b. The consonants ㄱ, ㄷ, ㅂ, and ㅈ become aspirated after ㅎ.

노랗고	[norakho]	yellow and
놓다	[notha]	to put something down
좋지?	[čočhi]	Isn't it nice?

c. The consonant ㅅ becomes tense after ㅎ.

| 좋소! | [čosso] | It's fine! |
| 좋습니다 | [čossŭmnida] | It's fine. |

6. The consonants ㄱ, ㄷ, ㅂ, ㅅ, and ㅈ become the tense consonants ㄲ, ㄸ, ㅃ, ㅆ, and ㅉ respectively when they follow any consonant except ㄴ, ㄹ, ㅁ, ㅇ, and ㅎ. (In some words they become tense after these consonants as well.)

학교	[hakʾkkyo]	school
받다	[patʾtta]	to receive
책방	[čhaekʾppang]	bookstore
밥상	[papʾssang]	table
학자	[hakʾčča]	scholar

7. Consonant clusters in the syllable final position are pronounced as a sequence of two consonants when followed by a vowel, but in isolation or followed by another consonant one of the consonants in the cluster becomes silent, thereby preventing a three-consonant sequence. When this reduction occurs, the following consonant is generally pronounced as tense (like a double letter).

a. ㄳ and ㄺ are pronounced [kʾ]:

| 삯 | [sakʾ] wage | 삯이다 | [sakʾsida] It is the wage. |
| 닭 | [takʾ] chicken | 닭이다 | [tagida] It is a chicken. |

But note the differences in pronunciation in the following examples :

삯   과   [삭꽈]
saks + kwa → [sak'kkwa]   wage and

닭   과   [닥꽈]
talk + kwa → [tak'kkwa]   chicken and

밝   고   [발꼬]
palk + ko → [palkko]   bright and

밝   지   [박찌]
palk + či → [pak'čči]   bright (neg.)

밝   는다   [방 는다]
palk + nŭnda → [pangnŭnda]   brightens

b. ㄼ and ㅄ are pronounced [p]:

밟다 [pap'tta]   밟으면 [palbŭmyŏn]
to step on   if stepped on

값 [kap']   값은 [kap'sŭn]
price   as for the price

없다 [ŏp'tta]   없어도 [ŏpssŏdo]
to not exist   even if there isn't

밟   고   [발꼬]
palp + ko → [palkko]   step on and

밟   지   [발찌] or [밥찌]
palp + či → [palčči] or [pap'čči]   step (neg.)

밟   는다   [밤는다]
palp + nŭnda → [pamnŭnda]   steps on

없   고   [업꼬]
ŏps + ko → [ŏp'kko]   there is not and

없   지만   [업찌만]
ŏps + čiman → [ŏp'ččiman]   although there isn't

없   는데   [엄는데]
ŏps + nŭnde → [ŏmnŭnde]   there isn't, but

c. ㄹㅁ is pronounced [m]:

닮다	[tamtta]	to resemble
닮아서	[talmasŏ]	as they resemble
젊다	[čŏmtta]	to be young
젊어서	[čŏlmŏsŏ]	as he is young

d. ㄴㅈ is pronounced [n]:

앉다	[antta]	to sit down
얹다	[ŏntta]	to put on top

Between vowels it is pronounced [nj]:

앉아요	[anjayo]	Please sit down.
얹어요	[ŏnjŏyo]	Please put it up (on the shelf).

e. ㄹㅌ is pronounced [l]:

핥다	[haltta]	to lick
훑다	[hultta]	to scrape

Between vowels it is pronounced [lth]:

핥아요	[halthayo]	Please lick.
훑어요	[hulthŏyo]	Please thrash.

f. ㄴㅎ and ㄹㅎ (consonant clusters with ㅎ) are pronounced [n] and [l] respectively, and the consonant following them becomes aspirated. When ㄴㅎ or ㄹㅎ is followed by a vowel, ㅎ is not pronounced.

많다	[mantha]	there are many
많고	[mankho]	there are many and
끓다	[kkŭltha]	to boil
끓고	[kkŭlkho]	it is boiling and
많아	[mana]	since there are many
많은	[manŭn]	many
끓어	[kkŭrŏ]	since it is boiling
끓은	[kkŭrŭn]	boiled

8. When two consonants come together, the following changes in pronunciation occur:

a. Consonants ㄱ, ㄷ, ㅂ, and ㅈ become aspirated (ㅋ, ㅌ, ㅍ, and ㅊ) before or after the consonant ㅎ.

ㄱ + ㅎ }
ㅎ + ㄱ } → ㅋ { 먹히다 [mŏkhida]   to be eaten
              { 놓고 [nokho]   put down and

ㄷ + ㅎ }
ㅎ + ㄷ } → ㅌ { 닫히다 [tathida → tačhida]   to be closed
              { 놓다 [notha]   to put down

ㅂ + ㅎ → ㅍ   접히다 [čŏphida]   to be folded

ㅈ + ㅎ }
ㅎ + ㅈ } → ㅊ { 잊히다 [ičhida]   to be forgotten
              { 놓자 [nočha]   Let's put it down.

b. When ㄱ, ㄷ, and ㅂ are followed by ㅁ and ㄴ, a nasal assimilation occurs.

ㅍ and ㅂ are pronounced [m].

앞문	[am mun]	front door
갑니다	[kam nida]	I am going.
밥 먹어	[pam mŏgŏ]	Eat dinner!

ㄷ, ㅅ, ㅆ, ㅈ, and ㅊ are pronounced [n].

닫니	[tan ni]	Are you closing?
낱말	[nan mal]	vocabulary
솟는다	[son nŭn da]	springs up
있는	[in nŭn]	existing
젖는다	[čŏn nŭnda]	gets wet
빛난다	[pin nan da]	shines

ㄱ, ㄲ, and ㅋ are pronounced [ng].

작년	[čang nyŏn]	last year
농작물	[nong čang mul]	crop
닦는다	[tang nŭn da]	polishes
부엌문	[pu ŏng mun]	kitchen door

c. ㄹ is pronounced [n] after any consonant except [n] as in 8d.

명랑	[myŏng nang]	cheerfulness
공로	[kong no]	contribution
삼리	[sam ni]	three li
함락	[ham nak]	fall under
국립	[kung nip]	national
독립	[tong nip]	independence
십리	[sim ni]	ten li

d. ㄴ is pronounced as [l] before or after ㄹ.

신라	[shil la]	Silla kingdom
천리	[chŏl li]	1,000 li
월남	[wŏl lam]	Vietnam
달나라	[tal la ra]	moon land

9. Syllable finals ㄷ and ㅌ are pronounced as ㅈ and ㅊ respectively when followed by the vowel 이 or a palatalized vowel (여, 야, 요, or 유).

맏이	[maji]	the first born
밑이다	[michida]	It is below.
걷히다*	[kŏchida]	to lift (e.g., clouds or fog)
닫혀서*	[tachyŏsŏ]	because it is closed

*See rule 8a for aspiration of ㄷ+ㅎ.

Note that the palatilization does not occur in words like

어디	[ŏdi]	where
잔디	[chandi]	lawn
티	[thi]	dust particle

10. The following vowel sequences are often contracted.

ㅗ + ㅏ → ㅘ   오아요→ 와요
[o] [a] [wa]   o-a-yo [wayo]   Please come.

                보아요→ 봐요
                po-a-yo [pwayo]   Please look.

ㅜ + ㅓ → ㅝ   주어요→ 줘요
[u] [ŏ] [wŏ]   ču-ŏ-yo [čwŏyo]   (Someone) gives.

                두어요→ 둬요
                tu-ŏ-yo [twŏyo]   Please put away.

ㅣ + ㅓ → ㅕ   지어요→ 져요
[i] [ŏ] [yŏ]   či-ŏ-yo [čyŏyo]   Please carry (on
                                          your back).

                가시었어요→ 가셨어요
                ka-si-ŏss-ŏ-yo   (Someone) left.
                [kasyŏssŏyo]

Lesson 1

제 일과 인사

USEFUL EXPRESSIONS

1. 안녕하십니까? How are you?
   An-nyŏng ha-sim-ni-kka?
2. 안녕하세요? How are you?
   An-nyŏng ha-se-yo?
3. 안녕히 가십시오. Good-bye (to the person leaving).
   An-nyŏng-hi ka-sip-si-o.
4. 안녕히 계십시오. Good-bye (to the person staying).
   An-nyŏng-hi kye-sip-si-o.
5. 고맙습니다. Thank you.
   Ko-map-sŭm-ni-da.
6. 감사합니다. Thank you
   Kam-sa-ham-ni-da.
7. 천만에요. You're welcome.
   Čhŏn-man-e-yo.
8. 질문 있어요? Do you have any questions?
   Čil-mun iss-ŏ-yo?
9. 네, 있어요. Yes, I do (I have).
   Ne, iss-ŏ-yo.
10. 아니요, 없어요. No, I don't have any.
    A-ni-yo, ŏps-ŏ-yo.
11. 이름이 무엇 이에요? What is your name?
    I-rŭm-i mu-ŏs-i-e-yo?
12. 다같이 하세요. Please say it all together.
    Ta kačh-i ha-se-yo.
13. 따라 하세요. Please repeat after me.
    Tta-ra ha-se-yo.
14. 다시 하세요. Please say it again.
    Ta-si ha-se-yo.

19

15. 크게 하세요.
    Khŭ-ge ha-se-yo.   Please speak louder.

16. 빨리 하세요.
    Ppal-li ha-se-yo.   Please speak faster.

17. 미안해요.
    Mi-an-hae-yo.   I am sorry. (polite informal)

18. 미안합니다.
    Mi-an-ham-ni-da.   I am sorry. (polite formal)

대화   DIALOGUE

김선생: 안녕하십^{2}니까?^{3}

이선생: 네, 안녕하십니까?

김선생: 요즈음 재미가 어떻습니까?

이선생: 좋습니다.^{3} 선생님은 어떻게 지내십니까?

김선생: 잘 지냅니다.

이선생: 그럼 안녕히 가십시오.^{3}

김선생: 네, 안녕히 가십시오.

NOTE: Superscripts in the dialogue refer to grammar and notes numbers.

낱말   VOCABULARY

제 일과	Lesson 1
인사	greeting
안녕하십니까? (안녕하다)	How are you? (polite formal)
안녕하세요? (안녕하다)	How are you? (polite informal)
안녕히 (안녕하다)	well, peacefully (to be well)
가십시오. (가다)	Please go. (to go)
계십시오. (계시다)	Please stay. (to stay)
고맙습니다. (고맙다)	Thank you. (to be grateful)
감사합니다. (감사하다)	Thank you. (to thank)
천만에요.	Not at all.
질문	question
네	yes

있어요. (있다)	There are. I have. (to exist) (See L3, GN6.)
아니요. (아니다)	No. (not to be)
없어요. (없다)	There aren't. I don't have. (not to exist)
이름	name
무엇	what
이에요. (이다)	It is. (to be)
다	all
같이	together
하세요. (하다)	Please do. (to do)
따라 (따르다)	following (to follow)
다시	again
크게 (크다)	loudly (to be loud)
빨리	quickly, fast, soon
미안해요. (미안하다)	(I am) sorry. (to be sorry) (polite informal)
미안합니다. (미안하다)	(I am) sorry. (polite formal)
김 선생	Mr./Mrs./Miss Kim (surname)
선생 (님)	teacher, you (hon.)
이	Lee, Yi (surname)
요즈음/요즘	these days
재미	interest, fun
어떻습니까? (어떻다)	How is it? (to be in some manner)
좋습니다. (좋다)	Fine, good. (to be good)
어떻게 (어떻다)	how
지내십니까? (지내다)	(How do you) pass the time? (to pass time)
잘	well
지냅니다. (지내다)	(I) pass the time.
그럼	well, then

NOTE: Words in parentheses are dictionary forms, grammatical information, or words necessary in English but not in Korean. "L3, GN6" refers to grammar and notes no. 6 of Lesson 3.

GRAMMAR AND NOTES

In this lesson we will study
1. General remarks on Korean
   a. word order
   b. absence of articles
   c. styles of speech
2. Honorific marker (for verbs) -(으)시
3. Sentence ending: polite formal style
   a. statement
   b. question
   c. request

1. General remarks on Korean

a. Word order

The basic word order is SUBJECT-OBJECT-VERB. The order SUBJECT-OBJECT is sometimes inverted (usually for emphasis), but the verb always comes at the end of the sentence.

제가	책을	읽습니다.
I (subj.)	book (obj.)	read (v.)
그것이	연필	입니다.
it (subj.)	pencil (comp.)	is (v.)

The modifiers, such as adjectives and adverbs, always precede the modified.

modifier	modified	modifier	modified
바쁜	시간	빨리	갑니다.
busy	time	quickly	goes
좋은	책	어떻게	지내십니까?
good	book	how	get along?
많은	학생	잘	지냅니다.
many	students	well	get along

b. Absence of articles

Korean has no articles, definite or indefinite, such as *the* and *a* in English. However, there are ways to indicate "definiteness" and "indefiniteness," as we will see in Lesson 2.

c. Styles of speech

There are four basic styles of speech in Korean: polite formal, polite informal, plain, and intimate. The speaker's choice of style is determined by the social relationship between the speaker and the addressee (hearer). Verb endings express the differences in the style of speech.

2. Honorific marker -(으)시

The presence or absence of -(으)시 marks the social relationship between the speaker and the person spoken of (referent). Attached to the stem of a verb, this marker forms an honorific stem indicating the speaker's deferential attitude toward the subject of the verb. (In the examples below, the polite formal ending is used.)

-시 is used after verb stems ending in a vowel.

-으시 is used after verb stems ending in a consonant.

Vowel stem	Consonant stem
가십니다 (S/he) is going	읽으십니다 (S/he) is reading
오십니다 (S/he) is coming	입으십니다 (S/he) is dressing

The order of honorific marker and polite formal endings is
VERB STEM-HONORIFIC MARKER-POLITE ENDING

VERB STEM	HONORIFIC MARKER	POLITE (QUESTION) ENDING	
안녕하	- 시	- ㅂ니까?	안녕하십니까? How are you?
가	- 시	- ㅂ니까?	가십니까? Are (you) going?
읽	- 으시	- ㅂ니까?	읽으십니까? Are (you) reading?
어떻게 지내	- 시	- ㅂ니까?	어떻게 지내십니까? How are you getting along?

3. Polite formal style

Statements, questions, and requests can be expressed in any of the four basic styles of speech. The polite formal style uses the following forms:

a. Statement

-ㅂ니다 is used after verb stems ending in a vowel.

Dictionary form

지내다	to pass	⟶ 지냅니다
이다	to be	⟶ 입니다
가다	to go	⟶ 갑니다
오다	to come	⟶ 옵니다

-습니다 is used after verb stems ending in a consonant.

좋다	to be good	⟶ 좋습니다
많다	there are many	⟶ 많습니다
있다	to exist	⟶ 있습니다
없다	to not exist	⟶ 없습니다

b. Question

The word order of question sentences is the same as that of statement (declarative) sentences. The endings have -까 instead.

	Statement	*Question*
이다 to be	이것이 펜 입니다. (this pen is) This is a pen.	이것이 펜 입니까? (this pen is) Is this a pen?
안녕하다 to be well	안녕하십니다. (is well) He/she is well.	그분은 안녕하십니까? (he/she is well) How is he/she? (polite formal)
좋다 to be good	그 책이 좋습니다. (the book is good) The book is good.	그 책이 좋습니까? (the book is good?) Is the book good?
있다 to exist	질문이 있습니다. (questions there are) There are questions.	질문이 있습니까? (questions are there?) Are there questions?

NOTE: -ㅂ니까 is used after verb stems ending in a vowel.
-습니까 is used after verb stems ending in a consonant.

c. Request

-십시오 is used after verb stems ending in a vowel.

-으십시오 is used after verb stems ending in a consonant.

Vowel stem

가다	to go	가십시오.	Please go.
하다	to do	하십시오.	Please do.

Consonant stem

읽다	to read	읽으십시오.	Please read.
앉다	to sit down	앉으십시오.	Please sit down.

연습 EXERCISES

A. 다음 인사에 대답하십시오. (Give appropriate responses to the following greetings.)

1. 안녕하십니까?
2. 요즘 어떻게 지내십니까?
3. 고맙습니다.
4. 안녕히 가십시오.

B. 다음 동사의 ㅂ/습니다, ㅂ/습니까?, (으)십시오 형을 쓰십시오. (Conjugate the verbs in the polite formal style.)

	ㅂ/습니다	ㅂ/습니까?	(으)십시오
5. 이다			
6. 가다			
7. 지내다			
8. 계시다*			
9. 있다			
10. 없다			
11. 고맙다			
12. 감사하다			

*시 is not repeated for 계시다; thus the (으)십시오 form is 계십시오.

Lesson 2

제 이과   이것이 무엇입니까?

대화 A

선생: 이것¹ 이² 무엇 입니까?³
학생: 그것은² 칠판 입니다.
선생: 이것은 무엇 입니까?
학생: 그것은 책 입니다.
선생: 저것은 무엇 입니까?
학생: 저것은 창문 입니다.
선생: 그것은 무엇 입니까?
학생: 이것은 연필 입니다.

Patterns

1. 이것이 무엇 입니까?
   저것 _____
   그것 _____

2. 이것은 책 입니다.
   저것은 책상 _____
   그것은 의자 _____
   _____ 문 _____
   _____ 칠판 _____

26

대화 B

선생: 이것이 연필 입니까?
학생: 네, 그것은 연필 입니다.
선생: 저것은 문 입니까?
학생: 아니요, 저것은 문이 아닙니다.
　　　저것은 창문 입니다.
선생: 이것은 책상 입니까?
학생: 아니요, 그것은 책상이 아닙니다.
　　　그것은 의자 입니다.

Patterns

1. <u>이것이</u> 연필 <u>입니까?</u>
　　<u>저것이</u> 문 _____
　　<u>그것이</u> 창문 _____
　　_____ 책상 _____
　　_____ 의자 _____

2. 이것은 연필이 아닙니다.
　　저것은 책_____
　　그것은 펜_____
　　_____ 교실_____
　　_____ 칠판_____

3. 이것은 <u>의자가</u> 아닙니다.
　　저것은 지우개_____
　　그것은 컴퓨터_____
　　이것은 시계_____
　　저것은 안경_____

낱말 VOCABULARY

제 이과	Lesson 2
이것	this, this thing
입니까? (이다)	Is (it)? (to be)
학생	student
그것	that, that thing, it

저것	that over there, that thing
칠판	chalkboard
입니다. (이다)	(It) is. (to be)
책	book
창문	window
연필	pencil
책상	desk (book-table)
의자	chair
문	door
펜	pen
교실	classroom
지우개	eraser
컴퓨터	computer
아닙니다. (아니다)	(It) is not. (not to be)
차	car, automobile
시계	watch, clock
안경	eyeglasses

GRAMMAR AND NOTES

In this lesson we will study
1. Demonstratives: 이- "this," 그- "that," 저- "that over there"
2. Postpositions
   a. subject marker -이/-가
   b. topic marker -은/-는
3. BE verb
   a. 이다   "to be," "to equal," "it is . . ."
   b. 아니다   "not to be," "it is not . . ."

1. Demonstratives

Korean demonstratives distinguish things three ways according to distance and visibility.

이-   indicates that the item is close to the speaker.

그-   indicates that the item is close to the addressee.

저- indicates that the item is away from both the speaker and the addressee.

이- and 저- are used only for items visible to the speaker and the addressee. 그- is also used to designate something known to both the speaker and the addressee, i.e., "the."

Demonstrative	Thing (item)
이- this	이것 this thing
그- that	그것 that thing, it
저- that over there	저것 that thing over there

2. Postpositions

Postpositions are markers attached to nouns, noun phrases, and verbal nouns to indicate their grammatical relationships in a sentence.

a. Subject marker: -이 or -가

Attached to a noun, these postpositions mark the noun as the subject of a sentence.

-가 is used after a noun ending in a vowel.

-이 is used after a noun ending in a consonant.

-가	-이
영희가　　　　옵니다. (Young-hie-SUBJ. comes) Young-hie comes.	그것이　　문 입니다. (that-SUBJ. door is) That is a door.
의자가　　　있습니다. (chair-SUBJ. there is) There is a chair.	책이　　　　있습니다. (book-SUBJ. there is) There is a book.
차가　　많습니다. (car-SUBJ. there are many) There are many cars.	연필이　　많습니다. (pencil-SUBJ. there are many) There are many pencils.

b. Topic marker and/or contrast marker: -은 or -는

Attached to a noun or a noun phrase, -은 or -는 indicates that the noun or the phrase is the topic of a sentence. In a sequence of sentences, or in a compound sentence, it also marks the contrast between the nouns or noun phrases.

-는   is used after a vowel.

-은   is used after a consonant.

Used as topic marker

-는   나는   학생 입니다.
          (I-TOPIC   student am)
          I am a student.

-은   저것은   칠판 입니다.
          (that-TOPIC chalkboard is)
          That is a chalkboard.

Used as contrast marker

A: 이것이   무엇 입니까?
     (this-SUBJ. what is)
     What is this?

B: 그것은   책상 입니다.
     (that-TOPIC desk is)
     That is a desk.

A: 저것은   무엇 입니까?
     (that-CONTRAST what is?)
     What is that, not this, over there?

B: 저것은   의자 입니다.
     (that-TOPIC chair is)
     That is a chair.

3. BE verb

a. BE verb 이다 "to be," "to equal," "it is . . ."

이다 expresses only one part of the meaning of "be" in English. It means "to be the equivalent of" or "to be equal to"; it does not mean "to exist," as in "I am in Berkeley" or "There are many students in this classroom." For the latter meaning, there is a different verb, 있다 (see Lesson 3).

나는 학생 입니다.   I am a student.

이것은 컴퓨터 입니다.   This is a computer.

Note that the complement noun preceding the verb 이다 takes neither the subject marker -이/-가 nor the topic marker -은/-는.

b. Negative BE verb 아니다　"not to be," "it is not . . ."
Unlike 이다, 아니다 requires the subject marker for the complement noun before it.

그것은 연필이 아닙니다.　That is not a pencil.
저것은 의자가 아닙니다.　That over there is not a chair.

연습　EXERCISES

A. 다음　질문에　대답하십시오. (Answer the following questions.)

　　1. 이것이 무엇 입니까?　(chalkboard)
　　2. 저것이 무엇 입니까?　(window)
　　3. 그것이 무엇 입니까?　(pencil)
　　4. 저것은 창문 입니까?　네, _____. 아니요, _____.
　　5. 이것은 책상 입니까?　네, _____. 아니요, _____.
　　6. 이 펜이 좋습니까?
　　7. 이 컴퓨터가 좋습니까?
　　8. 그 연필이 어떻습니까?
　　9. 그 책이 어떻습니까?
　　10. 그 지우개가 어떻습니까?

B. 다음　문장을　한국어로　번역하십시오. (Translate into Korean.)

　　11. How is this (thing)?　That (thing) is good.
　　　　How is that (thing)?　This (thing) is fine.
　　　　How is that over there?　That over there is fine.
　　12. How is this classroom?　This classroom is fine.
　　　　How is this window?　That window is fine.
　　　　How is this desk?　That desk is good.
　　13. What is this?　That is a pencil.
　　　　What is that?　This is a book.
　　　　What is that over there?　That over there is a chalkboard.
　　14. Is this a pencil?　No, that is not a pencil.
　　　　Is that a book?　No, this is not a book.
　　　　Is that a chalkboard?　No, this is not a chalkboard.

Lesson 3

제 삼과   어디에 있습니까?

김선생: 책이 어디에^1 있습니까?^{6}
스미스: (책은)^2 책상 위에 있습니다.
김선생: 가방은 어디에 있습니까?
스미스: (가방은) 의자 옆^{3}에 있습니다.
김선생: 칠판은 어디에 있습니까?
스미스: (칠판은) 책상 앞에 있습니다.
김선생: 공책은 어디에 있습니까?
스미스: (공책은) 책상 아래(에) 있습니다.
김선생: 연필은 어디에 있습니까?
스미스: (연필은) 가방 속에 있습니다.

Patterns

1. 책은 어디에 있습니까?
   연필_____
   가방_____
   공책_____
   도서관_____

2. 의자는 어디에 있습니까?
   기숙사_____
   철수_____
   컴퓨터_____

32

3. (책은) 책상 위에 있습니다.
　　　 가방 속＿＿＿＿＿＿
　　　 칠판 앞＿＿＿＿＿＿
　　　 의자 옆＿＿＿＿＿＿
　　　 책상 아래＿＿＿＿＿

대화　B

철수: 학교에 무엇이 있습니까?

혜경: 교실과[4] 도서관이 있습니다.

철수: 학교에 책방도[5] 있습니까?

혜경: 아니요. 책방은 없습니다.[6]

철수: 여기[7]에 무엇이 있습니까?

혜경: 체육관이 있습니다.

철수: 체육관 앞에는[8] 무엇이 있습니까?

혜경: (체육관 앞에는) 기숙사가 있습니다.
　　　 기숙사에는 식당도 있습니다.

Patterns

1. 도서관 안에(는) 무엇이 있습니까?
　　 학교 뒤＿＿＿＿＿＿＿＿＿＿＿＿＿
　　 기숙사 옆＿＿＿＿＿＿＿＿＿＿＿
　　 집 뒤＿＿＿＿＿＿＿＿＿＿＿＿＿

2. 가방 속에 연필이 있습니까?
　　 책상 아래＿＿＿＿＿＿＿＿＿
　　 칠판 앞＿＿＿＿＿＿＿＿＿

3. 도서관 안에 식당이 없습니다.
　　 기숙사 ＿＿＿＿＿＿＿＿＿＿
　　 책방 ＿＿＿＿＿＿＿＿＿＿

4. 여기에 식당도 있습니다.
　　 저기＿＿＿＿＿＿＿＿＿
　　 거기＿＿＿＿＿＿＿＿＿

5. 저기에 무엇과 무엇이 있습니까?
   <u>거기에 책과 공책이 있습니다.</u>
   _____ 기숙사와 식당_____
   _____ 책상과 의자_____
   _____ 차와 집_____

낱말 VOCABULARY

제 삼과	Lesson 3
김 선생	Mr. Kim
스미스	Smith
어디	where
있습니까? (있다)	Is there? (to exist, to have)
있습니다. (있다)	There is.
가방	bag, briefcase, handbag
공책	notebook
위	top, above
옆	side
앞	front
아래	below, under
속	inside, in
없습니다. (없다)	There is not. (I do not have. (to have not)
도서관	library
철수	Chul-soo (male name)
혜경	Hye-kyung (female name)
기숙사	dormitory
체육관	gymnasium
식당	cafeteria, restaurant
뒤	back, behind
안	inside
집	house
책방	bookstore
학교	school
여기 (에)	this place (here)

저기 (에)	that place (there) over there
거기 (에)	that place (there)
-와/과	and
-도	also

GRAMMAR AND NOTES

In this lesson we will study
1. Postposition: stative location marker -에 "at," "in," "on"
2. Omission of subject/topic pronouns
3. Location words 앞 "front," 옆 "side," 뒤 "back,"
   위 "above," 아래/밑 "below," 속/안 "inside"
4. Postposition -와 or -과 "and"
5. Postposition -도 "also," "too"
6. Verbs
   a. 있다 "to exist," "there is . . ."
   b. 없다 "not to exist," "there is not . . ."
7. Location pronouns 여기 "here," 거기 "there," 저기 "over there"
8. Location as topic: location noun + 에는
9. OR-questions

1. Stative location marker -에 "at," "in," "on"

-에 is used with stative verbs such as 있다 "to exist," 없다 "not to exist," and 살다 "to dwell." Attached to a place noun, it indicates someone or something is at, in, or on that place.

책은 어디에 있습니까?	Where is the book?
책상 위에 있습니다.	(It) is on the desk.
도서관에 식당이 없습니다.	There is no cafeteria in the library.
우리는 기숙사에 삽니다.	We live in the dormitory.

2. Omission of subject/topic pronouns

When the subject or topic of the sentence is well established and understood by the hearer, it may be omitted. In fact, you will not hear "I" or "you" in most conversations.

그 책은 어디에 있습니까?	As for the book, where is it?
(그것은) 책상 위에 있습니다.	(It) is on the desk.

3. Location words 앞 "front," 옆 "side," 뒤 "back," 위 "above," 아래/밑 "below," 속/안 "inside"

Location words come after the point of reference.

책상	<u>위</u>	(the) top of the desk
가방	<u>속</u>	(the) inside of the bag
의자	<u>옆</u>	beside the chair
학교	<u>앞</u>	(the) front of the school

4. Postposition -와 or -과 "and"

These postpositions are used between two or more nouns or noun phrases, but *not* between sentences. Also note that, unlike other postpositions,

-와   is used after a noun ending in a vowel.
-과   is used after a noun ending in a consonant.

-와

의자<u>와</u> 책상	chair and desk
너<u>와</u> 나	you and I
학교<u>와</u> 기숙사	school and dorm

-과

책<u>과</u> 공책	a book and a notebook
집<u>과</u> 나무	a house and a tree

5. Postposition -도 "also," "too"

When -도 is used after a noun or a noun phrase to indicate "also" or "too," it replaces the subject marker -이/-가, the topic marker -은/-는, and the direct object marker -을/-를 (see L4, GN6). But with the location marker -에, -도 follows -에.

책상 위에   연필<u>도</u>   있습니까?
(on the desk pencil-too is there?)
Is there a pencil too on the desk?

기숙사에   식당<u>도</u>   있습니까?
(in the dorm restaurant-also is there?)
Is there also a cafeteria in the dormitory?

기숙사<u>에도</u>   도서관이 있습니다.
(in the dorm-also library   there is.)
There is a library in the dorm also.

6. Verbs 있다 "to exist," "there is..."; 없다 "not to exist," "there is not..."

a. In English the verb "to be" expresses both "to be equal to" and "to exist." 있다 means only "to exist" or "there is."

책상 위에 책이 <u>있습니다</u>.	There is a book on the desk.
이 교실에 창문이 <u>있습니다</u>.	There is a window in this classroom.

b. 없다 expresses "not to exist" or "there is not..."

책상 위에 책이 <u>없습니다</u>.	There is no book on the desk.
그 교실에 창문이 <u>없습니다</u>.	There is no window in the classroom.

7. Location pronouns 여기 "here," 거기 "there," 저기 "over there"

here, this place   여기(에) = 이 곳에
there, that place   거기(에) = 그 곳에
there, that place over there   저기(에) = 저 곳에

As we learned in Lesson 2, the demonstratives 이-, 그-, and 저- come before -곳 "place" to make the place pronouns 이 곳 "here," 그 곳 "there," and 저 곳 "over there." Another set of place pronouns—여기, 거기, and 저기—is used more colloquially. The location marker -에 is optional with these pronouns, whereas -에 is required for 이 곳에, 그 곳에, and 저 곳에.

여기(에) 책이 많습니다.	There are many books here.
이 곳에 책이 많습니다.	There are many books at this place.
저기(에) 가방이 있습니다.	There is a bag over there.
저 곳에 가방이 있습니다.	There is a bag over at that place.

8. Location as topic: LOCATION NOUN +에는

As we learned in Lesson 2 (GN2b). -은/는 marks the topic of the sentence. -는 may follow after a location marker -에, thus making the location noun the topic of the sentence.

체육관 앞에는 무엇이 있습니까?	What is in front of the gymnasium? (As for in front of the gymnasium, what is there ?)
여기에는 무엇이 있습니까?	What is here? (As for here, what is there?)
저기에는 책상과 의자가 있습니다.	There are a desk and a chair over there. (As for over there, there are a desk and a chair.)

9. OR-questions

To make OR-questions such as "Is this a pencil *or* a pen?" simply put two questions one after the other.

학생입니까, 선생입니까?	Are you a student or a teacher?
이것이 책입니까, 공책입니까?	Is this a book or a notebook?
한국말이 어렵습니까, 쉽습니까?	Is Korean difficult or easy?
가방은 책상 위에 있습니까 책상 아래(에) 있습니까?	Is the briefcase on (top of) the desk or under the desk?

연습 EXERCISES

A. 다음 질문에 대답하십시오.
   1. 동생은 어디에 있습니까? (동생: "younger sibling")
   2. 집은 어디에 있습니까?
   3. 기숙사는 어디에 있습니까?
   4. 도서관에는 무엇이 있습니까?
   5. 이 교실(안)에 무엇이 있습니까?
   6. 책상 위에 무엇이 있습니까?
   7. 가방 속에 무엇이 있습니까?
   8. 학교 앞에 책방이 있습니까?
      네, _____
      아니요, _____
   9. 도서관에 식당이 있습니까?
      네, _____
      아니요, _____
  10. 학교에 체육관도 있습니까?
      네, _____
      아니요, _____

B. 다음 문장을 한국어로 번역하십시오. (Translate into Korean.)

11. *There is* a student *here.*
12. *There is* a teacher *here, also.* (Use honorific form.)
13. *There are* a student *and* a teacher *here.*
14. *There is* a student *in* the classroom.
15. *There is also* a teacher *in* the classroom.
16. *There are many* books *in* the library.
17. *There are no* notebooks *on* the desk.
18. *There is no* cafeteria *in* the library.
19. *Is there* a gymnasium *in* the university?
20. *Is this* a library *or* a gymnasium?
21. *Is he* a student *or* a teacher?
22. *Is* the bag *on* the desk *or under* the desk?
23. *Is* this a bookstore *or* a cafeteria?
24. *Where is* the gymnasium?
25. *Where is* the chair?

Lesson 4

제 사과   무엇을 공부하십니까?

대화

선생: 학생[1]은 이름이 무엇 입니까?
영식: 제[2] 이름은 김 영식 입니다.
선생: 대학생 입니까?[3]
영식: 네, 대학교에[4] 다닙니다.
선생: 대학교에서[5] 무엇을[6] 공부하십니까?
영식: 한국어를 공부합니다.
선생: 한국어는 재미있습니까?
영식: 네, 그러나 좀 어렵습니다.

Patterns

1. 학생은 이름이 무엇 입니까? (제 이름은) 김 영식 입니다.
   _____ 박 철수 _____
   _____ 존 스미스 ____

2. 학생 입니까?
   선생 _____?
   한국 학생 _____?
   대학생 _____?

3. 무엇을 공부하십니까?   영어를 공부합니다.
                          한국어_____.
                          수학_____.

4. 대학교에서 무엇을 공부하십니까?
   버클리_____?
   미국_____?
   한국_____?

5. 집에서 무엇을 보십니까?   책을 봅니다.
                            텔레비젼_____
                            영화_____

6. 어디에 다니십니까?   대학교에 다닙니다.
                            중학교_____
                            학교_____

7. 책방에서 무엇을 사십니까? 책을 삽니다.
                            가방_____
                            연필_____

8. 어디에 가십니까?   집에 갑니다.
                            학교_____
                            기숙사_____
                            식당_____

9. 어디에서 공부하십니까?   도서관에서 공부합니다.
                            식당_____
                            교실_____

10. 무엇이 어렵습니까?   한국어가 어렵습니다.
                            영어_____
                            수학_____

11. 무엇을 하십니까?   학교에 다닙니다.
                            텔레비젼을 봅니다.
                            책을 읽습니다.

12. 도서관에 책이 많습니다.
   기숙사에 학생_____
   학교에 차_____
   교실에 의자_____

낱말 VOCABULARY

제 사과	Lesson 4
공부하십니까? (공부하다)	Are (you) studying? (to study)
공부합니다.	(I) am studying.
김영식	Kim Young-shik (male name)
제/저	My/I (humble); 제가: I(subject); 저는: I (topic)
대학교	college, university
다닙니다. (다니다)	(I) attend. (to attend)
한국어	Korean language
재미있습니까? (재미있다)	Is (it) interesting? (to be interesting)
그러나	but, however
좀	a little, some, please
어렵습니다. (어렵다)	(It) is difficult. (to be difficult)
존	John
한국	Korea
영어	English
수학	mathematics
미국	the United States, America
버클리	Berkeley
중학교	middle school
대학생	college student
많습니다. (많다)	(There) are many. (to be many, much, a lot)
삽니다. (사다)	(I) buy. (to buy)
합니다. (하다)	(I) do. (to do)
봅니다. (보다)	(I) am looking. (to see)
신문	newspaper
읽습니다. (읽다)	(I) am reading. (to read)
텔레비젼	television
영화	movie
영화관	movie theater
극장	theater
뻐스/버스	bus

GRAMMAR AND NOTES

In this lesson we will study
1. Second-person terms of address
2. Humble form: 저 "I," 제 "I" or "my"
3. Omission of pronouns
4. Postposition: direction marker -에 "to"
5. Postposition: location marker -에서 "at," "in," "on"
6. Postposition: direct object marker -을/를
7. Descriptive verbs and action verbs

1. Second-person terms of address

To address a second person properly requires a good knowledge of Korean culture and of the person's position in the family, social rank, age, and so on. Simply stated, the second-person pronoun is often omitted in a dialogue (see point 2 below). When it is not, the addressee's occupation or title is commonly used for "you," as in this lesson's dialogue.

학생은 이름이 무엇입니까?

Here 학생 refers to "you (who are a student)" as a second person, not to a third-person "student." To indicate the third-person "student," add the demonstratives 이 학생, 그 학생, or 저 학생.

Another expression used for "you" in deference is 선생님 "teacher," as in

선생님 안녕하십니까?

which means "How are you (deferentially)?" or "How are you, teacher?"

2. Humble form: 저 "I," 제 "I" or "my"

One of the ways of being polite in speech is to use humble forms of words referring to oneself (the speaker) in deference to the addressee. 저 and 제 are two such words, meaning either "I" or "my."

저   is used with -는 "I (humble)"
제   is used with -가 "I (humble)"
제   also means "my (humble)" when followed by a noun.

제 이름은 김 영식입니다.*	My name is Young-shik Kim. (possessive)
저는 한국어를 공부합니다.	I am studying Korean. (topic)
제가 학생입니다.	I am the student. (subject)

* Notice that the Korean family name comes before the given name.

3. Omission of pronouns

As we saw in Lesson 3, the topic of a sentence is frequently omitted when it is understood by the speaker and the addressee. Pronouns such as "I" (first person is the speaker) or "you" (second person is the addressee) are commonly left out in conversation. Therefore, a question and an answer such as

대학생 입니까?	(Are . . . college student?)
네, 대학교에 다닙니다.	(Yes, . . . am attending college.)

are understood as "Are *you* a college student?" and "Yes, *I* am attending college," respectively. Throughout the lessons you will find that such pronouns are often absent.

4. Postposition: direction marker -에 "to"

Attached to a noun, -에 indicates the destination of verbs of motion such as 가다 "to go," 오다 "to come," and 다니다 "to attend."

저는 대학교에 다닙니다.	I attend college.
저는 버클리에 갑니다.	I am going to Berkeley.

5. Postposition location marker: -에서 "at," "in," "on"

-에서 is used with action verbs. Attached to a noun it indicates that someone or something is doing something at, in, or on that place.

대학교에서 무엇을 합니까?	What do you do in college?
대학교에서 공부를 합니다.	I study in college.
그 학생은 식당에서 일을 합니다.	The student works in a cafeteria.

6. Postposition : direct object marker -을/-를

Attached to a noun or noun phrase, -을/를 indicates that the noun or noun phrase is the direct object of the verb.

-를 is used after a noun ending in a vowel.

-을 is used after a noun ending in a consonant.

-를	-을
저는 한국어를 공부합니다.	무엇을 공부하십니까?
I am studying Korean.	What are you studying?
저는 친구를 만납니다.	저는 그림을 봅니다.
I am meeting a friend.	I am looking at a picture.
저는 편지를 씁니다.	저는 책을 읽습니다.
I am writing a letter.	I am reading a book.

7. Descriptive verbs and action verbs

Descriptive verbs are like adjectives in English; they denote qualities, "to be (large, small, young, etc.)." Like action verbs they take the full range of endings. One of the differences between descriptive and action verbs is in the present tense plain form: action verbs end in ㄴ/는다 whereas descriptive verbs end in 다 (as in the dictionary form).

DESCRIPTIVE VERBS

plain	*polite-formal*	*polite-formal question*
재미있다.	재미있습니다.	재미있습니까?
It is fun.	It is fun.	Is it fun?
어렵다.	어렵습니다.	어렵습니까?
It is difficult.	It is difficult.	Is it difficult?
춥다.	춥습니다.	춥습니까?
It is cold.	It is cold.	Is it cold?

ACTION VERBS

plain	polite-formal	polite-formal question
나는 공부한다. I am studying.	저는 공부합니다. I am studying.	공부하십니까? Are you studying?
나는 중학교에 다닌다. I attend middle school.	저는 중학교에 다닙니다. I attend middle school.	중학교에 다니십니까? Are you attending middle school?
나는 책을 읽는다. I am reading a book.	저는 책을 읽습니다. I am reading a book.	책을 읽으십니까? Are you reading a book?

연습 EXERCISES

A. 다음 질문에 대답하십시오.
1. 요즈음 집에서 무엇을 하십니까?
2. 대학교에서 무엇을 공부하십니까?
3. 도서관에서 무엇을 하십니까?
4. 책방에서 무엇을 사십니까?
5. 어디에서 책을 사십니까?
6. 요즘 무엇을 읽으십니까?
7. 어디에서 신문을 읽으십니까?
8. 어디에서 영화를 보십니까?
9. 어디에서 뻐스를 타십니까? (타다: to get on)
10. 요즘 어디에 다니십니까?

B. 다음 질문을 한국어로 번역하고 대답하십시오.
(Translate the following questions into Korean and answer them.)
11. *Are you* a college student?
12. *Do* you *study* Korean?
13. *Is* Korean *difficult?*
14. *Is* the movie *interesting?*
15. *Do* you *do* your homework *in* the library?
(homework: 숙제)

16. *Is there* a bookstore *in* the school?
17. *Where* do you get on the bus?
18. *Are* you (staying) *in* the dormitory?
19. *What* is the name of *that* student?
20. *What* does John study?

C. 읽기 (Reading)

　저는 대학생입니다. 한국어를 공부합니다. 한국어는 어렵습니다. 그러나 재미있습니다.

　저는 도서관에서 공부합니다. 도서관에는 책이 많습니다. 도서관에는 책방도 있습니다. 책방에서 책과 공책을 삽니다. 연필도 삽니다.

　저는 기숙사에 있습니다. 기숙사에는 식당도 있습니다. 식당에서 책도 봅니다.

D. 위의 읽기를 읽고 다음 질문에 대답하십시오.

(Answer the questions about the reading above.)

21. 한국어는 어떻습니까?
22. 도서관에는 무엇이 많습니까?
23. 어디에서 책과 공책을 삽니까?
24. 연필은 어디에서 삽니까?
25. 기숙사에는 식당도 있습니까?

Lesson 5

제 오과 누구십니까?

대화 A

선생: 저분[1]이 누구[2](이)*십니까?
영식: 제[3] 형 입니다.
선생: 형님도 학생 입니까?
영식: 네, 그렇습니다. 서울에서 대학에 다닙니다.
선생: 동생들[4]도 있[5]습니까?
영식: 아니요, 동생은 없습니다.

* (이) is usually omitted after nouns that end in a vowel.

Patterns

1. 저분이 누구십니까?
   이분_____
   그분_____

2. 동생이 있습니까?
   친구_____
   책_____
   집_____
   차_____

3. 형님도 학생입니까?
   누나_____
   오빠_____
   언니_____

4. 동생은 없습니다.
   오빠_____
   친구_____
   누나_____

5. 형님은 서울에서 대학에 다닙니다.
   친구_____
   동생_____
   영식_____

대화 B

김 선생: 이 책은 누구(의)[6] 것[7] 입니까?*
영식: 박 선생님(의) 것 입니다.
김 선생: 저 사전은 누구(의) 것 입니까?
영식: 저것도 박 선생님(의) 것 입니다.
　　　박 선생님은 책이 많습니다.
김 선생: 이 시계는 누구(의) 것 입니까?
영식: 제 것 입니다.
김 선생: 이 펜도 영식씨(의) 것 입니까?
영식: 아니요, 그것은 제 펜이 아닙니다.
　　　그것은 제 아버님(의) 것 입니다.

* (의) is usually omitted in spoken language.

Patterns

1. 이것은 누구(의) 신문입니까? 우리(의) 신문입니다.
   　　　　　　　　　할아버지_____
   　　　　　　　　　할머니_____
   　　　　　　　　　어머니_____
   　　　　　　　　　아저씨_____

2. 이 가방들은 누구(의) 것 입니까?
   　　　　　　　우리들(의) 것 입니다.
   　　　　　　저희들_____
   　　　　　　저 학생들_____
   　　　　　　저분들_____

3. 이 사전은 영식씨 (의) 것 입니까?
   _____ 박 선생님 _____
   _____ 아버지 _____
   _____ 어머니 _____
   _____ 오빠 _____

4. 그것도 박 선생님의 것입니다.
   그 펜_____
   그 시계_____
   그 책_____
   저 가방_____

5. 그것은 제 펜이 아닙니다.
   _____ 김 선생님의 펜_____
   _____ 형님의 것_____
   _____ 동생의 책_____
   _____ 영식의 시계_____

낱말 VOCABULARY

제 오과	Lesson 5
이분	this person (polite)
저분	that person (polite)
그분	that person, he/she (polite)
그렇습니다. (그렇다)	That is so; it is so; yes (to be so)
형	older brother (of a male); 형님 (hon.)
동생	younger brother or sister
나/저	I (plain)/I (humble) (See GN 3 in this lesson.)
너	you (plain)
우리들	we (plain)
저희(들)	we (humble)
누구	who
누구의	whose
누구의 것	whose, whose item
사전	dictionary
친구	friend

김	Kim (surname)
박	Park, Pak (surname)
-씨	Mr., Mrs., Miss
할아버지	grandfather; 할아버님 (hon.)
할머니	grandmother; 할머님 (hon.)
아버지 (아빠)	father (dad); 아버님 (hon.)
어머니 (엄마)	mother (mom); 어머님 (hon.)
언니	older sister (of a female)
누나	older sister (of a male); 누님 (hon.)
오빠	older brother (of a female)
아저씨	uncle
아주머니	aunt

GRAMMAR AND NOTES

In this lesson we will study
1. Third-person pronouns
2. Question words 누구 "who?" 무엇 "what?" 어디 "where?"
3. Pronouns: first, second, and third person, singular and plural
4. Plural marker -들 "-(e)s"
5. Verbs 있다 "to have," 없다 "to have not"
6. Postposition: possessive marker -의 "of," "-'s"
7. Dependent noun -것 "thing," "item"

1. Third-person pronouns

As we learned in Lesson 2 for "things" and Lesson 3 for "places," there are also three forms of third-person pronouns. There is no gender distinction in the pronouns, which mean literally "this person," "that person," and "that person over there." There are, however, two sets of pronouns showing different degrees of deference: honorific and plain.

	Person		Thing	Place
honorific	*plain*			
이 분	이 사람		이것	여기
그 분	그 사람		그것	저기
저 분	저 사람		저것	저기

2. Question words 누구 "who?" 무엇 "what?" 어디 "where?"

Question words also take postpositions to indicate their grammatical relations.

	Person		Thing		Place	
Subject	누가	who	무엇이	what	어디가	where
Direct object	누구를	whom	무엇을	what	어디를	where
Possessive	누구의	whose	무엇의	of what	어디의	of where

누<u>가</u> 이 선생 이십니까?
Who is Mr. Lee?

누구<u>를</u> 보십니까?
Whom do you see?

누구<u>의</u> 시계 입니까?
Whose watch is this?

무엇<u>이</u> 어렵습니까?
What is difficult?

무엇<u>을</u> 사셨습니까?
What did you buy?

어디<u>가</u> 기숙사 입니까?
Where (what place) is the dormitory?

어디<u>를</u>/어디<u>에</u> 가십니까?
Where are you going? (-를 or -에 is used for "going to.")

이것은 어디(<u>의</u>) 쌀입니까?
Where is the rice from? (This rice is product *of where?*)

저분이 누구 십니까?* (저분이 <u>누구</u> 이십니까?)
Who is that person?

* Notice that here, too, the verb 이다 does not take the subject marker and uses 누구, not 누가.

3. Pronouns: first, second, and third person, singular and plural

Korean pronouns, which are often omitted, have two or more forms of first-, second-, and third-person pronouns. The three possible forms are humble, plain, and honorific (hon.). The choice of pronoun is again based on the relationship between the speaker and the addressee and the social setting of the conversation.

	Subject	*Possessive*	*Possessive noun*
1st sg.	나 I (plain) 저 I (humble)	내/나의 my (plain) 제/저의 my (humble)	내것 mine (plain) 제것 mine (humble)
2d sg.	너 you (plain) 선생님 you (hon.)	네/너의 your (plain) 선생님의 your (hon.)	네것 yours (plain) 선생님의 것 yours (hon.)
3d sg.	그사람 he/she (plain) 그분 he/she (hon.)	그(사람)의 his/her (plain) 그분의 his/her (hon.)	그(사람)의 것 his/hers (plain) 그분의 것 his/hers (hon.)
1st pl.	우리(들) we (plain) 저희(들) we (humble)	우리(의), 우리들의 our (plain) 저희(의), 저희들의 our (humble)	우리것, 우리들의 것 ours (plain) 저희 것, 저희들의 것 ours (humble)
2d pl.	너희들 you (plain) 선생님들 you (hon.)	너희(의), 너희들의 your (plain) 선생님들의 your (hon.)	너희 것, 너희들의 것 yours (plain) 선생님들의 것 yours (hon.)
3d pl.	그(사람)들 they (plain) 그분들 they (hon.)	그(사람)들의 their (plain) 그분들의 their (hon.)	그(사람)들의 것 theirs (plain) 그분들의 것 theirs (hon.)

4. Plural marker -들 "-(e)s"

-들 is attached to a noun to indicate the plural form. The use of the plural ending is not always obligatory as in English; nouns without -들 may be plural as well. The plural marker is used optionally for emphasis and clarity, mostly for personal nouns and pronouns, as in:

동생들   younger siblings
우리들   we
그분들   they (hon.)

Compare:

학생들이 많다.   There are many students.
학생이 많다.   There are many students.

Both the singular 학생 and the plural 학생들 in the above examples mean "students" in English. The distinction between singular and plural is usually made by the context of the dialogue.

5. Verbs 있다 "to have," 없다 "to have not"

The verbs 있다 and 없다 are also used to indicate possession as in "to have" and "to have not" in English.

동생도 있습니까?   Do you have a younger
                    brother/sister also?

저는 동생이 없습니다.   I don't have a younger
                        brother/sister.

저는 한국어 책이 있습니다.   I have a Korean book.

6. Postposition: possessive marker -의 "of," "-'s"

Attached to a noun, -의 indicates that the noun is the possessor. The possessor always precedes the noun it possesses. Note that this -의 is pronounced [에] rather than [의].

존의 모자   John's hat
내 친구의 친구   my friend's friend; a friend of my friend

7. Dependent noun -것 "thing," "item"

Dependent nouns are nouns that cannot stand alone. -것 is a dependent noun that must be preceded by a demonstrative, the possessive 의, or another modifier.

Demonstratives	-의	*Possessive pronouns*
이것 this (thing)	우리의 것 ours	내것 mine (plain)
저것 that (thing)	누구의 것 whose	제것 mine (humble)
그것 that, it	친구의 것 friend's	네것 yours (plain)
		선생님의 것
		yours (hon.)

연습 EXERCISES

A. 다음 질문에 대답하십시오.
1. 그분은 누구십니까? (my older brother)
2. 그분은 무엇을 하십니까? (teaches)
    (to teach: 가르치다)
3. 그분도 동생이 있습니까? (yes)
4. 저분은 누구의 형님 이십니까? (my friend's)
5. 이 책은 누구의 것 입니까? (ours [humble])
6. 동생은 차가 있습니까? (no)
7. 이 차는 누구의 것입니까? (mine [humble])
8. 저 시계는 누구의 것입니까? (teacher's)

B. 다음 문장을 한국어로 번역하십시오.
9. This is *Mr. Lee's.*
10. This pencil is *David's.*
11. That briefcase is *the student's.*
12. These things are *my mother's.*
13. Those books are *mine.* (humble)
14. Those things *are not Mr. Lee's.*
15. That pen *is not Mr. Kim's.*
16. Those *are not yours.* (hon.)
17. The desk *is not Mr. Park's.*
18. *Whose* notebooks are these?

19. *Whose* dictionary is this?

20. *Whose* newspaper is this?

21. I *have* a younger brother. I *do not have* a younger sister.

22. I *have* a watch. I *do not have* a briefcase. (watch: 시계)

23. I *have* a Korean book. I *do not have* an English book.

24. I *have* a television. I *do not have* a magazine. (magazine: 잡지)

Lesson 6

제 육과   어디에 사십니까?

대화

김 선생: 요즈음 어디에 사[1]십니까?

이 선생: 기숙사에 삽니다.

김 선생: 아버님과 어머님께서[2]는 어디에 계십니까?[3]

이 선생: 로스앤젤레스에 계십니다.

김 선생: 부모님께서는 무엇을 하십니까?

이 선생: 아버님께서는 사업을 하시고[4] 어머님께서는
국민 학교에서 가르치십니다.

김 선생: 부인께서는 일을 하십니까?

이 선생: 네. 집사람은 백화점에서 일합니다.
김선생님 부인께서도 일을 하십니까?

김 선생: 아니요. 일을 안[5] 합니다. 학교에 다닙니다.

Patterns

1. <u>요즈음 어디에</u> 사십니까?
   _____ 계십니까?
   _____ 있습니까?

2. <u>김 선생님께서는 요즘</u> 무엇을 하십니까?
   _____ 사업 _____
   _____ 공부 _____
   _____ 일 _____

58

3. 학생은 무엇을 합니까?
   동생 _____
   친구 _____
   철수 _____

4. 그 학생은 어디에서 일합니까?
   <u>그 학생은</u> 대학교에서 일 합니다.
   _____ 국민학교_____
   _____ 백화점_____
   _____ 고등학교_____

5. 아버님께서는 무엇을 <u>하시고</u> 어머님께서는 무엇을 하십니까?
   형님은 무엇을 <u>하시고</u> 동생은 무엇을 합니까?
   언니는 서울에 <u>살고</u> 오빠는 나성에 삽니다.
   누님은 한국어를 <u>배우고</u> 저는 일본어를 배웁니다.

6. 집 사람은 일을 <u>안</u> 합니다.
   동생은 공부를 ____ 합니다.
   친구는 학교에 ____ 다닙니다.
   김 선생님은 사업을 ____ 하십니다.

7. 부인<u>께서도</u> 일을 하십니까?
   어머님_____ 사업을 하십니까?
   아버님_____ 서울에 계십니까?
   부모님_____ 로스앤젤레스에 사십니까?

낱말

제 육과	Lesson 6
사십니까? (살다)	... live? (to live)
삽니다. (살다)	(he/she) lives ... (to live)
계십니까? (계시다)	Is he/she here? (to exist) (hon.)
계십니다. (계시다)	He/she is (here). (hon.)
나성/로스앤젤레스	Los Angeles
사업	business
사업을 하다	to be in business
국민학교	elementary school

가르치십니다.	He/she is teaching.
(가르치다)	(to teach)
부인	wife (another person's) (hon.)
일을 하다	to work, to do work
집사람	wife (one's own)
백화점	department store
일본	Japan
일본어	Japanese language
배우다	to learn
고등학교	high school
부모(님)	parents (hon.)
알다	to know
들다	to lift, to raise, to hold
팔다	to sell
놀다	to play
살다	to live

GRAMMAR AND NOTES

In this lesson we will study
1. ㄹ irregular verbs
2. Postposition: honorific subject marker -께서
3. Honorific words
4. Coordinate connective and conjunction
   a. -고   "and"
   b. 그리고 "And (then)..."
5. Negative 안 "not"

1. ㄹ irregular verbs

All verb stems ending in ㄹ are irregular in that the ㄹ drops when followed by ㄴ/는, ㅂ/습, or (으)시.

	ㄹ drops			ㄹ remains
	-는	-ㅂ니다	-십니다	-고 (겠, 지, 면)
살다	사는	삽니다	사십니다	살고 (살겠다)
놀다	노는	놉니다	노십니다	놀고 (놀지)
팔다	파는	팝니다	파십니다	팔고 (팔면)
알다	아는	압니다	아십니다	알고 (알겠다)
들다	드는	듭니다	드십니다	들고 (들지)

2. Postposition: honorific subject marker -께서

Attached to a personal noun, -께서 indicates the speaker's deference toward the subject (person) of the verb. It is used for a person of higher social status than the speaker.

Higher status

아버지께서 일하십니다.
(father works)
My father is working.

어머니께서 무엇을 하십니까?
(mother what do)
What does your mother do?

Lower or equal status

동생이 일합니다.
(younger sibling works)
My younger sibling is working.

친구가 무엇을 합니까?
(friend what do)
What does your friend do?

The honorific subject marker -께서 can be used with the topic marker -는, but remember that the plain subject marker -이/가 cannot be used with the topic marker at the same time.

아버지께서는 책을 읽으십니다.
(as for father book read)
My father is reading a book.

동생은 책을 읽습니다.
(as for brother book read)
My brother is reading a book.

3. Honorific words

A number of nouns and verbs are inherently honorific and polite in meaning.

	NOUN			VERB	
	plain	*honorific*		*plain*	*honorific*
meal	밥	진지	to exist	있다	계시다
age	나이	연세	to sleep	자다	주무시다
name	이름	성함	to eat	먹다	잡수시다

아버지께서 진지를 잡수십니다.　My father is having a meal.

어머니께서 집에 계십니다.　My mother is in the house.

연세가 어떻게 되십니까?　How old are you?

성함이 어떻게 되십니까?　What is your name?

4. Coordinate connective and conjunction

a. -고　connects two clauses by attaching to the verb stem of the first.

영희는 공부합니다.　　영식이는 일합니다.*
1st sentence　　　　2d sentence

영희는 <u>공부하고</u> 영식이는 일합니다.
(Young-hie study-*and* Young-shik work)
Young-hie studies, and Young-shik works.

> 아버지께서는 사업을 하십니다.
> 1st sentence
> 어머니께서는 국민학교에서 가르치십니다.
> 2d sentence

아버지께서는 사업을 하시고 어머니께서는 국민학교에서 가르치십니다.
(father business does-HON-*and* mother at an elementary school teaches)
My father does/runs a business, and my mother teaches at an elementary school.

* See L17, GN1 for the use of the particle -이 for personal names.

b. When two sentences are independent, 그리고 is used at the beginning of the second sentence as a conjunction meaning "And (then)..."

아버지께서는 사업을 하십니다.	My father is in business.
그리고 어머니께서는 학교에서 가르치십니다.	And my mother teaches in school.

동생은 학교에서 놉니다.	My younger brother is playing at school.
그리고 저는 집에서 공부합니다.	And I am studying at home.

Most of the connectives have two sets, one for the clause-final position as in 4a and another for the sentence-initial position as in 4b.

5. Negative 안 "not"

안, like "not" in English, comes before a verb to make a negative sentence.

저는 학교에 <u>안</u> 갑니다.	I do not go to school.
저는 일을 <u>안</u> 합니다.	I do not work.
어머니는 사업을 <u>안</u> 하십니다.	My mother doesn't run a business.
동생은 일본어를 <u>안</u> 배웁니다.	My younger brother/sister is not learning Japanese.
저는 기숙사에서 공부를 <u>안</u> 하고 도서관에서 합니다.	I don't study in the dormitory, but I study in the library.

연습

A. 다음 질문에 대답하십시오.
1. 요즈음 어디에 사십니까?
2. 아버님께서는 어디에 계십니까?
3. 어머님께서는 무엇을 하십니까?
4. 선생님께서는 학교에서 무엇을 하십니까?
5. 요즈음 부인께서는 어디에 계십니까?
6. 아버님의 사업은 어떻습니까?
7. 동생은 어디에서 놉니까? (놀다)
8. 오빠는 어디에 삽니까? (살다)
9. 어디에서 공책을 팝니까? (팔다)
10. 언니는 무엇을 듣니까? (듣다)

B. 다음 문장을 한국어로 번역하고 대답하십시오.
11. Where does Mr. Lee live?
12. Where does your father live?
13. Do your parents live in San Jose?
14. What does your father do?
15. What does your mother do?
16. What does your wife do?
17. What do you do?
18. Where do you live?
19. What does your brother do?
20. Where does your father do/run his business?

C. 다음 문장을 한국어로 번역하십시오.
21. Mr. Kim teaches at a university, *and* Mr. Park teaches at an elementary school.
22. I read a book in the library, *and* my younger brother does his homework at home.
23. I attend a university, *and* my sister attends a middle school.
24. I get on the bus in front of the school, *and* my friend gets on the bus in back of the library.
25. I buy things in the bookstore, *and* my sister buys things in the department store. (things: 물건)

26. My father is in Los Angeies, *and* my brother is in San Francisco. (San Francisco: 샌프란시스코)
27. My father has a house *in* Los Angeles.
28. My friend has a car. My sister *also* has a car.
29. We buy books *and* magazines *in* the bookstore.
30. What do they sell *in* the department store?
31. I know Korean, *and* my friend knows Chinese.

D. 다음 빈 칸에 보기와 같이 알맞는 말을 써 넣으십시오. (Fill in the blanks with 께서는 ... 계십니다 or 은/는 ... 있습니다.)

보기: 어머님께서는 집에 계십니다.

32. 부인 _____ 집에 _____
33. 아버님 _____ 서울에 _____
34. 학생 _____ 기숙사에 _____
35. 김 선생님 ___ 교실에 _____
36. 동생 _____ 도서관에 _____

Lesson 7

제 칠과 언제 오셨습니까?

박 선생: 스미스 선생님은 어디에서[1] 오셨[2]습니까?
스미스: 저는 영국에서 왔습니다.
박 선생: 브라운 선생님도 영국에서 오셨습니까?
브라운: 아니요,[3] 저는 미국에서 왔습니다.
박 선생: 스미스 선생님은 언제[4] 한국에 오셨습니까?
스미스: 작년 9월[5]에[6] 왔습니다.
브라운: 저는 1985년 4월에 왔습니다.
박 선생: 영국에서는 무슨[4] 일을 하셨습니까?
스미스: 신문 기자로[7] 일했습니다.
박 선생: 브라운 선생님은 직업이 무엇 입니까?
브라운: 저는 학생 입니다. 대학교에서 경제학을
　　　　 공부합니다.
박 선생: 어느[4] 대학에 다니십니까?
브라운: 버클리 대학에 다닙니다.

Patterns

1. 오셨습니다.
　　가 _____
　　하 _____
　　읽으 _____
　　있으 _____

2. 선생님은 어디에서 오셨습니까?

　_____ 미국 _____
　_____ 영국 _____
　_____ 한국 _____
　_____ 중국 _____

3. 스미스 씨는 무슨 일을 하셨습니까?

　_____ 공부를 하셨습니까?
　_____ 책을 읽으셨습니까?

4. 언제 한국에 오셨습니까?

　____ 미국 _____
　____ 캐나다 _____
　____ 샌프란시스코 _____

5. 언제 신문기자로 일하셨습니까?

　_____ 대학교에 다니셨습니까?
　_____ 경제학을 공부하셨습니까?
　_____ 그 책을 읽으셨습니까?

6. 영국에서 왔습니다.

　서울_____
　멕시코_____
　일본_____
　소련_____

7. 신문 기자로 일했습니다.

　선생 _____
　의사 _____
　비서 _____

8. 어느 대학에 다니십니까?

　____ 식당에서 일하십니까?
　____ 기숙사에 계십니까?
　____ 책이 김 선생의 것입니까?
　____ 분이 안 선생이십니까?

9. 언제 미국에 오셨습니까?

　삼월에 왔습니다.
　유월에 _____
　시월에 _____
　십일월에 _____
　어제 _____
　오늘 _____

낱말

제 칠과	Lesson 7
언제	when
오셨습니까? (오다)	Did (you) come? (to come)
가셨습니까? (가다)	Did (you) go? (to go)
왔습니다	(I) came.
갔습니다	(I) went.
영국	England
미국	U.S.A.
무슨	what kind of, what sort of
무슨 일	what kind of work
기자	reporter
직업	occupation, job
경제학	economics
어느	which
나라	country, nation
작년	last year
1985년	the year 1985
9월	September
읽었습니까? (읽다)	Did (you) read? (to read)
상항/샌프란시스코	San Francisco
중국	China
캐나다	Canada
멕시코	Mexico
서울	Seoul
소련	U.S.S.R.
신문 기자	newspaper reporter
의사	medical doctor
비서	secretary
안 선생	Mr. Ahn
어제	yesterday
오늘	today
내일	tomorrow
생일	birthday
내년	next year
올해/금년	this year

Months of the year

1월	일월	January
2월	이월	February
3월	삼월	March
4월	사월	April
5월	오월	May
6월	유월 [yuwŏl]	June
7월	칠월	July
8월	팔월	August
9월	구월	September
10월	시월 [siwŏl]	October
11월	십일월	November
12월	십이월	December

Reading dates

In reading dates, month and day follow the year so that July 1, 1955, is read as "(one) thousand nine-hundred fifty-five *year,* seven *month,* one *day.*" Note that the word -년 "year" cannot be omitted as in English.

1986	천구백팔십육년
1950	천구백오십년
July 1, 1955	천구백오십오년 칠월 일일
October 9, 1988	천구백팔십팔년 시월 구일

GRAMMAR AND NOTES

In this lesson we will study
1. Postpositions: direction markers -에 "to," -에서 "from"
2. Past-tense markers -었- and -았-
3. Yes/no answers to negative questions
4. Question words
   a. 언제 "when?"
   b. 어느 "which?"
   c. 무슨 "what kind of?" "which?"
5. Sino-Korean numbers

6. Postposition: time marker -에 "in," "at," "on"
7. Postposition -(으)로 "as," "in the role of"
8. Chinese characters 一, 二, 三, 四, 五, 六, 七, 八, 九, 十
   (1 through 10)
9. Verb chart 1: present and past formal endings

1. Postpositions: direction markers -에 "to," -에서 "from"

As we saw in Lesson 4, a motion "to" or "toward" is indicated by -에 when used with the verbs 오다 "to come," 가다 "to go," and 다니다 "to commute" or "to attend." For such verbs -에서 indicates a motion "from" or "away from."

-에	-에서
언제 한국에 오셨습니까?	어디에서 오셨습니까?
(when Korea-to come?)	(where-from came?)
When did you come to Korea?	Where are you from?
우리는 중국에 갑니다.	우리는 중국에서 왔습니다.
We are going to China.	We are (came) from China.
우리는 대학에 다닙니다.	우리는 학교에서 옵니다.
We attend a college.	We are coming from school.

Here is a guide to some of the many uses of -에 and -에서:

-에 "in," "at," "on" is used with 있다, 없다, 살다, 계시다, 많다

-에 "to" is used with 가다, 오다, 다니나

-에서 "from" is used with 가다, 오다, 다니다

-에서 "in," "at," "on" is used with 놀다, 읽다, 공부하다, 살다 (살다 can be used with either -에 or -에서)

2. Past-tense markers -았- and -었-

Here we will introduce the basic rules for using the past-tense markers to form the past stems. (See L8, GN2 and 6 for more details.)

-았- is used after a verb whose stem vowel is either 아 or 오.

-었- is used after all other verbs.

	-았습니다		-었습니다
가다	갔습니다*	이다	이었습니다
사다	샀습니다*	다니다	다니었습니다
팔다	팔았습니다	계시다	계시었습니다
알다	알았습니다	배우다	배웠습니다*
오다	왔습니다*	읽다	읽었습니다
보다	보았습니다	있다	있었습니다
좋다	좋았습니다	먹다	먹었습니다
모르다	몰랐습니다	쓰다	썼습니다*
빠르다	빨랐습니다	기르다	길렀습니다
바쁘다	바빴습니다	서다	섰습니다*
		지내다	지냈습니다*

* Note that a contraction occurs when two vowels come together: 아 + 아 → 아; 오 + 아 → 와; 우 + 어 → 워; 어 + 어 → 어; 으 + 어 → 어; 이 + 어 → 여; 애 + 어 → 애 (optional).

The tense marker in an honorific-polite formal style comes after the honorific marker -(으)시-.

VERB STEM	- HON.	PAST	- POLITE -	SENTENCE ENDING
신문을 읽 -	으시 -	었 -	습 -	니까

Did (you) read the newspaper?

Note that the past-tense verb ending in the honorific-polite formal style is always 셨습니다. Since the tense marker follows the honorific marker 으시 or 시, it can only be 었, not 았.

The combination (으)시 and 었 becomes 셨, as in 하셨습니다. This contracted form has become a standard way of expressing the honorific past tense.

For additional verb forms, see verb chart 1 in GN9.

3. Yes/no answers to negative questions

Answers to positive questions are the same as in English. However, when a negative question is asked, 네 or 예 "yes" and 아니요 "no" answers should be interpreted as "Yes, that is correct" for 네 or 예, and "No, that is not correct" for 아니요.

학생이 아니십니까?	Aren't you a student?
아니요, 학생입니다.	Yes, I am.
네, 학생이 아닙니다.	No, I am not.
영국에서 안 오셨습니까?	Didn't you come from England?
아니요, 영국에서 왔습니다.	Yes, I came from England.
네, 영국에서 안 왔습니다.	No, I did not come (am not) from England.
동생이 없습니까?	Don't you have a younger brother?
아니요, 있습니다.	Yes, I do.
네, 없습니다.	No, I don't.

4. Question words

a. 언제 "when." This is the question word for time.

언제가 좋습니까?	When is a good time (for you)?
언제 오십니까?	When are you coming?
언제 공부하십니까?	When do you study?

b. 어느 "which." This question word, meaning "which (of several)," has to be followed by a noun.

어느것	which one
어느분	which person
어느 나라	which country
어느 학생	which student

c. 무슨 "what kind of," "which." This is also followed by a noun.

무슨 일	what kind of work
무슨 책	what kind of book, which book
무슨 공부	what kind of study

5. Sino-Korean numbers

There are two sets of numbers for counting, one of Korean origin and the other of Chinese origin. We refer to the latter as Sino-Korean numbers.

1	一	일	11	十一	십일	30	三十	삼십
2	二	이	12	十二	십이	40	四十	사십
3	三	삼	13	十三	십삼	50	五十	오십
4	四	사	14	十四	십사	60	六十	육십
5	五	오	15	十五	십오	70	七十	칠십
6	六	육	16	十六	십육	80	八十	팔십
7	七	칠	17	十七	십칠	90	九十	구십
8	八	팔	18	十八	십팔	100	百	백
9	九	구	19	十九	십구	1,000	千	천
10	十	십	20	二十	이십	10,000	萬	만

In general, Korean numbers are used with Korean words and Sino-Korean numbers are used with Sino-Korean words. For example, years, months, and dates are expressed in Sino-Korean numbers.

6. Postposition: time marker -에 "in," "at," "on"

When -에 is used after a time noun, it means "in," "at," or "on."

오월에 왔습니다.   I came in May.
월요일에 학교에 갑니다.   I go to school on Monday.
1975년에 났습니다.   I was born in 1975.

7. Postposition -(으)로 "as," "in the role of"

-로 is used after a noun ending in a vowel or ㄹ.
-으로 is used for all other nouns.

기자로 일합니다.   I work as a reporter.
학생으로 미국에 왔습니다. I came to the U.S. as a student.
비서로 일했습니다.   She worked as a secretary.

웨이터로 일했습니다.   He worked as a waiter.

평화사절로 외국에   He went to a foreign country
갔습니다.   as a peace delegate.

8. Chinese characters

We will introduce a number of Chinese characters for the Sino-Korean words introduced in each lesson. The Chinese character chart is read as follows:

a. In the second column, the first *hangŭl* word is the original Korean name for the number and the second is the Sino-Korean. For example, 하나 means "one" and the Sino-Korean character 一 is pronounced 일.

b. The order of strokes is shown from the third column.

一	하나 일 one	一					
二	두 이 two	－	二				
三	셋 삼 three	－	二	三			
四	넷 사 four	\	冂	四	四	四	
五	다섯 오 five	－	丁	五	五		
六	여섯 육 six	'	亠	六	六		
七	일곱 칠 seven	一	七				
八	여덟 팔 eight	ノ	八				
九	아홉 구 nine	ノ	九				
十	열 십 ten	一	十				

9. Verb chart 1: present and past formal endings

	현재 PRESENT		과거 PAST	
Dictionary form	*Polite formal*	*Plain**	*Polite formal*	*Plain*
가다 to go	갑니다 (plain) 가십니다 (hon.)	간다 가신다	갔습니다 가셨습니다	갔다 가셨다
가르치다 to teach	가르칩니다 가르치십니다	가르친다 가르치신다	가르쳤습니다 가르치셨습니다	가르쳤다 가르치셨다
다니다 to attend	다닙니다 다니십니다	다닌다 다니신다	다녔습니다 다니셨습니다	다녔다 다니셨다
공부(일, 사업) 하다 to do (study, work, business)	공부 일 합니다 사업 하십니다	공부 일 한다 사업 하신다	공부 일 하였습니다 (했습니다) 사업 하셨습니다	공부 일 하였다 (했다) 사업 하셨다
오다 to come	옵니다 오십니다	온다 오신다	왔습니다 오셨습니다	왔다 오셨다
보다 to see	봅니다 보십니다	본다 보신다	보았습니다 (봤습니다) 보셨습니다	보았다 (봤다) 보셨다
읽다 to read	읽습니다 읽으십니다	읽는다 읽으신다	읽었습니다 읽으셨습니다	읽었다 읽으셨다
살다 to live	삽니다 사십니다	산다 사신다	살았습니다 사셨습니다	살았다 사셨다
이다 to be	입니다 이십니다	이다 이시다	이었습니다 이셨습니다	이었다 이셨다
있다 to have	있습니다 있으십니다	있다 있으시다	있었습니다 있으셨습니다	있었다 있으셨다
있다 to exist	있습니다 계십니다	있다 계시다	있었습니다 계셨습니다	있었다 계셨다
좋다 to be good	좋습니다 좋으십니다	좋다 좋으시다	좋았습니다 좋으셨습니다	좋았다 좋으셨다
많다 to be many	많습니다 많으십니다	많다 많으시다	많았습니다 많으셨습니다	많았다 많으셨다
어렵다 ** to be difficult	어렵습니다 어려우십니다	어렵다 어려우시다	어려웠습니다 어려우셨습니다	어려웠다 어려우셨다
없다 to have not	없습니다 없으십니다	없다 없으시다	없었습니다 없으셨습니다	없었다 없으셨다

* See L11, GN2.   ** See L13, GN5.

연습

A. 다음 질문에 대답하십시오.
1. 스미스 선생은 직업이 무엇 입니까?
2. 브라운 선생은 어느 나라에서 오셨습니까?
   (나라: country)
3. 학생은 어디에서 고등학교에 다녔습니까?
4. 아버님은 어디에서 사업을 하셨습니까?
5. 언제 버클리에 오셨습니까?
6. 요즈음 무슨 책을 읽으셨습니까?
7. 요즈음 무슨 영화를 보셨습니까?
8. 1990년에는 어디에 사셨습니까?
9. 어머님은 국민학교 선생님이셨습니까?
10. 아버님은 무슨 일을 하셨습니까?
11. 1987년에 부모님께서는 어디에 계셨습니까?
12. 고등학교에서는 무엇을 공부했습니까?
13. 한국어는 어려웠습니까?

B. 다음 문장을 과거로 고치십시오. (Change the following sentences to the past tense.)
14. 동생이 집에 <u>갑니다</u>.
15. 형님은 차가 <u>있습니다</u>.
16. 그분은 신문 기자로 <u>일합니다</u>.
17. 브라운 씨는 <u>학생입니다</u>.
18. 저는 친구가 <u>많습니다</u>.
19. 철수는 로스엔젤레스에 <u>삽니다</u>.
20. 책상 위에 공책이 <u>없습니다</u>.
21. 친구는 대학교에 <u>다닙니다</u>.
22. 학생들은 도서관에서 신문과 잡지를 <u>읽습니다</u>.
23. 극장에서 영화를 <u>봅니다</u>. (극장: theater)
24. 아버님께서는 사업을 <u>하십니다</u>.
25. 김 선생님께서 서울에서 <u>오십니다</u>.
26. 어머님은 국민학교 선생님 <u>이십니다</u>.
27. 할아버님께서는 신문을 <u>보십니다</u>.
28. 유 선생님께서 한국어를 <u>가르치십니다</u>.
29. 이 선생님은 책이 <u>많으십니다</u>.

30. 박 선생님은 차가 <u>없으십니다</u>.
31. 스미스 선생님은 책을 <u>읽으십니다</u>.
32. 할머님께서는 L.A.에 <u>계십니다</u>.
33. 그분은 상항에 <u>사십니다</u>.

C. 다음 문장을 한국어로 번역하십시오.
    34. Mr. Yoon, when *did* you *come* to the United States?
    35. I *came in June* of 1985.
    36. *What kind of* work *did* you *do* in Korea?
    37. I *taught at* a university.
    38. What *is* your profession?
    39. I *am* a journalist.
    40. *Where did* you *attend* college?
    41. I *attended* college *in* England.
    42. I *worked as a secretary in* a department store.
    43. *Did* you *read* the newspaper?
    44. No, I *watched* television.

Lesson 8

제 팔과 출석

대화 A

김 선생: 오늘 아침에는 출석을 부르[1]겠어요.[2, 3] 죤슨 씨.
죤슨: 네.
김 선생: 브라운 씨는 오늘 왜[4] 안[5] 나오셨어요?
죤슨: 아파서[6] 못[5] 나왔어요.
김 선생: 이 책을 브라운 씨에게[7] 좀 전해 주시[8]겠어요?
죤슨: 네, 전하겠어요.
김 선생: 책을 보고[9] 다 같이 읽으세요.[10]

Patterns

1. 오늘 아침에는 출석을 부르겠어요.
   _____ 책을 읽겠어요.
   _____ 공부를 하겠어요.
   _____ 이 책을 전하겠어요.

2. 브라운 씨는 왜 안 나오셨어요?
   _____ 책을 안 읽었어요?
   _____ 공부를 안 했어요?
   _____ 버스를 안 탔어요?

3. 브라운 씨에게 전해 주십시오.
   친구 _____
   어머님 _____
   선생님 _____

78

4. <u>좀 전해 주시겠어요?</u>
　__ 읽어 _____
　__ 와 _____
　__ 가 _____
　__ 봐 _____

대화 B

영식: 오늘 저녁에는 무엇을 하겠어요?
미경: 집에서 숙제를 하겠어요.
영식: 숙제가 많아요?
미경: 숙제도 많고 내일은 시험도 있어서 아주 바빠요.
영식: 그럼 공부 많이 하세요.

Patterns

1. <u>브라운 씨는</u> 아파서 못 나왔어요.
　_____ 바빠서 영화를 못 가요.
　_____ 책이 없어서 못 읽었어요.
　_____ 숙제가 많아서 바빠요.
　_____ 시험이 있어서 공부해요.

2. <u>다 같이</u> 읽으세요.
　_____ 책을 보세요.
　_____ 나오세요.
　_____ 식당에 가세요.

낱말

제 팔과	Lesson 8
아침	morning
출석	attendance
부르겠어요. (부르다)	(I) will call. (to call)
존슨	Johnson
왜	why
안	(do) not
못	cannot
아파서 (아프다)	because (I am) sick (to be sick)
나왔어요. (나오다)	(He/she) came out. (to come out, to be present)
전해 주시겠어요? (전해주다)	Would (you) relay (it for me)? (to deliver for me)
전해 드리겠어요. (전해드리다)	(I) will deliver (it). (to deliver to an honorific person)
주다	to give
타다	to ride
저녁	evening, dinner
숙제	homework
시험	test, exam
아주	very
바빠요. (바쁘다)	(I) am busy. (to be busy)
공부 (工夫)	study
브라운	Brown
미경	Mi-kyung (female name)
백 (百)	hundred
천 (千)	thousand
책 (冊)	book
-년 (年)	year
-월 (月)	month
-일 (日)	day, date

GRAMMAR AND NOTES

In this lesson we will study
1. Irregular verbs with stems ending in -르
2. Sentence ending: polite informal style -어/아요
3. Future-tense marker -겠- "will," "shall"
4. Question word 왜 "why"
5. Negatives
   a. 안 + VERB "not," "do not"
   b. 못 + VERB "cannot," "not able to"
6. Causal connective -어/아서 "because," "since"
7. Postposition: indirect object marker
   a. -에게 (plain) "to (a person)"
   b. -께 (hon.) "to (an honorific person)"
8. Two-word verbs
   a. -어/아 주다 "to do something for someone" (plain)
   b. -어/아 드리다 (hon.)
9. Concurrent connective -고 "while ——ing"
10. Sentence ending: polite commands -(으)십시오 (hon. formal), -(으)세요 (hon. informal)
11. Chinese characters 百, 千, 冊, 工, 夫, 年, 月, 日
12. Verb chart 2: polite informal endings

1. Irregular verbs with stems ending in -르

Verb stems ending in -르 take another ㄹ before 어 or 아. But note that there is no change before 고.

	-었/았어요	-어/아서	-어/아요	-고
부르다 to call	불렀어요	불러서	불러요	부르고
모르다 to know not	몰랐어요	몰라서	몰라요	모르고
다르다 to be different	달랐어요	달라서	달라요	다르고
흐르다 to flow	흘렀어요	흘러서	흘러요	흐르고

2. Sentence ending: polite informal style -어/아요

This ending indicates that the speaker is polite but informal to the addressee. This style is most frequently used in everyday speech. Although there is no clear distinction between men's and women's speech, men tend to use the polite formal style more than women do, and women use the polite informal style more than men do.

Statements and questions in the polite informal style all have the same verb ending in writing, but they are spoken with different intonations. Statements have a level or falling intonation at the end of the sentence.

이 선생님은 안녕하세요.　　Mr. Lee is fine.

Questions have a rising intonation at the end of the sentence.

이 선생님, 안녕하세요?　　Mr. Lee, how are you?

Here are the rules for choosing between 아요 and 어요:

-아요 is used after a verb with 아 or 오 as the last stem vowel, whether the verb ends in a vowel or a consonant. If it ends in the vowel 아 or 오, the following changes occur:

아 + 아 → 아　　　　to go 가 + 아요 → 가요
오 + 아 → 와　　　　to come 오 + 아요 → 와요

If the verb stem ends in a consonant but the vowel is still 아 or 오, the ending will be -아요.

to be good 좋 + 아요 → 좋아요
to be plentiful 많 + 아요 → 많아요

-어요 is used after a verb with any other vowel as the last stem vowel.

먹 + 어요 → 먹어요　　가르치 + 어요 → 가르쳐요
읽 + 어요 → 읽어요　　가르치시 + 어요 → 가르치셔요
　　　　　　　　　　　(시 + 어 is contracted to 셔) or
있 + 어요 → 있어요　　가르치세요

If the verb stem ends in the vowel 으 or 우, the following changes occur :

으 + 어 → 어   to write 쓰 + 어요 → 써요
우 + 어 → 워   to give 주 + 어요 → 줘요

(See GN6 for further explanation.)

3. Future-tense marker -겠- "will," "shall"

Attached to a verb stem, -겠- indicates the future tense. Sometimes it also expresses intention or will.

출석을 부르겠어요.   (I) will call the roll.
내일 학교에 나오겠어요.   (I) will come (out) to school tomorrow.
내일 테니스(정구)를 치겠어요.   (I) will play tennis tomorrow.

-겠- takes the following place in verb endings :

V. STEM	(HON.)	FUTURE	ENDING	
이 책을 전해 주	시	겠	어요?	Would you deliver this book (for me)?
전해 주		겠	어요.	(I) will deliver (it).

4. Question word 왜 "why"

왜 usually comes at the beginning of a sentence, but it may come any place as long as it is before the verb.

왜 브라운 선생은 오늘 안 나왔어요?   Why is Mr. Brown
브라운 선생은 오늘 왜 안 나왔어요?   not here today?
왜 요즘 바쁘세요?   Why are you busy
요즘 왜 바쁘세요?   these days?

5. Negatives

a. 안 always precedes the verb it negates.

브라운 씨는 오늘 왜 <u>안</u> 나오셨어요?	Why didn't Mr. Brown come out (be present) today?
김 선생님은 상항에 <u>안</u> 가세요.	Mr. Kim does not go to San Francisco.
그분은 편지를 <u>안</u> 쓰세요.	He/she does not write letters.

b. 못 also comes before a verb like 안.

아파서 <u>못</u> 나왔어요.	Because (I) was sick, (I) could not come (out).
김 선생님은 상항에 <u>못</u> 가세요.	Mr. Kim cannot go to San Francisco.
그분은 편지를 <u>못</u> 쓰세요.	He/she cannot write letters.

Note that 못 is not used with 이다 or descriptive verbs (but -지 못하다 is used). See also L13, GN4.

6. Causal connective -어/아서 "because," "since"

This connective, meaning "because," "since," "as," or "for," links two clauses. (See L16, GN4 for sequential use.)

<u>아파서</u> 못 오셨어요.	(He) could not come because (he) was ill.
<u>추워서</u> 저는 안 가요.	I am not going because it is cold.
재미가 <u>있어서</u> 저는 경제학을 공부해요.	I study economics because it is interesting.

Note that, as with -고 "and," the tense is not indicated for the first clause to which the connective -어/아서 is attached. The tense for the first clause is determined by the tense of the second clause.

저는 <u>아파서</u>   공부를 못했어요.
(I *am* sick-because   study   could not)
Because I *was* sick I could not study.

Here are the rules for using -아서 or -어서 and 서:

-아서 is used after a verb with 아 or 오 as the last stem vowel, whether the verb ends in a vowel or a consonant. But if the verb ends in the vowel 아 or 오, the two vowels next to each other, 아 + 아서 or 오 + 아서, are contracted to 아서 or 와서 respectively.

자다 to sleep	자 + 아서 → 자서
오다 to come	오 + 아서 → 와서
보다 to see	보 + 아서 → 봐서 (optional)

-어서 is used after a verb with any other vowel as the last stem vowel, whether the verb ends in a vowel or a consonant. If the verb ends in 으 or 우, the two pairs of vowels 으 + 이 and 우 + 어 will become 어 and 워 respectively. Verbs ending in other vowels do not change.

먹다 to eat	먹 + 어서 → 먹어서
읽다 to read	읽 + 어서 → 읽어서
묶다 to tie	묶 + 어서 → 묶어서
쓰다 to write	쓰 + 어서 → 써서
춥다 to be cold	춥 + 어서 → 추워서 (See L13,GN5.)
두다 to put away	두 + 어서 → 둬서 (optional)
주다 to give	주 + 어서 → 줘서 (optional)

All verbs that have the vowel sequence 아 + 으 or 오 + 으 in the verb stem take -아서.

아프다 to be sick	아프 + 아서 → 아파서
바쁘다 to be busy	바쁘 + 아서 → 바빠서
빠르다 to be quick	빠르 + 아서 → 빨라서*
모르다 not to know	모르 + 아서 → 몰라서*
오르다 to rise	오르 + 아서 → 올라서*
고르다 to select	고르 + 아서 → 골라서*

*See GN1 for the doubling of ㄹ.

You may have noticed that the same rules apply to the past-tense markers (-었- and -았-), the polite informal endings (-어요 and -아요), and the -어/아서 connective. Although they are introduced in different lessons, the rules for choosing either -어 or -아 are founded on the same principle for all -어/아- based formations.

When some verbs such as 주다 or 보다 are used with -어/아 forms, they become auxiliary or modal verbs. See GN8.

7. Postposition: indirect object marker

a. -에게 (plain) "to (a person)"

브라운 씨에게 이 책을 전해 주시겠어요?	Would you give (deliver) this book to Mr. Brown?
제 친구에게 편지를 써요.	(I) am writing a letter to my friend.

b. -께 (hon.) "to (an honorific person)"

어머님께 카드를 보내요.	I am sending a card to my mother.
저는 선생님께 편지를 써요.	(I) am writing a letter to my teacher.

8. Two-word verbs

An action verb can be combined with another verb to take on a special aspect of the action, such as "beneficiary action," "continuous action," "gradual process," and so on.

a. -어/아 주다 "to do something for someone" (plain)

-어/아 주다 combined with an action verb indicates that the action is done for someone's benefit or sake, while the single verb indicates a simple action.

나는 책을 읽었다.	I read the book.
나는 책을 읽어 주었다.	I read the book (for someone).
이 책을 브라운 씨에게 전해 주시겠어요?	Would you please take this book to Mr. Brown (for me)?

b. -어/아 드리다 is the humble expression of -어/아주다 when the beneficiary of the action is an honorific person.

네, <u>전해 드리겠</u>어요.	Yes, I will deliver it to him (for you).
할아버님께 책을 <u>읽어드려</u>요.	I am reading a book to my grandfather.

9. Concurrent connective 고 "while ——ing"

Besides the meaning of "and," -고, when attached to the first clause verb, indicates an action concurrent with the verb in the second clause.

책을 <u>보고</u> 읽으십시요.	(Please read the book aloud while looking at it.) Please read the book.
뻐스를 <u>타고</u> 왔어요.	(I came riding the bus.) I came by bus.
안경을 <u>쓰고</u> 신문을 봤다.	I read the newspaper while wearing my glasses.
한국말을 <u>모르고</u> 한국에 갔다.	I went to Korea without knowing Korean.

10. Sentence ending: polite commands

-(으)십시오 is the politest form of request that goes with the 습니다 style. -(으)세요, the polite informal request, goes with the -어/아요 ending.

	-(으)십시오 *polite formal*	-(으)세요 *polite informal*
읽다 to read	읽으십시오. Would you please read?	읽으세요. Please read.
가다 to go	가십시오. Would you please go?	가세요. Please go.
쓰다 to write	쓰십시오. Would you please write?	쓰세요. Please write.
보다 to see	보십시오. Would you please look?	보세요. Please look.

(See also L1, GN2.)

11. Chinese characters

百	백 백 1,00	一	ア	ア	万	百	百		
千	천 천 1,000	ノ	二	千				
冊	책 책 book	丨	几	丹	冊	冊		
工	장인 공 workman	一	丁	工				
夫	지아비 부 husband man	一	二	夫	夫			
年	해 년 year	ノ	⺊	匕	午	在	年	
月	달 월 moon month	ノ	几	月	月			
日	날 일 sun day	丨	冂	日	日			

12. Verb chart 2: polite informal endings

Dictionary form	현재 present	과거 past	미래 future
가다 to go	가요(plain) 가세요(hon.)	갔어요 가셨어요	가겠어요 가시겠어요
가르치다 to teach	가르쳐요 가르치세요	가르쳤어요 가르치셨어요	가르치겠어요 가르치시겠어요
다니다 to attend	다녀요 다니세요	다녔어요 다니셨어요	다니겠어요 다니시겠어요
공부 일 사업 하다 to do (study, work, business)	공부 일 사업 해요 하세요	공부 일 사업 했어요 하셨어요	공부 일 사업 하겠어요 하시겠어요
오다 to come	와요 오세요	왔어요 오셨어요	오겠어요 오시겠어요
보다 to see	봐요 보세요	봤어요 보셨어요	보겠어요 보시겠어요
읽다 to read	읽어요 읽으세요	읽었어요 읽으셨어요	읽겠어요 읽으시겠어요
살다 to live	살아요 사세요	살았어요 사셨어요	살겠어요 사시겠어요
이다 to be	이에요 이세요	이었어요 이셨어요	이겠어요 이시겠어요
있다 to have	있어요 있으세요	있었어요 있으셨어요	있겠어요 있으시겠어요
있다 to exist	있어요 계세요	있었어요 계셨어요	있겠어요 계시겠어요
좋다 to be good	좋아요 좋으세요	좋았어요 좋으셨어요	좋겠어요 좋으시겠어요
많다 to be many	많아요 많으세요	많았어요 많으셨어요	많겠어요 많으시겠어요
어렵다 to be difficult	어려워요 어려우세요	어려웠어요 어려우셨어요	어렵겠어요 어려우시겠어요
없다 to have not	없어요 없으세요	없었어요 없으셨어요	없겠어요 없으시겠어요

모르다 to know not	⎰ 몰라요 ⎱ 모르세요	몰랐어요 모르셨어요	모르겠어요 모르시겠어요
부르다 to call	⎰ 불러요 ⎱ 부르세요	불렀어요 부르셨어요	부르겠어요 부르시겠어요
걷다 to walk	⎰ 걸어요 ⎱ 걸으세요	걸었어요 걸으셨어요	걷겠어요 걸으시겠어요

연습

A. 다음 질문에 대답하십시오.

1. 오늘 아침에는 누가 출석을 불렀어요?
2. 브라운 씨는 오늘 왜 못 나왔어요?
3. 누가 브라운 씨에게 책을 전해 주겠어요?
4. 미경이는 왜 바빠요?
5. 내일 왜 학교에 안 오겠어요?
6. 어제는 왜 숙제를 못했어요?
7. 오늘 저녁에는 무엇을 하시겠어요?
8. 집에서 무엇을 하시겠어요?
9. 12월에는 왜 바쁘세요?
10. 친구에게 무엇을 주겠어요?

B. "-어/아서"를 사용하여 보기와 같이 두 문장을 연결하십시오. (Combine the two sentences using the connective -어/아서.)

보기: 아파요. ⎫ → 아파서 학교에 못 가겠어요.
학교에 못 가겠어요. ⎭

11. 사람이 많아요. ⎫
버스를 못 타겠어요. ⎭

12. 시험이 있어요. ⎫
영화를 못 봤어요. ⎭

13. 친구가 로스앤젤레스에 있어요. ⎫
자주 못 봐요. (자주: often) ⎭

14. 한국어는 재미있어요. ⎫
공부해요. ⎭

C. "-고"를 사용하여 보기와 같이 두 문장을 연결하십시오.
(Combine the two sentences using -고.)

보기: 영어를 몰랐다. ⎫→ 영어를 모르고 영국에 갔다.
　　　영국에 갔다. ⎭

15. 비행기를 탔다. ⎫
　　 샌프란시스코에 왔다. ⎭

16. 모자를 썼다. ⎫
　　 정구를 쳤다. ⎭

17. 코트를 입었다. ⎫
　　 학교에 갔다. ⎭

18. 공부를 안했다. ⎫
　　 시험을 봤다. ⎭
　　 (시험을 보다: to take a test)

D. 다음 문장을 한국어로 번역하십시오.

19. When *will* you *go* to Russia?
20. Which book *will* you *read?*
21. Where *will* you *be* tomorrow?
22. *Will* you *call* the roll?
23. Please *teach* me (some) Chinese characters.
24. Please *watch* the house *(for me).*
25. Please *come* tomorrow *(for me).*
26. *Please read* the book *all together* (in unison).
27. *Please speak* in Korean.
28. *Please come* in the morning.
29. <u>Because</u> I am a student, I am busy.
30. <u>Because</u> I attend college, I study a lot.

Lesson 9

제 구과 무엇을 하고 있어요?

대화 A

영희: 스미스 씨는 무엇을 하고 있어요?¹

철수: 사무실에서 편지를 쓰고 있어요.

영희: 브라운 선생님은 무엇을 하고 계세요?

철수: 브라운 선생님은 밖에서 친구와 같이² 정구를 치고 계세요.

영희: 김 선생님도 테니스를 치고 계세요?

철수: 잘 모르겠어요.³

Patterns

1. <u>스미스 씨는 편지를 쓰고</u> 있어요.
   _____ 공부를 하_____
   _____ _ 논문을 쓰_____
   _____ 정구를 치_____

2. <u>아버님</u>께서는 무엇을 하고 계세요?
   어머님_____
   선생님_____

3. <u>친구는</u> 테니스를 치고 있어요.
   _____ 피아노_____
   _____ 타자_____

4. <u>밖에서</u> 동생과 같이 테니스를 치고 있어요.
   _____ 친구_____
   _____ 선생님_____
   _____ 형님_____
   _____ 부인_____

92

대화 B

영희: 오늘이 무슨 요일이에요?

철수: 화요일입니다. 내일 저와 같이 테니스를
치시겠어요?

영희: 내일은 못 치고 목요일이 좋겠어요.[4]

철수: 목요일은 제가 바빠서 못 치겠어요. 금요일은
어떠세요.

영희: 금요일도 괜찮아요.

Patterns

1. 오늘이 무슨 요일이에요? 월요일 이에요.
화_____
수_____
목_____

2. 저와 같이 테니스를 치시겠어요?
_____ 도서관에 가_____
_____ 영화를 보_____

낱말

제 구과	Lesson 9
사무실	office
편지	letter
쓰고 있다 (쓰다)	is writing (to write)
밖	outside
친구	friend

테니스/정구	tennis
치고 (치다)	playing (to hit, to play [tennis])
치고 계시다	is playing (hon.)
모르겠어요. (모르다)	I would not know. I don't know.
논문	thesis, paper
피아노	piano
타자기	typewriter
타자(를) 치다	to type
-요일	day (of the the week)
좋겠어요. (좋다)	(It) would be good.
어떠세요? (어떻다)	How is it? (see L25, GN3 for ㅎ- deletion)
괜찮아요. (괜찮다)	(It is) all right.
모레	the day after tomorrow
월요일 (月)	Monday
화요일 (火)	Tuesday
수요일 (水)	Wednesday
목요일 (木)	Thursday
금요일 (金)	Friday
토요일 (土)	Saturday
일요일 (日)	Sunday
주(일)	week
주중	weekdays, middle of the week
주말	weekend
다음 주일	next week
만 (萬)	ten thousand (10,000)

GRAMMAR AND NOTES

In this lesson we will study
1. Continuous action (present tense)
   a. -고 있다 (plain) "... is doing"
   b. -고 계시다 (hon.)
2. Postposition -와/과 같이 "together with," "with"
3. Expressions for
   a. "I don't know (politely)" 모르겠어요
   b. "Do you know/understand?" 아시겠어요?
4. Expressions for "... would be nice," "I would like ..." ... 좋겠어요
5. Expressions for "It's all right," "It's OK" 괜찮아요
6. Chinese characters 火, 水, 木, 金, 土, 萬

1. Continuous action (present tense)

These constructions are used to express a continuous action or event. When the subject is an honorific person, 계시다 is used.

a. -고 있다 (plain) "... is doing"

스미스 씨는 지금 무엇을 하고 있어요?	What is Mr. Smith doing now?
영희는 책을 <u>읽고 있어요</u>.	Young-hie is reading a book.
나는 지금 테니스를 <u>치고 있어요</u>.	I am playing tennis now.

b. -고 계시다 (hon.)

부모님께서는 테니스를 <u>치고 계세요</u>.	My parents are playing tennis.
선생님께서는 편지를 <u>쓰고 계세요</u>.	My teacher is writing a letter.

Postposition -와/과 같이 "together with," "with"

그분은 친구와 같이 테니스를 치고 계세요.	He is playing tennis with his friend.
나는 동생과 같이 일해요.	I work together with my brother.
편지와 같이 책을 보냈어요.	We sent the book with a letter.
저와 같이 집에 가시겠어요?	Would you go home with me?

3. Expressions for "I don't know (politely)" 모르겠어요, "Do you know/understand?" 아시겠어요?

a. 모르겠어요 may mean "I don't know," "I am not sure," or "I don't understand," depending on the context. This expression is commonly used without being offensive to the inquirer. By contrast, 몰라요, which also means "I don't know," might seem rude.

오늘이 몇일이에요?	What is the date today?
모르겠어요.	I don't know.
이것을 아시겠어요?	Do you understand this?
모르겠어요.	No, I do not understand.
금요일이 어때요?	How about Friday?
잘 모르겠어요.	I am not sure. (Literally, "I do not know well.")

b. 아시겠어요? similarly expresses "Do you know (something)?" or "Do you understand?" Since it is a polite question, "Would you know?" or "Would you understand?" would be closer to the true meaning.

그 뜻을 아시겠어요?	Would you understand the meaning?
네, 알겠어요.	Yes, I understand.
이분을 아시겠어요?	Would you know this person?
네, 알겠어요.	Yes, I know him.

4. Expressions for "... would be nice," "I would like ..." ... 좋겠어요

목요일이 <u>좋겠어요</u>.	Thursday would be nice.
저는 금요일이 <u>좋겠어요</u>.	I would like (it) on Friday. (Literally, "As for me, Friday would be nice.")

5. Expressions for "It's all right," "It's OK" 괜찮아요

This is a positive answer to "how about ...?" questions. It is not an enthusiastic answer like "Yes, it is good!"

일요일이 어때요?	How about Sunday?
괜찮아요.	It's all right.
요즈음 어떻게 지내세요?	How are you these days?
괜찮아요.	I am OK.
월요일도 괜찮아요?	Is Monday also OK?
괜찮아요.	It's fine.

6. Chinese characters

火	불 화 fire Tuesday	⼂	⼂ ⼃	少	火			
水	물 수 water Wednesday	丿	刁	汁	水			
木	나무 목 tree Thursday	一	十	才	木			
金	쇠 금 metal Friday	丿	人	仝	仐	仐	仐	金	金
土	흙 토 earth Saturday	一	十	土				
萬	만 만 10,000	丶	亠	丷	艹	茁	萬	萬	萬

연습

"읽기"

I. 저는 버클리 대학교에 다니고 있어요. 학교에서 한국어와
경제학을 공부해요. 저는 한국어가 재미있어요. 경제학은
어려워요. 금요일에는 경제학 시험이 있어서 목요일에는 테니스를
못 치겠어요. 요즈음 숙제도 많고 일도 많아요. 타자기가 없어서
리포트를 손으로 써요. 주말에는 박선생님의 사무실에 가서
타자를 쳐요. (영식)

II. 요즘 날씨가 좋아서 주말에 테니스를 쳤어요. 내일
아침에도 치겠어요. 친구와 같이 정구장에 가서 치겠어요.
토요일에는 부모님께서 집에 안 계셔서 동생을 봐 주겠어요.
동생과 같이 영화관에도 가겠어요. 오늘 저녁에는 할아버지께
편지를 쓰겠어요. 저는 바빠서 편지를 못 썼어요. 지금은
한국어와 수학 숙제를 하고 있어요. 동생은 친구와 같이
텔레비젼을 보고 있어요. (영희)

A. "읽기"를 읽고 다음의 질문에 대답하십시오.
1. 영식이는 무엇을 하고 있어요?
2. 한국어가 어떻습니까? 경제학은요?
3. 영식이는 무엇을 공부해요?
4. 목요일에는 왜 바빠요?
5. 타자기로 무엇을 해요?
6. 영희는 언제 테니스를 쳤어요?
7. 왜 영희는 동생을 봐 주어요?
8. 동생은 누구와 같이 텔레비젼을 보고 있어요?
9. 영희는 누구에게 편지를 쓰겠어요?
10. 왜 영희는 할아버지께 편지를 못 썼어요?

B. 다음 문장을 한국어로 번역하십시오.
11. What *is* Young-hie *doing* now?
12. She *is writing* a letter *in* the office.
13. *To* whom *is* she *writing* a letter?
14. She *is writing* a letter *to* her grandfather.
15. *With* whom *is* Mr. Brown *playing* tennis?
16. He *is playing* tennis *with* my older brother.

17. What *are* the students *doing outside?*
18. They *are also playing* tennis (outside).
19. *Do* you *understand* the question? (Use -겠.)
20. No, I *am not sure.* (I don't know.) (Use -겠.)
21. *What day of the week* do you have the quiz?
22. We have the quiz on *Fridays.*

Lesson 10

제 십과 지금 몇 시에요?

대화

영희: 실례지만[1] 지금 몇[2] 시에요*?

철수: 지금 열두시[3] 에요.

영희: 벌써 점심 때[4]가 됐어요?

철수: 네. 점심 식사하러[5] 나가시겠어요?

영희: 저는 한시 반에 약속이 있어서 지금
　　　나가기[6]가 어렵습니다.

철수: 자, 그럼, 먼저 갑니다.

*이에요 becomes 에요 after a word ending in a vowel.

Patterns

1. <u>실례지만</u> 지금 몇 시에요?
　　_____ 저 분이 누구세요?
　　_____ 저 학생은 누구세요?
　　_____ 저 남자는 누구에요?
　　_____ 저 여자는 누구에요?

2. 토요일이<u>지만</u>　학교에 나갔어요.
　　약속이 있____　못 가요.
　　점심 때가 됐____　식당에 못 갔어요.
　　여섯시가 됐____　집에 못 갔어요.

3. 벌써 점심 때가 됐어요?
   ____ 방학 _____
   ____ 저녁 _____
   ____ 시험 _____
   ____ 크리스마스 ____

4. 몇 시 에요?
   __ 살이에요?
   __ 일_____
   __ 월_____
   __ 년_____

5. 식사하러 나가겠어요.
   일하_____
   테니스 치_____
   영화를 보_____
   저녁을 먹_____

6. 지금 나가기가 어렵습니다.
   신문을 읽_____
   편지를 쓰_____
   타자를 치_____

7. 뻐스를 타기가 쉽습니다.
   일을 다니_____
   한국말을 배우_____
   테니스를 치_____

8. 지금 열두시에요.
   ____ 한시에요.
   ____ 두시에요.
   ____ 세시 반이에요.
   ____ 네시 십오분이에요.
   ____ 다섯시 십분 전이에요.

9. 한 시간 공부했어요.
   두 _____
   여덟 _____
   열 _____

낱말

제 십과	Lesson 10
지금	now
몇-	how many (question word referring to numbers)
시 (時)	o'clock; time
몇 시	what time
실례지만(실례이다)	I am sorry... (to be discourteous) but
열두시	twelve o'clock
벌써	already
점심	noon, lunch
점심 때	lunchtime
됐어요/되었어요.(되다)	(It) became. (to become)
식사하러 (식사하다)	(in order) to have a meal (to eat)
나가시겠어요? (나가다)	Will (you) go out? (to go out)
한시	one o'clock
반 (半)	half
약속	promise, appointment
자	well, then
먼저	ahead, first
미안하지만 (미안히다)	I am sorry but...(to be sorry)
방학	school vacation
크리스마스	Christmas
-살	—— year(s) old (두살: two years old)
-개	—— item(s), piece(s) (세개: three items)
보러 (보다)	(in order) to see, (to see)
먹으러 (먹다)	(in order) to eat, (to eat)
배우기 (배우다)	learning (to learn)
쉽습니다. (쉽다)	(It) is easy. (to be easy)
-장	piece (of paper, or flat item)

오전	morning, A.M.
오후	afternoon, P.M.
-분 (分)	minute
남자 (男子)	man, male
여자 (女子)	woman, female
시간	time, hour

GRAMMAR AND NOTES

In this lesson we will study
1. Concessive connective -지만 "even though," "although," "but"
2. Question word 몇 - "how many?"
3. Telling time
4. Dependent noun -때 "time," "when," "during"
5. Sentence connective (으)러 "in order to," "for," "for the sake of"
6. Nominalizer V. STEM + 기
7. Korean numbers and noun counters
8. Chinese characters 男, 女, 子, 時, 半, 分

1. Concessive connective -지만 "even though," "although," "but"

Attached to the verb of the first clause, -지만 expresses the idea "although," or "even though."

실례(이)지만 　지금 　몇시(이)에요?
(am sorry-*but* 　now 　what time is it?)
Excuse me, but what time is it now?

그분을 모르지만 　　　만나겠어요.
(do not know him-*although* 　will meet.)
Although I do not know him, I will meet him.

토요일이지만 집에 있겠어요.　It is Saturday, but I will stay home.

약속이 있었지만 못 갔어요.　Although I had an appointment, I could not go.

2. Question word 몇- "how many?"

This question word for quantity is used when the answer requires a number.

몇 시 지금 몇 시에요?	what time What time is it?
몇 개 몇 개 있어요?	how many (items) How many do you have?
몇 사람 몇 사람이 있어요?	how many persons How many people are there?
며칠* 며칠 계세요?	how many days How many days will you be there?
몇 일* 오늘은 몇 일이에요?	what day (date) What is the date today?
몇 살 몇 살이에요?	how many years old How old are you?
몇 월 몇 월이에요?	what month What month is it now?
몇 년 몇 년이에요?	what year What year is it?
몇 장 편지를 몇 장 썼어요?	how many sheets How many (sheets of) letters did you write?

* Note the differences in spelling between "how many days" 며칠 and "what date" 몇일.

3. Telling time

The time is always read hour first, minute second, and second last. For telling the time, both Korean and Sino-Korean numbers are used.

a. Hours are read in Korean numbers (See GN7).

한시	one o'clock	일곱시	seven o'clock
두시	two o'clock	여덟시	eight o'clock
세시	three o'clock	아홉시	nine o'clock
네시	four o'clock	열시	ten o'clock
다섯시	five o'clock	열한시	eleven o'clock
여섯시	six o'clock	열두시	twelve o'clock

b. Minutes and seconds are read in Sino-Korean numbers.

9:05	아홉시 오분	2:15	두시 십오분
8:20	여덟시 이십분	4:45	네시 사십오분
12:06:27	열두시 육분 이십칠초	3:01:10	세시 일분 십초

Time words such as 시 "hour," 분 "minute," and 초 "second" must not be omitted as they are in English (e.g., "ten thirty").

c. Half past the hour can be read in two ways, using 반 "half" or 삼십분 "thirty minutes."

2:30   두시 반 or 두시 삼십분
4:30   네시 반 or 네시 삼십분

d. Before or to the hour is expressed by 전 "before."

3:55   네시 오분 전 (= 세시 오십오분)
9:50   열시 십분 전 (= 아홉시 오십분)

e. A.M. and P.M. are expressed by 오전 "before noon" and 오후 "after noon." They always precede the time.

2:15 A.M. 오전 두시 십오분   2:15 P.M. 오후 두시 십오분
7:00 A.M. 오전 일곱시   7:00 P.M. 오후 일곱시

f. The optional "exactly" is expressed by 정각.

8:00 A.M. exactly   오전 여덟시 정각
12:00 P.M. exactly   오후 열두시 정각

4. Dependent noun -때 "time," "when," "during"

A number of special nouns, which we call "dependent nouns," cannot be used by themselves. The dependent noun -때 always follows a time noun such as 점심 "lunch," 세 살 "three years old," 방학 "vacation," and so on. (-것 is also a dependent noun, since it cannot be used alone. See L5, GN7.)

점심 때	lunchtime
저녁 때	in the evening (evening time)
세 살 때	when (I) was three (three years old)
방학 때	vacation time
점심 때 그분을 만났다.	I met him during the lunch hour.
저녁 때 책을 읽는다.	In the evening I read books.
세 살 때 중국에 있었다.	When I was three, I was in China.
크리스마스 때 스키를 갔다.	During Christmas time I went skiing.
방학 때 한자를 배우겠다.	During the vacation I will learn Chinese characters.

5. Sentence connective -(으)러 "in order to," "for," "for the sake of"

Attached to a verb stem, -(으)러 indicates "purpose" or "goal" and is used with verbs of directional motion such as 가다 "to go," 오다 "to come," and 다니다 "to attend."

-러 is used after a verb stem ending in a vowel or ㄹ.
-으러 is used for all other verb stems.

점심 <u>먹으러</u>   같이   나가시겠어요?
(lunch eat-*in order to* with   go out?)
Would you like to go out (with me in order) to have lunch?

영어를 <u>배우러</u>   미국에   가겠어요.
(English learn-*in order to*   U.S.   will go)
I will go to the U.S. to learn English.

동생은 <u>놀러</u>   나갔어요.
(younger brother play-*in order to*   went out)
My younger brother went out to play.

6. Nominalizer V. STEM + 기

Attached to a verb stem, this suffix turns a verb into a noun. Nouns made from verbs, or verbal nouns, are used as the subject of descriptive verbs such as "difficult," "easy," "interesting," "good," and so on, or as the direct object of transitive verbs such as "do." But not all transitive verbs can use the noun form of -기.

Verb		*Verbal noun*	
나가다	to go out	나가기	going out
쓰다	to write	쓰기	writing
읽다	to read	읽기	reading
걷다	to walk	걷기	walking
말하다	to speak	말하기	speaking
듣다	to hear	듣기	hearing/to hear

<u>나가기가</u> 어렵다.	It is difficult to go out.
한글은 <u>쓰기가</u> 어렵다.	Korean is difficult to write.
지금 <u>말하기가</u> 어렵다.	It is hard to talk now.
노어는 <u>배우기가</u> 어렵다.	Russian is hard to learn.
그 음악은 <u>듣기가</u> 좋다.	That music is nice to listen to.
길을 <u>걷기가</u> 어렵다.	It is difficult to walk on the street.
이 책은 <u>읽기가</u> 쉽다.	It is easy to read this book.

7. Korean numbers and noun counters

In addition to Sino-Korean numbers (see L7), there is a set of native Korean numbers, 1 to 99. In general, Korean numbers are used with native Korean words and Sino-Korean numbers are used with Sino-Korean words. Sometimes, however, the two sets of numbers are used strictly by the rules of convention. The use of Korean numbers for hours and Sino-Korean numbers for minutes and seconds is one such example. Sino-Korean numbers are preferred for numbers above 20.

Arabic numerals	Korean numerals	Time (o'clock)	Hour(s)	Minute(s)	Second(s)
1	하나	한시	한 시간	일분	일초
2	둘	두시	두 시간	이분	이초
3	셋	세시	세 시간	삼분	삼초
4	넷	네시	네 시간	사분	사초
5	다섯	다섯시	다섯 시간	오분	오초
6	여섯	여섯시	여섯 시간	육분	육초
7	일곱	일곱시	일곱 시간	칠분	칠초
8	여덟	여덟시	여덟 시간	팔분	팔초
9	아홉	아홉시	아홉 시간	구분	구초
10	열	열시	열 시간	십분	십초
11	열 하나	열한시	열 한 시간	십일분	십일초
12	열 둘	열두시	열 두 시간	십이분	십이초
20	스물			이십분	이십초
30	서른			삼십분	삼십초
40	마흔			사십분	사십초
50	쉰			오십분	오십초
60	예순			육십분	육십초
70	일흔			칠십분	칠십초
80	여든			팔십분	팔십초
90	아흔			구십분	구십초
100	백			백분	백초

As in many Asian languages, Korean uses "noun counters" or "classifiers," which are added to the number when counting things. These counters are usually dependent nouns that cannot be used alone. The counting numbers are usually Korean numbers.

-살 "years old" is always used with Korean numbers.

-개 "item" or "piece" is used with Korean numbers for small quantities and Sino-Korean numbers for large quantities.

-사람 "person" is used with Korean numbers.

Note the phonetic change of 하나 into 한, 둘 into 두, 셋 into 세, and 스물 into 스무 when used with counters.

-살	*Age*	사람	*Person*	-개	*Item*
한 살	1 year old	한 사람	1 person	한 개	1 item
두 살	2 years old	두 사람	2 persons	두 개	2 items
열다섯 살	15 years old	열 사람	10 persons	일곱 개	7 items
스무 살	20 years old	서른 사람	30 persons	마흔 세 개	43 items
여든 살	80 years old				

8. Chinese characters

男	남자 남 male man	丶	冂	日	田	田	甼	男	
女	여자 여 female woman	く	女	女					
子	아들 자 son child	了	了	子					
時	때 시 time hour	刂	日	日丷	日丷	昨	時	時	時
半	반 반 half	丶	丷	丷	半	半			
分	나눌 분 divide minute	丿	八	分	分				

연습

A. 다음 질문에 대답하십시오.
   1. 영희는 왜 지금 나가기가 어려워요?
   2. 지금 몇 시에요?
   3. 몇 시에 점심 식사를 하세요?
   4. 점심을 먹으러 어디에 가요?
   5. 왜 한국 신문을 읽기가 어려워요?
   6. 오늘은 몇 월, 몇 일이에요?
   7. 학생은 몇 살이에요?
   8. 몇 시에 약속이 있어요?
   9. 어제는 몇 시간 공부했어요?
   10. 이 교실에 여학생이 몇 사람 있어요?
       남학생은요?

B. 다음 문장을 끝마치십시오. (Complete the sentences.)
   11. 어제는 월요일이었지만 _____
   12. 내일은 주말이지만   _____
   13. 친구와 약속이 있지만 _____
   14. 시간이 없었지만   _____
   15. 숙제가 많겠지만   _____
   16. 방학 때가 됐지만   _____
   17. 공부를 많이 했지만   _____
   18. 한국어는 어렵지만   _____
   19. 쓰기는 쉽지만   _____
   20. 요즘은 바쁘지만   _____

C. 지금 몇 시에요?
   21. It is 3:04 P.M.   24. It is 2:36 A.M.
   22. It is 12:07 A.M.   25. It is 6:30 A.M.
   23. It is 5:20 P.M.   26. It is 10:45 A.M.

D. 다음 문장을 한국어로 번역하십시오.
   27. Will you go to a Korean restaurant *to have dinner* with me? (Use -[으]러)
   28. I will go to the library *to read* the newspaper.
   29. I will go to Japan *to learn* Japanese.

30. Hangŭl is easy *to read and write.* (Use -기.)
31. *Although it is difficult to learn Korean,* it is fun. (Use -기 and -지만.)
32. I have an appointment at *2:00 P.M.*
33. Please go *ahead.*
34. Please read *ahead.*
35. It *is (has become)* already *5:00 P.M.* (Use 되다.)
36. It *is* already December.
37. It *is* already vacation time.
38. Where did you live *when* you were *ten years old?*

Lesson 11

제 십일과 소풍

어제는 날씨도 좋고 노는[1] 날이어서 친구와 같이 시외에 나갔다.[2] 남대문에서 뻐스를 타고 한 시간 동안 갔다. 우리는 관악산 앞에서 내려서 걷기[3] 시작했다.[4] 산에는 큰 나무들과 바위들이 많이 있었다. 또한 맑은 공기와 시원한 바람이 참 상쾌했다. 점심을 먹고 좀 쉰 후에[5] 돌아왔다.

철수: 주말을 어떻게 지내셨어요?

브라운: 토요일에는 영화를 보고 일요일에는 관악산에 갔어요.

철수: 관악산이 멀어요?

브라운: 아니요. 뻐스로 한 시간쯤 가요.

철수: 등산하는 사람들이 많았어요?

브라운: 네, 날씨가 좋아서 사람들이 꽤 많았어요.

Patterns

1. 오늘은 노는 날이다.
   _____ 쉬_____
   _____ 공부하_____
   _____ 일하_____
   _____ 등산 가_____

112

2. 맑은 공기
   시원한 바람
   상쾌한 바람
   좋은 날씨
   큰 나무
   등산하는 사람들

3. 쉰 후에 돌아왔다.
   일한 _____
   점심을 먹은 ____
   좀 걸은 _____
   잘 논 _____

4. 걷기 시작했다.
   뛰_____
   한자를 배우_____
   돌아오_____
   뻐스에서 내리_____

5. 뻐스를 타고 한 시간 동안 갔다.
   기차_____
   비행기_____
   배_____
   자동차_____

6. 점심을 먹고 좀 쉬었다.
   숙제를 하_____
   한 시간 (동안) 뛰_____
   일을 하_____

7. 몇 시간 걸었어요?
   한 시간 걸었어요.
   두 시간 반 ____
   세 시간 _____

8. 주말을 어떻게 지내셨어요?
   관악산에 _____ 가셨어요?
   시외에 _____ 나가셨어요?
   어려운 일을 _____ 시작하셨어요?

낱말

제 십일과	Lesson 11
소풍	picnic
날씨	weather
시외 (市外)	suburb (literally "outside the city")
남대문 (南大門)	Nam-dai-moon, Great South Gate
-동안	duration, period, while
시작하다	to start, to begin
산 (山)	mountain
크다	to be big
나무	tree
바위	rock
또한	also
맑다	to be clear
공기	air
시원하다	to be (refreshingly) cool
바람	wind
참	very
상쾌하다	to be refreshing
점심	lunch
-후	after
돌아오다	to come back
관악산	Kwan-ak Mountain
멀다	to be far
-쯤	about
등산하다	to go mountain climbing
꽤	quite, somewhat
걷다	to walk
뛰다	to run
내리다	to get off
기차	train
비행기	airplane
배	ship, boat

자동차	car
시간 (時間)	time (period), hour, class (한국어 시간: Korean class)
공원	park

GRAMMAR AND NOTES

In this lesson we will study
1. Verbal modifiers (similar to relative clauses)
    a. Action-verb modifiers -는 and -ㄴ/은
    b. Descriptive-verb modifiers -ㄴ/은
2. Sentence endings: plain-style statements
    a. Present tense -다, -ㄴ다, -는다
    b. Past tense -었다, -았다, -ㅆ다
3. Irregular ㄷ/ㄹ alternating verbs
4. Construction of -기 시작하다 "begin to," "start to"
5. Expression for "after doing ... " -ㄴ/은 후(에)
6. Chinese characters 山, 市, 外, 大, 門, 間
7. Verb chart 3: verbal modifiers

1. Verbal modifiers (similar to relative clauses)

There are no relative pronouns in Korean. The work of English relative clauses is done by verbal modifiers. These verb forms modify or describe nouns and noun phrases. In a sentence the modifier generally precedes the modified.

There are distinct verbal modifiers for present, past, and future tenses. In this lesson we will discuss only present and past verbal modifiers. (For future verbal modifiers, see L15, GN1.)

a. Action-verb modifiers -는 and -ㄴ/은

Action verbs have -는 and -ㄴ/은 verbal modifier forms. -는 forms indicate present tense or continuous actions without specific reference to time, as in the English -ing form of verbs. -ㄴ/은 forms indicate simple past tense.

	-는 *present/continuous*	-ㄴ/은 *past*
놀다* to play	노는 날 (playing day) holiday	논 날 (rested day) day off (in the past)
지나가다 to go by	지나가는 사람 person passing by	지나간 사람 person who passed by
일하다 to work	일하는 학생 working student	일한 학생 student who worked

*놀다: ㄹ drops before ㄴ, ㅅ, or ㅂ (see L6, GN1).

노는 날 소풍을 갔다.	We went on a picnic for the holiday (playing day).
논 날이 없다.	I have never been absent. (There is no day I rested.)
지나가는 사람이 많다.	There are many passers by. (There are many people who go by.)
지나간 사람이 많다.	There are many people who went by (here).
저 학생이 도서관에서 일하는 학생이다.	He is the student who works in the library (present).
저 학생이 도서관에서 일한 학생이다.	He is the student who worked in the library (past).
교실에서 책을 읽는 학생에게 이 신문을 전해 주세요.	Please give this newspaper to the student who is reading a book in the classroom.

b. Descriptive-verb modifiers -ㄴ/은

The descriptive-verb modifiers, like English adjectives, always precede nouns. The present- and past-tense forms are the same. Both are formed by adding -ㄴ or -은 after the stem. (-는 is not used for descriptive verbs.) For additional modifier forms, see verb chart 3 in GN7.

Descriptive verb	Modifier form	Example
시원하다 to be cool	시원한 cool	시원한 날씨 cool weather
작다 to be small	작은 small	작은 아이 small child
맑다 to be clear	맑은 clear	맑은 공기 clear air

2. Sentence endings: plain-style statements

So far we have learned two styles of speech, *polite formal* and *polite informal.*

The third style, *plain,* has the simplest verb endings. This style is used among children, with close friends who are social equals, and by a social superior to a social inferior.

a. Present tense -다, -ㄴ다, -는다

-다 is used after a descriptive-verb ending.

-ㄴ다 is used after an action-verb stem ending in a vowel.

-는다 is used after an action-verb stem ending in a consonant.

Descriptive verb	Action verb	
-다	-ㄴ다	-는다
이것은 크다.	우리는 학교에 간다.	우리는 책을 읽는다.
This is big.	We go to school.	We read books.
저것은 작다.	저기에 차가 온다.	우리는 점심을 먹는다.
That is small.	There is a car coming.	We are eating lunch.
공기가 시원*하다.	나는 한국어를 공부*한다.	
The air is cool.	I study Korean.	
날씨가 상쾌하다.	우리는 네 시간 일한다.	
It is refreshing.	We work four hours.	

* Note that the verb 하다 "to do" ends in -하다 for descriptive verbs and -한다 for action verbs.

b. Past tense -았다, -었다, -ㅆ다

Past-tense sentence endings follow the rules of 아/어 (see L7, GN3 and 9):

-았다 is used after a verb whose stem vowel is 아 or 오; contractions occur when two vowels come together.

-었다 is used after a verb whose stem vowel is other than 아 and 오; contractions occur when two vowels come together.

-ㅆ다 is used after verbs ending in 아 or 어 as a result of vowel contractions.

Unlike the present tense, the past tense does not distinguish between descriptive verbs and action verbs.

Descriptive verbs	*Action verbs*	
-았다/었다	-았다/었다	-ㅆ다
그 산이 멀었다. (멀다)	우리는 걸었다. (걷다)	우리는 책방에서 책을 샀다.(사다)
The mountain was far.	We walked.	We bought books in a bookstore.
공기가 맑았다 (맑다)	나는 책을 읽었다.(읽다)	나는 뻐스를 탔다.(타다)
The air was clean.	I read the book.	I got on the bus.
날씨가 좋았다. (좋다)	나는 수요일에 일을 안했다.(하다)	나는 다섯시에 돌아 갔다.(가다)
The weather was nice.	I didn't work on Wednesday.	I returned at 5:00.

Honorific plain statements are expressed by -(으)신다 for present tense and by -(으)셨다 for past.

부모님은 소풍을 <u>가신다</u>.	My parents are going on a picnic.
부모님은 소풍을 <u>가셨다</u>.	My parents went on a picnic.

선생님은 산에서 <u>돌아오신다</u>.	My teacher returns from the mountain.
선생님은 산에서 <u>돌아오셨다</u>.	My teacher returned from the mountain.

그분들은 공원에서 <u>걸으신다</u>.	They are walking in the park.
그분들은 공원에서 <u>걸으셨다</u>.	They walked in the park.

3. Irregular ㄷ/ㄹ alternating verbs

In some verbs with the stem ending in ㄷ, ㄷ changes to ㄹ when a vowel suffix such as -었/았, -으시, or -으면 follows. ㄷ remains when a consonant suffix follows.

a. With vowel suffixes:

	-은 (v. mod., past)	-었/았 (past)	-으시 (hon.)	-으면 (if)	-으러 (in order to)
듣다 to hear	들은	들었다	들으시	들으면	들으러
걷다 to walk	걸은	걸었다	걸으시	걸으면	걸으러
묻다 to ask	물은	물었다	물으시	물으면	물으러

b. With consonant suffixes:

	-기 (nominalizer)	-겠 (future)	-는 (v. mod., present)
듣다	듣기	듣겠다	듣는
걷다	걷기	걷겠다	걷는
묻다	묻기	묻겠다	묻는

c. The regular verbs that do not alternate include 받다 "to receive," 얻다 "to obtain," and 닫다 "to close."

4. Construction of -기 시작하다 **"begin to," "start to"**

The verb 시작하다 "to begin" is always preceded by the nominalizer -기 if it is not preceded by a noun.

우리는 걷기 시작했다.	We began to walk.
우리는 쉬기 시작했다.	We started to rest.
그분은 세시에 일하기 시작했다.	She started to work at 3 o'clock.

5. Expression for "after doing ... " -ㄴ/은 후(에)

-후 "after" is always used with the past-tense verbal modifiers -ㄴ or -은, even if the event is in the future.

소풍에서 돌아온 후에 한 시간 동안 쉬었다.	After I came back from the picnic, I rested for an hour.
소풍에서 돌아온 후에 한 시간 동안 쉬겠다.	After I come back from the picnic, I will rest for an hour.

버스를 <u>탄</u> <u>후</u>에 책을   After getting on the bus,
읽기 <u>시작했다</u>.   I started to read the book.

피아노를 한 시간   Every day after playing piano
친후에 저녁을 <u>먹는다</u>.   for an hour, I eat dinner.

The word 후 is also used with nouns or noun phrases to indicate "after."

열두시 <u>후</u>에 점심을   I will eat lunch after 12
먹겠어요.   o'clock.

이년 후에 한국에   I will go to Korea in two
가겠어요.   years.

6. Chinese characters

山	뫼 산 mountain	ㅣ	凵	山				
市	저자 시 시장 city	﹑	亠	宀	市	市		
外	바깥 외 outside	ノ	夕	夕	列	外		
大	큰 대 big great	一	大	大				
門	문 문 door	｜	冂	冂	冂	冂	門	門	門
間	사이 간 space	冂	門	門	閒	閒	間		

7. Verb chart 3: verbal modifiers

	dictionary form	present v.mod.	past v.mod.
	ACTION VERBS		
to go	가다	가는	간
to work	일하다	일하는	일한
to buy	사다	사는	산
to sleep	자다	자는	잔
to do	하다	하는	한
to pass the time	지내다	지내는	지낸
to stand	서다	서는	선
to come	오다	오는	온
to see	보다	보는	본
to write	쓰다	쓰는	쓴
to call	부르다	부르는	부른
not to know	모르다	모르는	모른
to stay (hon.)	계시다	계시는	계신
to get off	내리다	내리는	내린
to become	되다	되는	된
to jump	뛰다	뛰는	뛴
to rest	쉬다	쉬는	쉰
to eat	먹다	먹는	먹은
to walk	걷다	걷는	걸은
to play	놀다	노는	논
to blow	불다	부는	분
to live	살다	사는	산
to know	알다	아는	안
to exist/have	있다	있는	있은
to read	읽다	읽는	읽은
to sit	앉다	앉는	앉은

	DESCRIPTIVE VERBS	
	dictionary form	*past & present v. mod.*
to be refreshing	상쾌하다	상쾌한
to be cool	시원하다	시원한
to be	이다	인
to be fast	빠르다	빠른
to be big	크다	큰
to be small	작다	작은
to be far	멀다	먼
to be cold	춥다	추운
to be difficult	어렵다	어려운
to be good	좋다	좋은
to be red	빨갛다	빨간*
to be yellow	노랗다	노란
to be blue	파랗다	파란
to be white	희다/하얗다	흰/하얀
to be black	까맣다	까만
to be in some manner	어떻다	어떤
to be plenty	많다	많은
to be clear	맑다	맑은

* See irregular ㅎ- deleting verbs in L24, GN3.

연습

A. "소풍"을 읽고 다음 질문에 대답하십시오.
   1. 브라운 씨는 어제 어디에 나갔어요?
   2. 어디에서 뻐스를 탔어요?
   3. 어디에서 뻐스를 내렸어요?
   4. 산에는 무엇이 많이 있었어요?
   5. 언제 돌아왔어요?
   6. 언제 등산을 하기가 좋아요?
   7. 언제 한국어 공부를 시작했어요?
   8. 언제 일을 하기 시작했어요?

9. 점심을 먹은 후에 어디에 가겠어요?

10. 한국어 시간 후에 무엇을 하겠어요?

B. 다음 문장을 끝마치십시오. (Complete the sentences.)

11. 재미없는 영화지만 _____

12. 기숙사에 사는 학생들은 _____

13. 나무가 없는 산에는 _____

14. 날씨가 좋은 날에는 _____

15. 나무와 바위들이 많은 산에서 _____

16. 한국에 계신 부모님께 _____

17. 친구가 많은 학생 _____

18. 비행기를 타고 _____

19. 집에 돌아온 후 _____

20. _____ 기 시작했다.

C. 다음 문장을 한국어로 번역하십시오.

21. I *began to study* Korean in August.

22. *After I did* my homework, I went outside.

23. What will you do *after eating* dinner?

24. Which (one) is the book *that you bought* yesterday?

25. *After walking* for an hour, I rested for half an hour.

26. *After learning Korean* for one year, I will go to Korea.

27. It was *difficult to walk* because there were many rocks.

28. The wind was *cool and refreshing*.

29. The air is *clear* in the mountains.

30. The air is clear *where there are* many trees.

Lesson 12

제 십이과 박물관

어느 일요일 오후, 우리는 골든게이트 공원에 있는
아세아 미술관을 찾기로 했다.[1] 이 유명한 박물관에는
동양의 좋은 그림과 예술품이 많이 있다[2]고 들었기
때문이다.[3] 그러나 우리는 길을 잘 몰라서 지나가는
사람에게 물어 보기[4]로 했다.

철수: 골든게이트 공원을 어떻게 갑니까?

행인: 이 길로 똑바로 가서 오가에서 왼쪽으로[5] 가세요.
　　　그러면 곧 공원이 나옵니다.

철수: 공원에서 박물관까지[6] 멀어요?

행인: 아니요. 한 십분만[7] 걸으면[8] 됩니다.

철수: 고맙습니다.

행인: 천만에요. 구경 잘 하십시오.

Patterns

1. 공원에 있는 아세아 미술관에 갔다.
   　학교＿＿＿＿＿＿＿＿＿＿＿＿＿＿＿
   　샌프란시스코＿＿＿＿＿＿＿＿＿＿＿
   　서울＿＿＿＿＿＿＿＿＿＿＿＿＿＿＿
   　북경＿＿＿＿＿＿＿＿＿＿＿＿＿＿＿

2. 박물관을 찾기로 했다.
   　백화점＿＿＿＿＿＿＿＿＿＿＿＿＿
   　파고다 공원＿＿＿＿＿＿＿＿＿＿
   　기숙사에 있는 친구＿＿＿＿＿＿
   　사무실에 계신 선생님＿＿＿＿＿

3. 그 뉴스를 들었기 때문이다.
   그 영화를 못 봤_____
   그 길을 몰랐_____
   날씨가 좋았_____
   그 책이 재미있_____

4. 예술품이 많이 있다고 한다.
   그 그림이 좋다_____
   시간이 없다_____
   공원이 가깝다_____
   그 남자가 학생이라_____
   그 집이 친구의 집이라____

5. 예술품이 많이 있다고 들었다.
   그 그림이 유명하다_____
   십분만 걸으면 된다_____
   길을 잘 모른다_____
   오가에서 왼쪽으로 가면 된다_____
   곧 공원이 나온다_____

6. 지나가는 사람에게 물어 봤다.
   한국어 책을 읽어 _____
   아세아 미술관을 찾아 _____
   명동 거리를 걸어 _____
   한글로 편지를 써 _____

7. 왼쪽으로 가세요.
   오른쪽_____
   남쪽_____
   동쪽_____
   서쪽_____
   북쪽_____
   저쪽_____
   이쪽_____

8. 십분만 걸으면 돼요.
   지나가는 사람에게 물어 보면 ____
   책만 읽어보면 _____
   왼쪽으로 가면 _____
   아세아 미술관만 보면 _____

9. 공원에서 박물관까지 멀어요?
   서울___ 부산_____
   여기___ 나성_____

10. 세시부터 네시까지 박물관을 구경했어요.
    일월___ 삼월___ 도쿄에 있었어요.
    1980년___ 1990년___ 가르쳤어요.

낱말

제 십이과	Lesson 12
박물관	museum
어느	some ——, one —— (어느날: one day)
아세아 미술관	Asian Art Museum
동양 (東洋)	Orient
찾다	to seek, to find, to visit
유명(有名)한	famous (유명하다: to be famous)
그림	painting (좋은 그림: nice/good painting)
예술품	art objects, artwork
듣다	to hear, to listen
-기 때문에	because (때문에: because)
길	road, street, way
지나가다	to pass by, to go by
묻다	to ask, to inquire, to question
어디로	to where, to which direction
행인	passerby, pedestrian
똑바로	straight ahead, straight
왼쪽	left side, leftward
오른쪽/바른쪽	right side, right direction
곧	immediately, right away
나오다	to come out, to appear
멀다	to be distant, to be far
-만	only
-(으)면	if, when

-(으)면 되다	will do if
천만 (千萬)에요	not at all
구경	sightseeing
구경하다	to sightsee, to see (scenery, a movie, etc.)
서울	Seoul
북경	Beijing
파고다 공원	Pagoda Park
가깝다	to be close, to be near
명동거리	Myung-dong Blvd. (a busy section of downtown Seoul)
동쪽 (東)	east
서쪽 (西)	west
남쪽 (南)	south
북쪽 (北)	north
-까지	until, up to
부산	Pusan
나성	Los Angeles
-부터	from
도쿄	Tokyo

GRAMMAR AND NOTES

In this lesson we will study
1. Construction of v. STEM + 기로 하다 "to decide to," "to plan to"
2. Reported speech
   a. -(이)라고 하다 "They say that something/someone is ... "
   b. -다고 하다 "It is said that ... "
3. Constructions for "because"
   a. V .+ 기 때문이다 "It is because ... "
   b. N. + 때문이다 "It is because of (something)"
   c. V. + 기 때문에 "because ... "
   d. N. + 때문에 "because of (something)"

4. Two-word verb -어/아 보다 "to try to," "to have an experience of"
5. Postposition: direction marker -(으)로 "to," "through," "toward"
6. Postposition -까지 "to," "up to," "until," "by"
7. Postposition -만 "only," "just"
8. Conditional connective -(으)면 "if," "when"
9. Points of the compass
10. Chinese characters 東, 西, 南, 北, 洋, 有, 名

1. Construction of V. STEM + 기로 하다 "to decide to," "to plan to"

Attached to a verb, this construction indicates a decision to do something. The verb ending is usually used in the past-tense form -기로 했다.

우리는 그분에게 물어 보기로 했다.	We decided to ask him.
우리는 로스앤젤레스에 살기로 했다.	We decided to live in Los Angeles.
그들은 공원을 구경하기로 했다.	They decided to go sightseeing in the park.
나는 그분의 이야기를 듣기로 했다.	I decided to listen to his story.
우리는 동양 박물관을 보기로 했다.	We planned to see the Oriental Museum.

2. Reported speech

These constructions indicate that the information given in the statement is a reported event rather than the speaker's firsthand knowledge.

a. -(이)라고 하다 "They say that something/someone is . . . " This construction is used after a sentence ending in 이다 "to be" for present tense *only*. The past tense 이었다 does not change to -라고 하다. See **b** below.

Simple statement	Reported speech
이것들은 좋은 그림들<u>이다</u>.	이것들은 좋은 그림들<u>이라고</u> <u>한다</u>.
These are nice paintings.	(They) say that these are nice paintings.
그 박물관은 디영 박물관 <u>이다</u>.	그 박물관은 디영 박물관 <u>이라고 한다</u>.
The museum is called the de Young Museum.	(They) say that the museum is called the de Young Museum.
그것은 한국 영화<u>(이)다.</u>	그것은 한국 영화<u>(이)라고</u> <u>한다</u>.
It is a Korean movie.	(They) say that it is a Korean movie.
그것이 아세아 미술관<u>이다</u>.	그것이 아세아 미술관<u>이라고</u> <u>한다</u>.
It is the Asian Art Museum.	(They) say that it is the Asian Art Museum.

b. -다고 하다 "It is said that ... "

This construction is used after other verbs and after 이다 "to be" in all but the present tense.

Simple statement	Reported speech
그사람은 유명한 예술가 <u>이었다</u>.	그 사람은 유명한 예술가<u>이</u> <u>었다고 한다</u>.
He was a famous artist.	(They) say that he was a famous artist.
공원에서 박물관을 <u>찾았다</u>.	공원에서 박물관을 <u>찾았다고</u> <u>한다</u>.
They found the museum in the park.	(They) say that they found the museum in the park.
좋은 그림이 많이 <u>있다</u>.	좋은 그림이 많이 <u>있다고</u> <u>한다</u>.
There are many good paintings.	(They) say that there are many nice paintings.
공원이 여기에서 <u>멀다</u>.	공원이 여기에서 <u>멀다고 한다</u>.
The park is far from here.	(They) say that the park is far from here.

그 소식을 <u>들었다</u>.	그 소식을 <u>들었다고 한다</u>.
They heard the news.	(They) say that they heard the news.

3. Constructions for "because"

When 때문 comes after a verb, the verb must be changed to a verbal noun with -기 (see L10, GN6), after which 때문 follows. It indicates a causal effect.

a. V. + 기 때문이다 "It is because ... "

우리는 박물관을 찾기로 했다.	We decided to visit the museum.
그 박물관에는 좋은 그림들이 많이 있다고 <u>들었기</u> <u>때문이다</u>.	It is because we heard that there are many good paintings in the museum.
우리는 공원에서 산책하지 못 했다.	We could not take a walk in the park.
길을 <u>몰랐기 때문이다</u>.	It is because we did not know our way around.

b. N. + 때문이다 "It is because of (something)"

공원에 못 간다.	I cannot go to the park.
<u>숙제 때문이다</u>.	It is because of homework.
박물관에 갔다.	We went to the museum.
유명한 예술품 <u>때문이다</u>.	It is because of the famous arts (and crafts).

c. V. + 기 때문에 "because"

뻐스를 타<u>기</u> 어려웠<u>기</u> <u>때문에</u> 백화점에 못 갔다.	We could not go to the department store because it was difficult to ride the bus.
공원이 유명하<u>기 때문에</u> 사람들이 많다.	There are many people in the park because it is famous.

d. N. + 때문에 "because of (something)"

친구 때문에 한국어를 공부한다.	(I) study Korean because of my friend.
안개 때문에 샌프란시스코를 구경 못 했다.	We could not sightsee (in) San Francisco because of the fog.
시험 때문에 등산을 못 갔다.	I could not go hiking because of the exam.

4. Two-word verb -어/아 보다 "to try to," "to have an experience of"

A number of verbs have special idiomatic meanings when used together with another verb, such as 보다 "to see," 버리다 "to throw away," and 주다/드리다 "to give." (See L8, GN8.) 보다, which means "to see" by itself, indicates "to try to do something" (in the sense of "try having the experience of") when used in a two-word combination.

-어/아 보다 follows the rules for -어/아. (See L8, GN2, 6, and 8.)

-아 보다 is used after verbs with 아 or 오 in the last syllable.

-어 보다 is used after all other verbs.

-아 보다		-어 보다	
타 보다	try riding	써 보다	try writing
자 보다	try sleeping	물어 보다	try asking
와 보다	try coming	읽어 보다	try reading
가 보다	try going	입어 보다	try wearing (try on)
찾아 보다	try finding (look for)	가지어 보다 (가져 보다)	try having (have had)

나는 지하철을 타 봤다.	I have ridden the subway.
나는 뉴욕에 가 봤다.	I have been to New York.
나는 그 책을 읽어 봤다.	I have read the book.
나는 차를 가져 봤다.	I have owned (had) a car.
나는 그 옷을 입어 봤다.	I tried on the dress.

나는 그 의자에 <u>앉아 봤다</u>.   I tried sitting in the chair.

나는 영희에게 <u>물어 봤다</u>.*   I asked Young-hie the
                                 question.

나는 한국에서 친구를   I looked for/visited my
<u>찾아 봤다</u>.*   friend in Korea.

* 찾아보다 and 물어보다 here have the idiomatic meanings of
"to visit" and "to ask," respectively.

5. Postposition: direction marker -(으)로 "to," "through," "toward"

When used with the verbs "coming" or "going," -(으)로
indicates the direction of motion. -쪽 is often used with 으로.

-로 is used after a noun ending in a vowel or ㄹ.

-으로 is used after all other nouns.

<u>-로</u>	<u>-으로</u>
나는 서울<u>로</u> 간다.	동쪽<u>으로</u> 가세요.
I am going to Seoul.	Please go to the east.
나는 기숙사<u>로</u> 왔다.	이쪽<u>으로</u> 오십시오.
I came to the dorm.	Come this way, please.

어디로 "(to) where ... ?" is used for asking directions on a
bus or train, or asking "Where are you heading?" as in:

이 버스는 어디로 가지요?   Where does this bus go?
동대문<u>으로</u> 갑니다.   This goes to the East Gate.
지금 어디로 가세요?   Where are you heading now?
집<u>으로</u> 가요.   I am going home.

6. Postposition -까지 "to," "up to," "until," "by"

Attached to a noun or a noun phrase, -까지 indicates
"extent," with the meaning of "up to," "until," or "by (noon)."
It can be used for both time and place. (See L19, GN6.)

선생님은 오후 여섯시<u>까지</u>   The teacher was in the
연구실에 계셨다.   office until 6 o'clock in the
                   afternoon.

내일 오전 여섯시<u>까지</u> 오십시오.	Please come by 6 A.M. tomorrow.

-<u>까지</u> is often used in conjunction with -에서 and/or -부터 to indicate "from."

공원<u>에서</u> 박물관<u>까지</u> 멀어요?	Is it far from the park to the museum?
어제는 세시 <u>(에서)부터</u> 아홉시<u>까지</u> 도서관에서 공부했다.	I studied in the library from 3 to 9 o'clock yesterday.

7. Postposition -만 "only," "just"

-만 limits the effect of the predicate to the noun, noun phrase, or verbal noun to which -만 is attached. Unlike other postpositions, -만 does not have to replace the postpositions for subject, topic, direct or indirect object, and so on.

십분<u>만</u> 걸으십시오.	Walk only 10 minutes.
일본에서 온 한국 사람<u>만</u> 있다.	There are only Koreans from Japan.
그는 말을 안하고 듣기<u>만</u> 한다.	He only listens without talking.

When used with other postpositions, -만 precedes -이, -은, and -을.

박물관에는 동양화<u>만이</u> 있다.	In the museum, there are only Oriental paintings.
서양화<u>만은</u> 없다.	Only the Western paintings are not there.
우리<u>만이</u> 서울을 구경했다.	Only we (not other people) did the sightseeing in Seoul.
우리는 유명한 예술품<u>만을</u> 샀다.	We bought only famous art objects (not insignificant ones).

-만 follows the postpositions -에, -에게/-께, and -(으)로.

이 길로만 가세요.	Just follow this road.
동쪽으로만 가면 뉴욕이 나온다.	If you go only eastward, New York will appear.
오늘은 공원에만 갔다.	Today, we went only to the park.
선생님께만 묻기로 했다.	I decided to ask my teacher only (not anyone else).

Compare the paired sentences in the following examples.

나만 동양 박물관에 갔다.	Only I (not other people) went to the Oriental Museum.
나는 동양 박물관에만 갔다.	I went only to the Oriental Museum (not to other places).
나만 친구에게 편지를 썼다.	Only I wrote a letter to my friend.
나는 친구에게만 편지를 썼다.	I wrote letters only to my friend (not to other people).

8. Conditional connective -(으)면 "if," "when"

-(으)면 is used to construct a conditional clause, which must precede the main clause.

-면 is used after a verb ending in a vowel or ㄹ.

-으면 is used after all other verbs.

봄이 되면 꽃이 핀다.	When spring comes, flowers bloom.
답을 알면 대답하세요.	If you know the answer, please respond.
좋은 그림을 보면 사기로 했다.	We have decided to buy a painting if we see a good one.
멀면 뻐스를 타겠다.	If it is far, I will take the bus.

보스톤에서 친구를 <u>찾으면</u> 주말을 지내겠다.	If I find my friend in Boston, I will stay over the weekend.
길을 <u>모르면</u> (나에게) 물어 보세요.	If you do not know your way, please ask (me).
십오분 <u>걸으면</u> 돼요.	If you walk 15 minutes, it will do.

9. Points of the compass

An important thing to remember with the directions is the order of east, west, south, north. Any combination of directions usually follows this order.

동(東)	east	동북(東北)	northeast
서(西)	west	서북(西北)	northwest
남(南)	south	동남(東南)	southeast
북(北)	north	서남(西南)	southwest

-쪽 is usually attached to the direction words and indicates "side," "in the direction of," "way," or "-ward."

동쪽	east, eastern, eastward
서쪽	west, western, westward
오른쪽/바른쪽	right side, rightward, (to) the right
왼쪽	left side, leftward, (to) the left
이쪽	this way, this side
그쪽	that way, that side
저쪽	over that way, over that side

10. Chinese characters

東	동녘 동 east	一	冂	戸	自	車	東	東	
西	서녘 서 west	一	厂	冂	丙	西	西	
南	남녘 남 south	一	十	宀	冇	肉	肉	南	南
北	북녘 북 north	丨	才	才	圵	北	
洋	바다 양 sea ocean	丶	冫	氵	氵	沪	洰	洋
有	있을 유 exist have	一	厂	才	冇	有	有	
名	이름 명 name	丿	勹	夕	夕	名	名	

연습

A. 다음 질문에 대답하십시오.

1. 일요일 오후에 무엇을 하기로 했습니까?

2. 아세아 미술관에는 무엇이 많이 있습니까?

3. 왜 미술관에 가기로 했습니까?

4. 왜 지나가는 사람에게 물어 봤어요?

5. 공원은 멀다고 했어요? (가깝다: to be near)

6. 몇 분만 걸으면 된다고 했어요?

7. 학생은 상항에 있는 아세아 미술관에 가 봤어요?

B. 다음 문장을 끝마치십시오.

    8. _____ 찾기로 했다.

    9. _____ 일하기로 했다.

  10. _____ 배우기로 했다.

  11. _____ 묻기로 했다.

  12. _____ 걷기로 했다.

C. 다음 문장을 보기와 같이 -어/아 보다 형으로 고치십시오. (Change the following sentences into experiential -어/아 보다 sentences.)

보기: 아세아 미술관을 구경했다.→ 아세아 미술관을 구경해 봤다.

  13. 한국어 책을 읽는다. →

  14. 타이프를 친다. →

  15. 지나가는 사람에게 길을 묻는다. →

  16. 그 길로 걷는다. →

  17. 한국 음악을 들었다. →

  18. 바트를 탔다. →

  19. 식당에서 일했다. →

  20. 영어를 가르쳤다. →

  21. 한국음식을 먹었다. →

D. 다음 문장을 한국어로 번역하십시오.

  22. *They say that* he is a good student.

  23. *I heard that* economics is difficult.

  24. John *tasted (had the experience of eating)* Korean food. (food: 음식)

  25. *We have been* to China.

  26. *We have not been* to Russia. (Russia: 소련, 러시아)

  27. *How do we get to* San Jose? (*Which direction is* San Jose?)

  28. Go *that way.* Go *south.*

  29. If you walk *just* two blocks, you will find the park (the park will appear). (block: 블록)

  30. If you don't know the direction (way), please *try asking* Young-hie.

  31. Where is the *famous* Statue of Liberty? (Statue of Liberty: 자유의 여신상)

32. *Because* I don't know Korean well, I *decided to* study it.

33. *Because* my house is far from school, I take the bus.

E. 다음 지도를 보고 질문에 대답하십시오.
(Answer the questions about the following map.)

34. 우체국이 어디에 있어요?

35. 서울역은 어디로 가요?

36. 여관에서 공원을 어떻게 가요?

37. 은행 옆에 무엇이 있어요?

38. 다방과 이발소 사이에 무엇이 있어요?
(사이: in between)

39. 박물관은 병원에서 멀어요?

40. 주차장은 어느 쪽에 있어요?

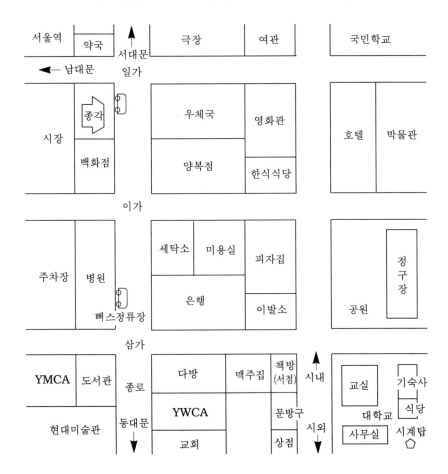

지도 낱말

지도	map
시계탑	clock tower
책방/서점	bookstore
문방구	stationery store
다방/코오피 숍	tearoom, coffee shop
교회	church
양복점	tailor shop (for men)
현대 미술관	modern art gallery
호텔	hotel
이발소	barbershop
미용실/미장원	beauty shop
시장	market
은행	bank
우체국	post office
피자집	pizza house
맥주집	beer house
뻐스정류장	bus stop
주차장	parking lot
비행장/공항	airport
동대문	Great East Gate
서대문	Great West Gate
서울역	Seoul train station
종로	Chong-no (the name of a street in Seoul)
종로 일가	the 1st street of Chong-ro
양장점	tailor shop (for women)
여관/모텔	inn/motel
세탁소	laundry, cleaner
약국/약방	pharmacy
상점	store

Lesson 13

제 십삼과 날씨

데이빗 : 한국의 날씨는 어떻지요?[1]

영식 : 한국은 계절마다[2] 기후가 아주 다릅니다. 봄에는
따뜻하지만 여름에는 덥고 비가 많이 옵니다.
겨울에는 눈도[3] 오고, 바람도 불고, 매우
춥습니다.

데이빗 : 여행하기가 제일 좋은 계절은 언제입니까?

영식 : 가을입니다. 가을은 춥지[4]도 덥[5]지도 않기 때문에
여행하기가 좋습니다. 그리고 경치도
아름답습니다.

Patterns

1. 한국<u>의</u> 기후는 어떻지요?
   제주도_____
   여름_____
   겨울_____

2. 계절<u>마다</u> 아주 다릅니다.
   사람_____
   여름_____
   집집_____

3. 토요일<u>마다</u> 테니스를 친다.
   일요일____ 교회에 간다.
   여름_____ 비가 많이 온다.

4. 눈도 오고 바람도 불지요.
   비__ 오고 눈__ 오지요.
   친구__ 오고 동생__ 오지요.
   봄__ 좋고 가을__ 좋지요.

5. 춥지도 덥지도 않지요.
   좋____ 나쁘_____
   슬프____ 기쁘_____

6. 덥지 않기 때문에 여행하기가 좋습니다.
   춥_____ 공부하기가 _____
   눈이 오_____ 일하기가 _____
   바람이 불_____테니스 치기가 ____

7. 따뜻하기 때문에 걷기가 좋지요.
   시원하_____
   경치가 아름답_____
   날씨가 좋_____

8. 제일 좋은 계절은 봄입니다.
   ____ 더운 ____은 여름입니다.
   ____ 아름다운 ____은 가을 입니다.
   ____ 추운 ____은 겨울입니다.

9. 제일 비가 많이오는 계절은 여름입니다.
   ____ 눈이 많이오는 ____은 겨울입니다.
   ____ 바람이 많이 부는 ____은 봄입니다.

낱말

제 십삼과 (第十三課)	Lesson 13
계절 (季節)	season
기후	weather, climate
다르다	to be different
봄	spring
여름	summer
가을	fall, autumn
겨울	winter
따뜻하다	to be warm
덥다	to be hot

비가 오다	to rain (the rain comes)
눈이 오다	to snow (the snow comes)
바람이 불다	to be windy, the wind blows
여행하다	to travel
여행을 가다	to go on a trip
제일 (第一)	the first, the most
경치	scenery
아름답다	to be beautiful
제주도	Cheju Island (southernmost island of Korea)
나쁘다	to be bad
슬프다	to be sad
기쁘다	to be glad, to be joyful, to be happy
한국 (韓國)	Korea

GRAMMAR AND NOTES

In this lesson we will study
1. Sentence endings: polite informal style -지요 and plain -지
   a. confirming statement
   b. tentative statement
   c. casual question
   d. propositive statement ("let's")
   e. request ("won't you?")
2. Postposition -마다 "each," "every"
3. Postposition -도 ...도 "both ... and," "neither ... nor," "as well as"
4. Negative verb base -지 with
   a. 않다 "do not"
   b. 못하다 "cannot"
5. Irregular ㅂ verbs
6. Chinese characters 韓, 國, 第, 季, 節, 課

1. Sentence ending -지요 for polite informal style, -지 for plain or intimate style

-지요 or -지 is used in several ways: as a confirming statement, a tentative statement, a casual question, a propositive statement such as "Let's ..." or "Shall we ...?" and a request such as "Wouldn't you ...?"

The intonation (like that of the -어/아요 ending) and the context in which the sentences are spoken mark the differences in meaning. The -지/-지요 ending also indicates some degree of intimacy between the speaker and the addressee.

a. A *confirming statement*, usually spoken with a level or falling intonation, is made as a response to a question.

여행을 끝냈어요?	Are you finished with your traveling?
네, 여행을 다 끝냈지요.	Yes, (I say that I) finished with my traveling.
바쁘세요?	Are you busy?
할 일이 많지요.	(I say that there) is a lot of work to be done.
가을에 날씨가 좋아요?	Is the weather nice in the fall?
네, 가을은 춥지도 덥지도 않지요.	Yes, (I say that) the fall is neither cold nor hot.

An emphatic response of agreement is also expressed with a level or falling intonation.

물론 이지요!	Of course it is!
좋지요!	(That's) great!

b. A *tentative statement*, which is also spoken with a level or falling intonation, takes -겠 before -지(요).

그분도 서울에 가시겠지요.	(I presume/suppose) he/she will go to Seoul, too.
산에 눈이 많겠지요.	(I suppose there) is a lot of snow on the mountains.
경치도 좋겠지요.	(I presume) also the scenery is beautiful.

c. A *casual question* is spoken with a rising intonation. It is similar to an English tag question, as in "You went to school, didn't you?" It may also indicate an after-thought question, as in "By the way ...?"

한국의 여름은 아주 덥지요?	It is very warm in Korea in the summer, isn't it?
가을이 여행하기가 제일 좋지요?	Fall is the best season to travel, isn't it?
토요일마다 테니스를 치지요?	You play tennis every Saturday, don't you?
언제 오시지요?	(By the way) when are you coming?
무엇을 찾으시지요?	(May I ask) what you are looking for? (meaning, May I help you?)

d. A *propositive statement* is spoken with a level or falling intonation.

같이 가시지요.	Let's go together. (polite proposition)
여기 같이 앉으시지요.	Let's sit here together. (polite)
내일 같이 가시지요.	Let's go tomorrow. (polite)

e. A *request* is spoken with a rising intonation like a casual question. Only the context in which it is spoken distinguishes a request from a casual question.

내일 오시지요? (request)	Won't you come tomorrow?
어제 오셨지요? (casual question)	You came yesterday, didn't you?

2. Postposition - 마다 "each," "every"

-마다 comes immediately after a noun or a noun phrase.

계절마다	every season, each season
사람마다	everybody
날마다 (or 매일)	every day
주(일)마다 (or 매주)	every week

| 달마다 (or 매월) | every month |
| 해마다 (or 매년) | every year |

Note that some nouns may reduplicate before -마다. Usually the noun is one syllable, and reduplication is optional.

집마다 or 집집마다	every house
곳마다 or 곳곳마다	every place, everywhere
나는 여름마다 쉰다.	I rest (do not work) every summer.
주말마다 집에 간다.	I go home every weekend.
날마다 한국어 시간이 있다.	I have Korean class every day.
집집마다 나무가 많다.	There are many trees around every house.

3. Postposition -도 … 도 "both … and," "neither … nor," "as well as"

-도 is used after a noun, after a verbal noun (v. + 기) or negative -지 ending (v. + 지), and after -에 or -으로 but not after -이/-가, -은/는, or -을/ -를.

N. + 도 … N. + 도

봄도 여름도 좋다.	Both spring and summer are fine.
봄도 여름도 춥지 않다.	Neither spring nor summer is cold.
여행도 관광도 많이 했다.	We did a lot of traveling as well as sightseeing.
여행도 관광도 못 했다.	We could neither travel nor sightsee.

V. + 기 + 도 … V. + 기 + 도

| 철수는 웃기도 잘 하고 울기도 잘 한다. | Chul-soo laughs as easily as he cries. |

V. + 지 + 도 … V. + 지 + 도

| 오늘은 비가 오지도 않고 바람이 불지도 않는다. | Today, it is neither rainy nor windy. |

N. + 에 + 도 … N. + 에 + 도

집에도 안가고 학교<u>에도</u>   I went neither home nor to
안갔다.   school.

N. + (으)로 + 도 … N. + (으)로 + 도

이리<u>로도</u> 가보고 저리<u>로도</u>   I went here and there.
가 봤다.

4. Negative verb base -지

-지 is always used with a negative verb such as 않다 or 못하다 (and 말다). Note that there is a difference in present tense between action verbs and descriptive verbs. There is no such difference in past and future tense forms.

a. V. STEM + 지 않다

Present	*Past*	*Future*
-지 않다 is used with *descriptive* verbs.	-지 않았다	-지 않겠다
-지 않는다 is used with *action* verbs.	-지 않았다	-지 않겠다

Descriptive verbs

춥지 않다.	It is not cold.
쉽지 않다.	It is not easy.
좋지 않았다.	It was not good.
상쾌하지 않았다.	It was not refreshing.
많지 않겠다.	It will not be much.
덥지 않겠다.	It will not be hot.

Action verbs

가지 않는다.	(I) do not go.
불지 않는다.	(It) does not blow.
읽지 않았다.	(I) did not read.
여행하지 않았다.	(I) did not travel.
구경하지 않겠다.	(I) will not sightsee.
다니지 않겠다.	(I) will not attend.

In addition to indicating simple future tense, 겠 has the meaning of conjecture, especially when used with descriptive verbs. It can be translated as "I think," "probably," "I guess," etc.

b. V. STEM + 지 못하다

	Present	Past	Future
-지 못하다 is used for descriptive verbs.		-지 못했다	-지 못하다
-지 못한다 is used for action verbs.		-지 못했다	-지 못하겠다

Descriptive verbs

빠르지 못하다.   (It) is not fast.

상쾌하지 못했다.   (It) was not refreshing.

Action verbs

가지 못한다.   (I) cannot go.

잘 하지 못했다.   (I) could not do well.

먹지 못하겠다.   (I) will not be able to eat.

For descriptive verbs, the use of 못하다 is limited.

5. Irregular ㅂ verbs

Many of the verb stems that end in ㅂ alternate with 우, depending on what follows after the stem.

a. When the ㅂ verb is followed by a vowel connective or suffix:

춥 + 으면 →	(추우 + 면)	<u>추우면</u>	if it is cold ...
춥 + 으세요 →	(추우 + 세요)	<u>추우세요</u>.	(He) is cold.
춥 + 어도 →	(추우 + 어도)	<u>추워도</u>	although it is cold, ...
춥 + 어서 →	(추우 + 어서)	<u>추워서</u>	because it is cold, ...
춥 + 었지만 →	(추우 + 었지만)	<u>추웠지만</u>	it was cold, but ...

b. When the ㅂ verb is followed by a consonant connective or suffix:

춥 + 지만 →	춥지만	it is cold, but ...
춥 + 고 →	춥고	it is cold, and ...
춥 + 겠다 →	춥겠다	It will be cold. (It must be cold.)
춥 + 다 →	춥다	It is cold.
춥 + 기 때문에 →	춥기 때문에	because it is cold, ...

Although only some of the action verbs ending in ㅂ have alternating forms, the majority of descriptive verbs ending in ㅂ alternate.

Alternating verbs

춥다	to be cold (descriptive)
덥다	to be warm (des.)
어렵다	to be difficult (des.)
쉽다	to be easy (des.)
아름답다	to be beautiful (des.)
돕다*	to help (action)
뜨겁다	to be hot to the touch (des.)
즐겁다	to be joyful, merry (des.)
무섭다	to be scary (des.)

Nonalternating verbs

잡다	to catch (action)
접다	to fold (action)
입다	to dress (action)
뽑다	to pull (action)
업다	to piggyback (action)
좁다*	to be narrow (des.)

* Note that some action verbs alternate and some descriptive verbs do not.

6. Chinese characters

韓	나라 한 한나라 한 Korea	車	卓	卓	卓	卓	卓	韓	韓
國	나라 국 country	丨	冂	冂	同	戻	國	國	國
第	차례 제 order —th	ノ	ベ	ケ	竺	竺	竺	笃	第
季	계절 제 (아우) season	一	二	千	禾	禾	季	季	
節	절기 절 마디 season	ケ	竹	竺	笁	管	管	節	節
課	과목 과 lesson	丶	二	三	言	言	訂	課	課

연습

A. 다음 질문에 대답하십시오.
 1. 샌프란시스코의 기후는 어떻지요?
 2. 로스앤젤레스의 기후는 어떻지요?
 3. 왜 한국은 가을이 여행하기가 제일 좋은 계절입니까?
 4. 더운 계절에는 무엇을 하기가 좋아요?
 5. 추운 계절에는 무엇을 많이 해요?
 6. 미국 동부에는 경치가 아름다운 계절이 언제이지요?
  (동부: east coast)
 7. 바람도 불고 비가 오는 계절은 언제이지요?
 8. 주말마다 무엇을 하세요?
 9. (학생은) 어느 계절이 좋아요?
 10. 여름방학마다 일을 하시겠어요?

B. 다음 문장을 보기와 같이 -지요 형으로 바꾸십시오. (Change the formal endings to informal -지요 forms.)

> 보기: 기후가 다릅니다. → 기후가 다르지요.

> 11. 여름에는 비가 많이 옵니다.
> 12. 여름에는 아주 덥습니다.
> 13. 바람이 많이 붑니다.
> 14. 벌써 봄이 되었습니다.
> 15. 경치가 아름답습니다.

C. 다음 빈 칸에 알맞는 말을 써 넣으십시오. (Fill in the blanks.)

> 16. 사업 때문에 _____ 지 못 한다.
> 17. 시험 때문에 _____ 지 못 했다.
> 18. 바람이 불기 때문에 _____ 지 못 한다.
> 19. 날씨가 춥기 때문에 _____ 지 못 하겠다.
> 20. 날씨가 덥기 때문에 _____ 지 못 하겠다.
> 21. 해가 났기 때문에 _____ 지 못 했다.
> 22. 구름이 끼었기 때문에 _____ 지 못 한다.
>   (해: sun, 구름: cloud, 나다: to come out, (구름이) 끼다: to be overcast)

D. 다음 문장을 보기와 같이 -지 못하다 형으로 고치십시오. (Change the following sentences to negative sentences using -지 못하다.)

> 보기: 가을에 여행을 간다. → 가을에 여행을 가지 못한다.

> 23. 겨울에는 스키를 탔다. (스키: ski)
> 24. 아침에 공원에서 걷는다.
> 25. 일요일에 도서관에서 공부한다.
> 26. 주말에 박물관을 구경했다.

E. 다음 문장을 보기와 같이 -지 않다 형으로 고치십시오. (Change the following sentences to negative sentences using -지 않다.)

> 보기: 아침에 바람이 분다. → 아침에 바람이 불지 않는다.

> 27. 가을에 경치가 좋다.
> 28. 산에 눈이 많이 왔다.
> 29. 오늘은 춥다.
> 30. 시험이 쉽다.

F. 다음 문장을 한국어로 번역하십시오.

31. *Every* winter a lot of snow falls in the mountains.

32. It's rainy *every day*.

33. There are lots of people playing tennis in *every* park.

34. Are *neither* (your) mother *nor* father in Japan?

35. It is *neither* cold *nor* hot in San Francisco.

36. (*I presume that*) you have been to Pusan and Taegu, *haven't you*?

37. They taught *both* Chinese and Korean in high school.

38. We take (read) *neither* newspapers *nor* magazines.

39. *Every summer vacation*, we take a trip to the Orient.

40. I cannot go home *every weekend*. (Use -지 못한다.)

Lesson 14

제 십사과 한국의 기후

한국의 기후는 사철이 있는 대륙성 기후이다. 봄, 여름,
가을, 겨울이 분명하다. 여름에는 장마철이 있어서 비가
많이 오고 태풍도 분다. 반대로 겨울에는 매우 춥고
지방에 따라[1] 눈도 많이 온다. 그러나 봄이 되면 새싹이
돋고 꽃이 피기 시작한다. 가을에는 하늘이 푸르고
높아지[2]며[3] 단풍이 들어[4] 경치가 아름답다.

Patterns

1. 사철이 있는 <u>대륙성 기후이다.</u>
   봄이 따뜻한 ＿＿＿＿＿＿＿
   겨울이 추운 ＿＿＿＿＿＿＿
   여름에 비가 오는 ＿＿＿＿＿

2. <u>지방에 따라</u> 눈이 많이 온나.
   ＿＿＿＿＿＿ 말이 다르다.
   ＿＿＿＿＿＿ 꽃과 나무가 많다.
   ＿＿＿＿＿＿ 태풍이 분다.

3. <u>봄이 되면</u> 새싹이 돋는다.
   ＿＿＿＿＿ 꽃이 핀다.
   ＿＿＿＿＿ 날씨가 따뜻하다.
   ＿＿＿＿＿ 공기가 상쾌하다.

4. 하늘이 높아<u>진다.</u>
   공기가 맑아＿＿＿
   기후가 따뜻해＿＿
   날씨가 추워＿＿
   날씨가 더워＿＿

5. 하늘이 높아지며 단풍이 든다.
   ＿＿＿＿＿＿＿＿ 날씨가 추워진다.
   ＿＿＿＿＿＿＿＿ 비가 오기 시작한다.
   ＿＿＿＿＿＿＿＿ 나뭇잎이 떨어진다.
   ＿＿＿＿＿＿＿＿ 공기가 맑아진다.

6. 춥고 바람이 분다.
   푸르고 아름답다.
   새싹이 돋고 꽃이 핀다.
   해가 나고 따뜻하다.
   비가 오고 바람이 분다.

낱말

제 십사과 (第十四課)	Lesson 14
사철	four seasons
철	season
하늘	sky
대륙 (大陸)	continent
대륙성 (大陸性)	continental
분명하다 (分明)	to be clear, to be distinctive
장마철	monsoon season
태풍	typhoon
반대로	on the other hand, on the contrary
지방 (地方)	local area, countryside
새싹	new bud, sprout
돋다	to come out, to bud
푸르다	to be green, to be blue
높아지다 (높다)	to become high, to become tall (to be tall or high)
단풍	fall colors, maple
꽃	flower
단풍이 들다	to turn to fall colors (for trees, hills, and mountains)
꽃이 피다	to bloom, to blossom

-에 따라 (따르다)	depending on, according to (to follow)
잎	leaf
떨어지다	to fall
경치 (景致)	scenery

GRAMMAR AND NOTES

In this lesson we will study
1. Expressions for
    a. "according to," "depending on" -에 따라(서)
    b. "following" -을/를 따라
2. Construction of D. V. + 어/아지다 "to become ... (by itself)," "to turn into"
3. Concurrent connective
    a. -(으)며 "and"
    b. -(으)면서 "while," "at the same time," "as"
4. Causal/sequential connective -어/아(서): deletion of 서
5. Chinese characters 景, 致, 明, 地, 方, 性, 陸

1. Expressions for
a. "according to," "depending on" N. + 에 따라(서)
b. "following" N. + (을/를) 따라

a. -에 따라(서) means "according to," "depending on."

학교에 따라(서) 학비가 다르다.	The tuition varies according to the school.
지방에 따라(서) 눈도 많이 온다.	Depending on the region, there can be (is) heavy snowfall.
계절에 따라(서) 기후가 변한다.	The weather changes according to the season.

b. -을/를 따라 indicates "one follows something or someone."

김 선생(을) 따라 학생들은 교실로 들어갔다.	The students went into the classroom following Mr. Kim.

따뜻한 기후를 따라 사람들이 플로리다로 간다.	People go to Florida following the warm weather.
저를 <u>따라</u> 오세요.	Please follow me. (come following me)
저를 <u>따라</u> 읽으세요.	Please read after me.

2. Construction of D. V. + 어/아지다 "to become ... (by itself)," "to turn into"

When used with descriptive verbs, 어/아지다 changes them into action verbs indicating that the condition is gradually changing.

높다	to be high	높아지다	to become high, tall
따뜻하다	to be warm	따뜻해지다	to become/get warm
크다	to be big	커지다	to become big, to grow tall
쉽다	to be easy	쉬워지다	to become easy
빨갛다	to be red	빨개지다	to become red, to blush

가을에는 하늘이 높아진다.	The sky becomes clear blue in the fall. (In the fall, the sky becomes blue.)
한국어는 두 달 배우면 쉬워진다.	Korean becomes easier after studying two months. (Korean will become easier if you study for two months.)
봄이 되면 날씨가 따뜻해진다.	When it becomes spring, the weather will be warm.

3. Concurrent connective -(으)며 "and," "while," "at the same time," "as"

-(으)며 has two distinct meanings, "and" and "while." The proper meaning is understood from the context of the sentence.

-며 is used with verb stems ending in a vowel or ㄹ.

-으며 is used with all other verb stems.

a. "and"

To avoid repeating -고, -(으)며 is used for the same meaning of "and."

가을에는 하늘이 푸르고 높아지며 바람도 분다.	In the fall the sky is blue and becomes high and the winds blow. (In the fall the sky becomes clear and blue, and it is windy.)
영식이는 공학을 공부하며 그의 아내는 인류학을 공부한다.	Young-shik studies engineering, and his wife studies anthropology.

b. "while," "at the same time," "as"

-(으)며 is also a short form of -(으)면서, which indicates two actions going on at the same time.

해가 나며 (나면서) 비가 온다.	It is raining while the sun shines (while being sunny).
이야기 하며 (하면서) 걸었다.	We walked as we talked.
책을 읽으며 (읽으면서) 라디오를 듣는다.	I listen to the radio while reading a book.

But for "and" only -(으)며 is used.

하늘이 높고 푸르며 경치가 아름답다.	The sky is deep blue and the scenery is beautiful.
바람이 불고 추우며 눈이 온다.	It is windy, cold, and snowing.

4. Causal/sequential connective -어/아(서): deletion of 서

The causal/sequential connective -어/아서 can be used without 서:

단풍이 들어서 경치가 아름답다. → 단풍이 들어 경치가 아름답다.

The scenery is beautiful because the leaves are turning to fall colors.

시간이 <u>없어서</u> 안 물어 봤다. → 시간이 <u>없어</u> 안 물어 봤다.
Because I didn't have time, I didn't ask.

그는 숙제가 <u>많아서</u> 집에 있다. → 그는 숙제가 <u>많아</u> 집에 있다.
Since he has a lot of homework, he is staying at home.

나는 <u>바빠서</u> 극장에 안 갔다. → 나는 <u>바빠</u> 극장에 안 갔다.
Because I was busy, I did not go to the movies.

As a consequence of dropping -서, the verb stems ending in 어 or 아 may not have any trace of -어/아서 (see vowel contraction rules L7, GN2):

한국에 <u>가서</u> 사세요. → 한국에 <u>가</u> 사세요.
Go to Korea and live (there).

우리는 친구를 <u>만나서</u> 다방에 갔다. → 우리는 친구를 <u>만나</u> 다방에 갔다.
We met our friend and went to a tearoom.

5. Chinese characters

景	별 경 bright	冂	日	旦	旦	昮	昮	景	
致	이를 치 reach	厶	五	至	圣	至	到	到	致
明	밝을 명 bright	日	明	明	明	明			
地	땅 지 earth	一	十	土	圹	坦	地		
方	방향 방 direction	丶	亠	方	方				
性	성품 성 character	丨	忄	忄	忄	忏	性	性	
陸	육지 육 대륙(륙) land	孑	阝	阝	阝	陸	陸	陸	陸

연습

A. 다음 질문에 대답하십시오.
  1. 대륙성 기후는 어떻습니까?
  2. 사철은 무슨 계절들을 말합니까?
  3. 미국의 기후는 지방에 따라 어떻게 다릅니까?
  4. 장마철에는 날씨가 어떻습니까?
  5. 가을에는 왜 경치가 아름답습니까?

B. 다음을 영어로 번역하십시오. (What are the meanings of the following phrases?)
  6. 사철이 있는 대륙성 기후
  7. 높고 푸른 하늘
  8. 비가 많이 오는 계절
  9. 태풍이 부는 지방
  10. 눈이 많이 오고 추운 날씨
  11. 사철이 분명한 기후
  12. 단풍이 든 산
  13. 경치가 아름다운 곳
  14. 꽃이 많은 공원
  15. 새싹이 돋는 봄

C. 다음 문장을 한국어로 번역하십시오.
  16. We talked *while* taking a walk.
  17. It rained *while* the sun was shining (the sun was out).
  18. The *sky is clear* and the *air refreshing*.
  19. It is nice to travel in the season *when there are no* typhoons.
  20. In the fall the sky becomes clear *and* the trees turn to fall colors.
  21. *While reading* the newspaper, I heard the rain fall (the sound of rain coming). (sound: 소리)
  22. *They say that* China has continental weather.
  23. In Korea the four seasons are *distinct*.
  24. When do the flowers *start to* bloom in San Francisco?

25. We can't go on a picnic *if* there is a typhoon (if a typhoon blows).

D. 다음 문장을 끝마치십시오. (Complete the sentences using the following phrases.)

26. 계절에 따라 _____
27. 날씨에 따라 _____
28. 지방에 따라 _____
29. 사람에 따라 _____
30. 기후에 따라 _____
31. 가을이 되면 _____
32. 겨울이 되면 _____
33. 봄이 되면 _____
34. 여름이 되면 _____
35. 태풍이 불면 _____
36. 날씨가 추워지며 _____
37. 새싹이 돋으며 _____
38. 태풍이 불며 _____
39. 장마철이 있으며 _____
40. 경치가 아름다우며 _____

Lesson 15

제 십오과   한국어 시간

대화

영희: 실례지만 duty 를 한국말로 무엇 이라고 해요?

선생: 할[1] 일 또는[2] 임무라고 합니다.

영희: 할 일과 임무는 똑 같은 뜻이에요?

선생: 네, 할 일은 순수한 한국말 이고 임무는
　　　중국어에서 나온 말입니다.

영희: 한 가지 더 여쭈어 보겠어요. 한국에서는
　　　중학교에서 한자를 배워요?

선생: 네. 얼마[3] 동안[4] 안 가르쳤는데[5] 다시 가르치기로
　　　됐다[6]고 해요.

영희: 전부 몇 자나[7] 배우나요?[8]

선생: 중학교에서 약 900자, 고등학교에서 900자,
　　　합해서 1,800자쯤[9] 배운다고 해요.

Patterns

1. 할 일이 많다.
　　볼 영화_____
　　읽을 책_____
　　배울 한자_____
　　버릴 것_____

160

2. <u>얼마 동안</u> 안 가르쳤다.
　　_____ 안 배웠다.
　　_____ 기다렸다.
　　_____ 중학교에 다녔다.
　　_____ 중국에 있었다.

3. <u>이것은 얼마</u> 지요?
　　_____ 얼마나 해요?
　　_____ 얼마나 걸려요?

4. 전에는 가르쳤<u>는데</u> 지금은 안 가르쳐요.
　　한자를 배웠<u>는데</u> 잘 모르겠어요.
　　고등학교에 다녔<u>는데</u> 한자를 안 배웠어요.
　　순 한국말<u>인데</u> 외국어 같아요.

5. 다시 <u>가르치기로 되었다</u>.
　　한자를 다시 배우_____
　　선생님께 여쭈어 보_____
　　일요일에 피크닉을 가_____

6. 몇 <u>자나</u> 배우나요?
　　몇 사람 ____ 있나요?
　　몇 개 _____ 샀나요?
　　몇 시 _____ 됐나요?

7. <u>Duty</u> 를 한국말로 무엇이라고 해요?
　　Birthday _____
　　Weather _____
　　Physics _____
　　Economics _____
　　Wind _____
　　Snow _____

8. 몇 자쯤 배워요?　　　　　　　1800자쯤 배워요.
　　언제쯤 오시겠어요?　　　　　월요일쯤 가겠어요.
　　며칠쯤 뉴욕에 계시겠어요?　한 일 주일쯤 있겠어요.
　　몇 시쯤 갈까요?　　　　　　여섯시쯤 오세요.
　　언제쯤 여쭈어보겠어요?　　내일쯤 여쭈어 보겠어요.

낱말

제 십오과 (第十五課)	Lesson 15
한국어 (韓國語)	Korean language
시간	hour, class (한국어 시간: Korean class)
실례	discourtesy
실례이지만 (실례지만)	I am sorry but ..., excuse me.
할 (하다)	to be done (future)
또는	or
임무	duty
똑	exactly
같은 (같다)	like, same (to be alike, to be the same)
뜻	meaning
순수한 (순수하다)	pure (to be pure)
나온 (나오다)	came out, originated (to come out, to originate)
-가지	item, type, thing (한 가지: one item, one type, one thing)
여쭈다	to tell, to ask (to hon. person)
중학교 (中學校)	middle school
고등학교	high school
한자 (漢字)	Chinese character
얼마(나)	how much, how long
-기로 되다	it turns out that
전부	all, total
자 (字)	character, letter
몇 자(나)	how many characters
약	about, approximately
합하다	to add, to put together, to combine
-쯤	about, approximately
버리다	to throw away, to discard
기다리다	to wait
걸리다	to take (time)

전에	before, previously
외국어	foreign language
순-	pure- (prefix)
물리학	physics
생일	birthday

GRAMMAR AND NOTES

In this lesson we will study
1. Verbal modifier (similar to relative clause): future modifier -ㄹ/을
2. Coordinate conjunction 또는 "or," "in addition," "either ... or"
3. Question word 얼마
   a. "how much?" "how long?"
   b. indefinite pronoun
4. Dependent noun 동안 "during," "while"
   a. N. + 동안
   b. V. MOD. + 동안
5. Consequence connective "ㄴ/은데/는데 "but," "however," "for," "and," "so," "while," "since," "when," "as"
   a. descriptive verbs
   b. action verbs
6. Construction of V. STEM + 기로 되다 "it turns out that," "is supposed to"
7. Postposition -(이)나 "to the extent of," "to what extent?"
8. Question ending -나? plain/intimate, -나요? polite informal
9. Dependent noun -쯤 "about," "around," "approximately"
10. Chinese characters 中, 學, 校, 漢, 字, 語

1. Verbal modifier (similar to relative clause): future modifier -ㄹ/을

In addition to the past and present modifiers -는 and -ㄴ/은 (see L11, GN1), there is the future modifier -ㄹ/을.

	Future	*Present/ongoing*	*Past*
일하다 to work	할일 work to do	하는일 work (one) does	한일 work (one) did
배우다 to learn	배울 것들 things to learn	배우는 것들 things (one) learns	배운 것들 things (one) learned
살다 to live	살집 house to live in	사는 집 house where (one) lives	산집 house where (one) lived
듣다 to listen, to hear	들을 이야기 a story that (one) will hear	듣는 이야기 a story that (one) is listening to	들은 이야기 a story that (one) heard

Some nouns with the future modifier -ㄹ/을 have idiomatic meanings, as in the following examples.

할 일	duty, work to do
저는 할 일이 많아요.	I have a lot to do.
쓸 돈	spending money
저는 쓸 돈이 없어요.	I have no money to spend.
볼 사람	person to see
볼 사람이 없어요.	I have no one to see.
갈 길	road to travel (destination)
갈 길이 멀다.	I have a long way to go (travel).

2. Coordinate Conjunction 또는 "or," "in addition," "either ... or"

또는 can be used at the beginning of a sentence or in the middle of a sentence.

At the beginning of a sentence:

Los Angeles 는 L.A.라고 한다.	Los Angeles is known as
또는 나성이라고 한다.	L.A. Or it is known as *nasŏng.*

그는 영어로 Ken 이라고 한다. 또는 한국어로 규식이라고 한다.	He is called Ken in English. Or he is Kyu- shik in Korean.

In the middle of a sentence (as a sentence connective), it connects two nouns, noun phrases, or clauses:

할 일 <u>또는</u> 임무라고 한다.	It is known as *halil* or *immu*.
Korean 은 한국말 <u>또는</u> 한국어 라고 한다.	Korean is called *hankuk- mal* or *hankuk-ŏ*.

3. Question word 얼마

얼마 is often used with -나 for "amount" and 동안 for "duration of time."

a. 얼마 as a question word: "how much?" "how long?"

얼마나 (see GN7)

중국어는 얼마나 어려워요?	How difficult is Chinese?
이 책은 얼마나 해요?	How much is this book?*
얼마나 걸려요?	How long does it take?

Two expressions are commonly used for "How much is it?"

얼마나 해요?	How much is (does) it?
얼마에요?*	How much is it?

* Note that -나 is not used with 이다, and 이 in 얼마 + 이에요 is dropped.

b. 얼마 as an indefinite pronoun

얼마동안 한자를 안 가르쳤다.	For some time they didn't teach Chinese characters.
공원에 사람이 <u>얼마</u> 없다.	There are not many people in the park.

4. Dependent noun 동안 "during," "while"

동안 is always preceded by a noun or a verbal modifier to indicate the duration of time.

a. N. + 동안

방학 <u>동안</u>	during the vacation (방학: school vacation)
한 시간 <u>동안</u>	for one hour
여름 방학 <u>동안</u>	during the summer vacation
가을 학기 <u>동안</u>	during the fall semester
얼마 <u>동안</u>	for a while, for some time

b. V. MOD. + 동안

한자를 배우는 <u>동안</u>	while learning Chinese characters
선생님께 여쭈어 보는 <u>동안</u>	while asking our teacher questions
내가 영어 공부 하는 <u>동안</u>에 동생은 일본어를 공부했다.	While I was studying English, my brother studied Japanese.
한 시간 <u>동안</u>에 그는 백화점과 도서관과 책방에 갔다.	In one hour, she went to the department store, the library, and thc bookstore.

5. Consequence connective -ㄴ/은데/는데 "but," "however," "for," "and," "so," "while," "since," "when," "as"

-ㄴ/은데/는데 has various meanings of conjunction, but its main function is to introduce an event or a fact for the sentence that follows.

a. Descriptive verbs

Present tense

-ㄴ데 is used after a stem ending in a vowel, e.g., 크(다) → 큰데.

-은데 is used after a stem ending in a consonant, e.g., 많(다) → 많은데.

한자는 <u>어려운데</u> 재미있다.	Chinese characters are difficult but interesting.
토마토가 <u>빨간데</u> 맛이 없다.	The tomatoes are red, but they have no taste.
그는 미국 사람<u>인데</u> 한국말을 잘 한다.	Even though he is American, he speaks Korean well.
<u>추운데</u> 그는 옷을 많이 안 입었다.	It is cold, but he is not wearing a lot of clothes.
그것이 순 한국 낱말<u>인데</u> 나는 몰랐다.	Although it is a pure Korean word, I did not know it.

Past tense

-는데 is used after the past-tense marker -았/었:

크(다) → 컸는데

작(다) → 작았는데

| 한자는 <u>어려웠는데</u> 재미 있었다. | Chinese characters were difficult but interesting. |
| 토마토가 <u>빨갰는데</u> 맛이 없었다. | Although the tomatoes were red, they had no taste. |

b. Action verbs

-는데 is used after action verbs in both past and present tenses:

| 가(다) → 가는데 (present) | 갔는데 (past) |
| 읽(다) → 읽는데 (present) | 읽었는데 (past) |

Present tense

지금 일본어를 안 <u>가르치는데</u> 다시 가르치기로 됐다.	We are not teaching Japanese now, but it is decided that we will be teaching it again.
그는 공부를 많이 안 <u>하는데</u> 시험을 잘 본다.	Although he does not study a lot, he does well in his exams.
집에 <u>가는데</u> 같이 가시겠어요?	As I am on my way home, would you like to go together (with me)?

Past tense

작년에 일본어를 안 가르쳤는데 다시 가르치기로 됐다.	We did not teach Japanese last year, but it is decided that we will teach it again.
그는 공부를 많이 안 했는데 시험을 잘 봤다.	Although he did not study a lot, he did well in his exams.
친구의 집에 갔는데 아무도 없었다.	I went to my friend's house, but there was nobody (there).

6. Construction of v. STEM + 기로 되다 "it turns out that," "is supposed to"

Attached to a verb stem, -기로 되다 describes an event that is a result of some decision. -기로 되다 is usually used in the past tense.

힌자를 다시 가르치기로 됐다.	It's been decided that Chinese characters will be taught again.
나는 서울에 가기로 됐다.	I am supposed to go to Seoul.
그는 다음 학기부터 독일어를 가르치기로 됐다.	He is to teach German beginning next semester.

(Compare -기로 되다 with -기로 하다 in L12, GN1.)

7. Postposition -(이)나 "to the extent of," "to what extent?"

-(이)나 is usually used with the question words 얼마- and 몇- to express "to what extent?" or "to what degree?":

한자를 몇 자쯤이나 배웠어요?	How many characters did you learn?
백 자쯤 배웠어요.	We learned about 100 characters.
며칠이나/얼마나 계시겠어요?	How many days (how long) will you stay?
사흘 있겠어요.	I will stay for three days.

When -이나 is used for a statement or a response to a question, however, it expresses "more than the expected amount."

Note that the responses above do not use -(이)나, but the responses in the following examples do:

고등학교에서 한자를 많이 배웠어요?	Did you learn many Chinese characters in high school?
네, 이천 자나 배웠어요.	Yes, we learned 2,000 characters (quite a few).
한국어를 오랫동안 가르치셨어요?	Did you teach Korean for a long time?
네, 십오 년이나 가르쳤어요.	Yes, I taught for 15 years (a long time).

8. Question ending -나? plain/intimate, -나요? polite informal

This question ending is used with all verbs in present, past, and future forms to express "I wonder if ...?"

	Plain	Polite	Honorific	
Present	배우나?	배우나요?	배우시나요?	Are you learning?
Past	배웠나?	배웠나요?	배우셨나요?	Did you learn?
Future *intention* (-겠-)	배우겠나?	배우겠나요?	배우시겠 나요?	Will you learn?

The future form -겠나요 is not often used. The ending -을/ ㄹ까요 is more often used for future tense.

9. Dependent noun -쯤 "about," "around," "approximately"

-쯤 is attached directly to a noun to indicate an approximation.

두 시쯤	about two o'clock
저녁 때쯤	around dinnertime
열 사람쯤	approximately ten people
1마일쯤 가면 됩니다.	It will be about one mile.

10. Chinese characters

中	가운데 중 mid–	丶	冂	口	中			
學	배울 학 study	乛	F	F	臼	閁	𦥯	學
校	학교 교 school	一	十	木	术	柊	栌	校
漢	한수 한 (물) Han dyn.	丶	氵	汀	汢	芦	漢	漢
字	글자 자 letter character	丶	宀	宀	字	字		
語	말씀 어 language	丶	言	言	訂	許	語	語

연습

A. 다음 질문에 대답하십시오.
1. 영어로 "생일"을 무엇이라고 해요?
2. 한국어로는 guest 와 customer 가 똑 같아요?
3. 미국에서는 고등학교에서 무슨 외국어를 배우나요?
4. 중국어를 몇 년이나 배웠나요?
5. 얼마 동안 미국에 사셨나요?
6. 저 책은 얼마나 해요?
7. 얼마 동안 영어를 가르치셨어요?
8. "임무"가 영어로 무슨 뜻이에요?
9. 왜 한자를 안 배웠어요?
10. 미국에서는 중학교에서 한국어를 가르치나요?

B. 다음 문장을 영어로 번역하십시오.
11. 한국에서 친구가 오면 들을 이야기가 많겠다.
12. 할 일이 많아서 소풍을 안 가기로 했다.
13. 일곱과 열 둘을 합하면 얼마 (이)에요? (얼마나 돼요?)
14. 그분은 팔월부터 한국어를 배웠는데 잘 한다. (부터: from)
15. 아침마다 신문을 볼 시간이 없다.
16. 집에 가면 부모님께 여쭈어 볼 것이 많다.
17. 친구가 얼마 동안 서울에 살았는데 지금은 부산에 있다고 한다.
18. 영식이는 언제쯤 학교에 다시 나오기로 됐다고 해요?
19. 한자를 몇 자나 배웠어요?
    전부 합해서 500자쯤 배웠어요.
20. 두 가지 질문이 있어요.

C. 다음 문장을 보기와 같이 미래형으로 바꾸십시오.
   (미래형 : future form)
  보기: 한국어를 가르치시는 분이 누구십니까? → 한국어를
        가르치실 분이 누구십니까?

21. 한자를 배우는 학생이 많아요. →
22. 그 이야기를 들은 사람이 없다. →
23. 일하는 사람들이 오지 않는다. →
24. 여름에는 여행하는 학생들이 많다. →

D. 다음 문장을 보기와 같이 바꾸십시오.
   (Change the sentences into reported speech using
   -라고 해요 or -다고 해요.)

   보기: Duty 는 한국말로 임무(이)다 → Duty 는 한국말로
   임무(이)라고 해요.

   25. 임무는 중국어에서 나온 말이다 →

   26. 임무와 할일은 같은 뜻이다 →

   27. 중학교에서 한자를 배운다 →

   28. 고등학교에서 외국어를 가르친다 →

E. 다음 문장을 한국어로 번역하십시오.

   29. *How do you say* 할 일 or 임무 in English?

   30. Do "duty" and "responsibility" *have the same
       meaning?*

   31. Are there many Chinese *borrowed* (Sino-Korean)
       words in the Korean language? (Use -나요?)

   32. Do students learn a foreign language *in middle
       school?* (Use -나요?)

   33. *Which* foreign languages do they teach in high
       school?

   34. (*It turns out that*) we *are supposed to* learn about
       100 Chinese characters in one year.

   35. (*It turns out that*) we *are supposed to* ask (hon.) our
       teacher in Korean.

   36. *How long* did you stay in New York?

   37. Do you have many *things to buy?*

   38. Who is the *person who will teach* Korean to us?

   39. I borrowed this book from the library *and (by the
       way)* it is very interesting (to borrow: 빌리다)

   40. He lived in Japan for ten years, *but (by the way)* he
       cannot speak Japanese.

Lesson 16

제 십육과   한글에 대하여[1]

한글이 만들어지[2]기 전[3]에는 한국 사람들은 한자를 빌려[4]
썼다. 그러나 한국어와 중국어는 다르기 때문에 한자는
한국어를 표현하기[5]에 적당하지 않았다. 또한 한자는
배우기가 어려웠기 때문에 많은 사람들이 글을 쓰지
못했다. 세종대왕께서는 이것을 깨달으시고 학자들과
같이 한국어에 맞는 한글을 만드셨다. 그리고 백성들에게
이 새로운 문자를 가르치려고[6] 여러가지 책을 지으[7]셨다.

최선생 : 한국 사람들은 왜 한자를 빌려 썼어요?
  학생 : 한글이 생기기 전에는 문자가 없었기 때문
         이에요.
최선생 : 한국말은 중국말과 비슷한 언어 인가요?[8]
  학생 : 아니요. 두 나라 말은 아주 달라요. 그래서
         한자를 쓰기가 어려웠어요.
최선생 : 그럼 우리는 왜 지금도 한자를 쓰지요?
  학생 : 한국어에는 중국어에서 빌려온 낱말들이 많이
         있기 때문이에요.

Patterns

1. 한국 사람들은 한자를 <u>빌려 썼다</u>.
   나는 연필을 _____
   친구는 내 차를 _____
   그들은 돈을 _____

2. <u>도서관에서</u> 책을 빌려 봤다.
   <u>친구에게서</u> 돈을 빌려 썼다.
   _____ 차를 빌려 탔다.
   _____ 옷을 빌려 입었다.

3. 한글은 한국어를 표현하기에 <u>적당하다</u>.
   그 책은 한국어를 배우기에 _____
   그 종이는 편지를 쓰기에 _____
   그 도서관은 공부하기에 _____

4. <u>한글은 한국어를 표현하기에</u> 적당하다.
   _____ 좋다.
   _____ 편리하다.
   _____ 알맞다.

5. <u>새로운 문자를 가르치려고</u> 책을 지었다.
   _____ 배우려고 공부했다.
   _____ 쓰려고 노력했다.
   _____ 만들려고 생각했다.

6. 한국어와 중국어는 다르기 <u>때문에</u> 한글을 만들었다.
   형과 동생이 비슷하기 _____ 쌍둥이라고 한다.
   한자는 많기 _____ 배우기(가) 어렵다.
   문자가 없었기 _____ 쓰지 못했다.
   배우기가 어려웠기 _____ 안 배웠다.
   사람들이 글을 쓰지 못했기 _____ 한글을 가르쳤다.

낱말

제 십육과 (第十六課)	Lesson 16
한글	Korean writing system
-에 대하여	concerning, about
만들어지다	to be made
빌리다	to borrow
빌려 쓰다	to borrow and use
빌려 주다	to lend
지으셨다. (짓다)	(He) made. (hon.) (to make)
글	writings, character
표현하다 (表現)	to express

때문에	because of
-기 때문에	because of ——ing
적당하다	to be appropriate, to be suitable
깨달으시고 (깨닫다)	realizing (to realize, to recognize, to understand)
학자 (學者)	scholar
맞는 (맞다)	suitable (to fit, to be correct)
알맞다	to be suitable, appropriate, just right
만드셨다. (만들다)	(He) made. (hon.) (to make)
세종대왕	The great King Sejong (the fourth king of the Yi dynasty, 1392–1910)
왕 (王)	king
대왕 (大王)	great king
백성 (百姓)	common people
새로운 (새롭다)	new (to be new)
문자	writing system, letter
여러가지	various kinds
비슷하다	to be similar
언어 (言語)	language
편리하다	to be convenient
노력하다	to make an effort, to try hard, to endeavor
또한	also
생각하다	to think, to consider
쌍둥이	twins

GRAMMAR AND NOTES

In this lesson we will study
1. Expressions for "concerning," "about" -에 대하여
2. Passive construction: ACTION VERB + 어/아 지다
   "to be ——ed"
3. Constructions for "before"
   a. v. + 기 전에 "before doing"
   b. N. + 전에 "before (some event)"
4. Sequential use of the connective -어/아서 "and,"
   "and then"
5. More on nominalization: v. STEM + 기
6. Purposive connective -(으)려고 "in order to," "for the
   purpose of," "for the sake of"
7. Irregular ㅅ verbs
8. Question ending ㄴ/은 + 가요? "Is it true that ...?"
   (polite informal)
9. Chinese characters 言, 姓, 表, 現, 王, 者

1. Expressions for "concerning," "about" -에 대하여

-대하여 derives from the verb 대하다 "to be about
(something)," but the verb is rarely used by itself; it is usually
used in a postpositional phrase, -에 대하여, or in an adjectival
(verbal modifier) phrase, -에 대한. Both come after a noun or
a verbal noun.

-에 대하여	
한글에 대하여	about *hangŭl*
낱말의 뜻에 대하여	about the meaning of the word
우리 학생에 대하여	concerning our students
한국에 대하여 썼다	(We) wrote about Korea.
세종대왕에 대하여 여쭈어 봤다.	(We) asked about King Sejong (respectfully).
우리는 중국어 표현에 대하여 배웠다.	We learned about Chinese expressions.

-에 대한

세종대왕에 대한 글	writings about King Sejong
사랑에 대한 표현	expressions of love
한국 역사에 대한 책들	books on Korean history

2. Passive construction: ACTION VERB + 어/아지다 "to be ——ed"

Some transitive verbs take on a passive meaning by combining with the auxiliary verb 지다. (Cf. L14, GN2 for DESCRIPTIVE VERB + 어/아지다.)

만들다 "to make," 만들어 지다 "to be made"

한글은 1446년에 <u>만들어졌다</u>. Hangul was invented (made) in 1446.

주다 "to give," 주어지다 "to be given"

큰 책임이 우리에게 <u>주어졌다</u>. A big responsibility is given to us.

지우다 "to erase," 지워지다 "to be erased"

글자가 <u>지워졌다</u>. The characters were erased.

3. Constructions for "before"

Unlike the time expression for "after doing...," which uses the past-tense modifier forms, the expression for "before doing..." uses the verbal noun -기 form. (Cf. L11, GN5.)

a. V. + 기 전에 "before doing"

-기 전에 is used *without* a tense marker before a past event or a future event.

한글이 <u>만들어지기 전에</u>는 학자들은 한자를 썼다.	Before *hangŭl* was invented, scholars used Chinese.
그 책을 <u>사기 전에</u>는 도서관에서 빌려봤다.	Before I bought the book, I borrowed it from the library.
내 친구를 찾아 <u>보기 전에</u> 전화를 하겠다.	Before visiting my friend, I will call him.

b. N. + 전에 "before (some event)"

크리스마스 전에 집에 가겠다.	I will go home before Christmas.
겨울방학 전에 시험이 있다.	There is an exam before the winter vacation.

4. Sequential use of the connective -어/아서 "and," "and then"

We have learned that -어/아서 indicates cause (see L8, GN6). It also indicates a sequence of events when the events occur one after another.

그들은 한자를 빌려서 썼다.	They borrowed Chinese characters and used (them).
나는 편지를 써서 보냈다.	I wrote a letter and then sent it.
미국으로 돌아와서 그 책상을 만들었다.	After I came back to the U.S., I made the desk.

When used with the verbs 가다 "to go" and 오다 "to come," -어/아서 usually indicates a sequence of events similar to the connective -고 "and" or "and then." The tense of the first clause is determined by the tense of the second clause.

저는 브라운 씨 집에 가서 그 책을 전하겠어요.	I will go to Mr. Brown's house *and* give (deliver) the book.
우리는 집에 와서 편지를 쓰겠어요.	We will come home *and then* write the letter.
우리는 식당에 가서 친구들을 만나요.	We are going to the cafeteria *and* (will) get together with friends (there).
저는 집에 와서 공부 했어요.	I *came* home and *studied*.
편지를 써서 부쳤어요.	I *wrote* a letter and then *mailed* it.

5. More on nominalization: V. STEM + 기

-기 nominalizes verbs into verbal nouns (see L10, GN6), which are similar to English gerunds (e.g., "learning") or infinitives (e.g., "to learn"). They can be a subject or a direct object and are used to construct the meaning "for ——ing" or "for ... to."

a. -기 used as a subject:

잘 쓰기가 어렵다.	It is difficult to write well.
쓰기가 쉽다.	It is easy to write.
글자를 만들기가 어렵다.	It is hard to make characters.

b. -기 used as a direct object:

나는 장래 외교관이 되기를 희망한다.	I hope to become a diplomat in the future.
그는 내년에 한국에 가기를 원한다.	He wishes to go to Korea next year.

c. -기에 used to construct "for ——ing" or "for ... to":

이 아파트는 한 사람이 살기에 적당하다.	This apartment is adequate for one person to live in.
한글은 한국어를 표현 하기에 좋다.	*Hangŭl* is good for expressing Korean.
겨울은 여행하기에 나쁘다.	Winter is not good for traveling.

6. Purposive connective -(으)려고 "in order to," "for the purpose of," "for the sake of"

Attached to a verb stem, -(으)려고 indicates a goal, intention, or purpose. The verb stem preceding -(으)려고 does not take tense markers.

-려고 is used after the verb stems that end in a vowel or ㄹ.

-으려고 is used after all other verb stems.

우리는 중국에 <u>가려고</u> 중국어를 공부해요.	We study Chinese intending to go to China.
안 선생에게 <u>드리려고</u> 이 선물을 샀어요.	We bought this gift for (in order to give it to) Mr. Ahn.
한국어를 <u>배우려고</u> 한국에 가려고 해요.	We plan to go to Korea (in order) to learn Korean.
한국 음식을 <u>먹으려고</u> 식당에 갔다.	We went to the restaurant (in order) to eat Korean food.

Often an extra ㄹ is inserted before -(으)려고 and 려고 is pronounced 라고 in spoken language.

중국에 <u>갈라고</u> 중국어를 공부해요.	Intending to go to China, we study Chinese.
안 선생에게 <u>줄라고</u> 이 선물을 샀어요.	Intending to give this gift to Mr. Ahn, I bought it.
한국어를 <u>배울라고</u> 한국에 가려고 해요.	In order to learn Korean, we plan to go to Korea.

7. Irregular ㅅ verbs

Some verb stems with ㅅ drop the ㅅ before a vowel suffix:

		-어/아서	-(으)면	-지
낫다	to get well	나(아)서	나으면	낫지
짓다	to make, to build	지어서	지으면	짓지
긋다	to draw (a line)	그어서	그으면	긋지
잇다	to connect	이어서	이으면	잇지

Some ㅅ verbs do not change:

		-어/아서	-(으)면	-지
벗다	to take off (undress)	벗어서	벗으면	벗지
웃다	to laugh	웃어서	웃으면	웃지
빗다	to comb	빗어서	빗으면	빗지
씻다	to wash (body)	씻어서	씻으면	씻지
빼앗다	to take away	빼앗아서	빼앗으면	빼앗지

8. Question ending ㄴ/은 + 가요? "Is it true that ...?" (polite informal)

-가요 is preceded by a verbal modifier, ㄴ or 은, and has the meaning "Is it true that ...?" or "Is it the case that ...?" It is used for descriptive verbs in the present tense. For descriptive verbs in the past tense and action verbs in the past and present tenses use the -나(요)? ending for the same meaning (see L15, GN8).

한국어는 중국어와 비슷한 언어 <u>인가요</u>?	(Is it true that) Korean is similar to Chinese?
한자는 배우기가 <u>어려운가요</u>?	(Is it true that) Chinese characters are difficult to learn?
한국어는 중국어와 <u>다른가요</u>?	Is Korean different from Chinese?
서울은 교통이 <u>편리한가요</u>?	Is transportation convenient in Seoul?

9. Chinese characters

言	말씀 언 language	`	二	三	言	言	言	
姓	이름 성 surname	〈	女	女	女	妒	姓	姓
表	거죽 표 surface	一	二	丰	主	表	表	表
現	나타날현 appear	二	干	王	珇	玔	珇	現
王	임금 왕 king	一	二	干	王			
者	사람 자 person	一	十	土	尹	者	者	者

연습

A. 다음 질문에 대답하십시오.

1. 한글이 만들어지기 전에 한국 사람들은 무슨 글을 썼나요?

2. 한자는 왜 한국어를 표현하기에 적당하지 않았나요?

3. 세종대왕께서는 무엇을 깨달으셨어요?

4. 왜 한국어에는 중국어에서 나온 낱말이 많이 있어요?

5. 학생은 왜 한국어를 공부해요?

6. 대학교에 오기 전에 한국어를 배웠나요?

7. 우리는 그동안 한자를 몇 자나 배웠지요?

B. 다음 문장을 끝마치십시오.

8. 한글이 만들어지기 전에 _____

9. 대학교에 오기 전에 _____

10. 한글을 배우기 전에 _____

11. 내 잘못을 깨닫기 전에 _____
    (잘못: mistake, error)

12. 그 친구를 만나기 전에 _____

13. 이 아파트는 혼자 _____ 기에 적당하다.
    (혼자: alone)

14. 이 공원은 _____ 기에 좋다.

15. 이 은행은 _____ 기에 편리하다.

16. 이 책은 _____ 기에 알맞다.

17. 우리 직장은 _____ 기에 불편하다.
    (불편하다: to be inconvenient; 직장: job site)

C. 다음 동사의 -은/ㄴ가요 형을 쓰십시오.

18. 이다 → 인가요.

19. 다르다 →

20. 비슷하다 →

21. 적당하다 →

22. 편리하다 →

23. 불편하다 →

24. 좋다 →

25. 어렵다 →

D. 다음 문장을 한국어로 번역하십시오.

26. Because Korean had no writing system, Koreans *borrowed (and used)* Chinese characters.
27. That book *is not suitable* for students.
28. She *expresses* (herself) well in writing.
29. We play tennis *before eating* dinner.
30. This pen *is good to write* with.
31. I am learning Korean *with the intention* of going to Korea next summer.
32. I study physics *because it is interesting.*
33. He is *the person who wrote (authored) many books.* (Use 짓다.)
34. Do you know *an appropriate expression?*
35. Why were many people *unable to write?*

Lesson 17

제 십칠과　친구

영식이는[1] 오늘 일본에 있는 친구 창호에게 편지를
쓰기로 했다. 창호는 영식이와 같이 고등학교를 졸업한
후, 일본으로 가서 지금은 도쿄에서 어느[2] 대학교를
다니고 있다. 창호는 정치학을 전공하며, 장래 외교관이
되기를 희망하고 있다.[3] 영식이는 올 여름 한국으로 가는
길에[4] 일본에서 창호를 만나려고 한다.[5]

Patterns

1. 일본에 있는 친구
   서울 _____
   미국 _____
   한국 _____
   중국 _____

2. 창호에게 편지를 쓰기로 했다.
   동생_____
   친구_____
   어머님_____
   선생님_____

3. 편지를 쓰기로 했다.
   여행을 가_____
   일본에 들르_____
   친구를 만나_____
   정치학을 전공하_____

4. 장래 외교관이 되기를 희망하고 있다.
   ____ 의사 _____
   ____ 선생 _____
   ____ 변호사 _____
   ____ 사업가 _____
   ____ 과학자 _____
   ____ 예술가 _____

5. 일본으로 가서 대학교를 다니고 있다.
   중국_____
   영국_____
   소련_____
   불란서_____
   독일_____

6. 한국에 가는 길에 일본에 들르려고 한다.
   중국_____
   하와이_____
   미국_____

7. 그는 정치학을 전공하며 외교관이 되기를 희망하고
   있다.
   ____ 경제학 ____ 사업가_____
   ____ 수학 ____ 교수_____
   ____ 물리학 ____ 과학자_____
   ____ 공학 ____ 엔지니어_____
   ____ 영문학 ____ 작가_____

낱말

제 십칠과 (第十七課)	Lesson 17
일본 (日本)	Japan
창호	Chang-ho (male name)
쓰기 (쓰다)	writing (to write)
졸업하다	to graduate
도쿄 (東京 : 동경)	Tokyo
정치학 (政治學)	political science

전공하다	to major
장래	future
외교관 (外交官)	diplomat
희망하다	to hope, to wish
희망	hope
만나다	to meet
가는 길에	on the way (going to)
오는 길에	on the way (coming to)
의사	doctor
변호사	lawyer, attorney-at-law
사업가	businessman
건축가	architect
과학자	scientist
공학	engineering
엔지니어	engineer
영문학	English literature
예술가	artist
미술가	(fine) artist
음악가	musician
들르다	to stop by, to drop by
선생 (先生)	teacher
교수	professor
작가	author
불란서	France
독일	Germany

낱말 연습

1. 일본에 가 봤어요?
   일본은 어디에 있어요?
2. 편지 쓰기를 좋아하세요?
3. 학생은 졸업이 언제 이지요?
   무슨 학교를 졸업했어요?

4. 정치학을 공부했어요?
   정치학을 전공하세요?
   정치학을 영어로 무엇 이라고 해요?

5. 대학에서 무엇을 전공하세요?
   전공이 어려워요? 쉬워요?
   학생들은 전공이 같아요?

6. 외교관은 무엇을 하는 사람 이에요?
   형님은 외교관으로 중국에 갔어요.

7. 장래 무엇이 되기를 희망하세요?
   외교관이 되기를 희망해요.

8. 시장에 가는 길에 친구를 만났다.
   집에 오는 길에 도서관에 갔다.
   뉴욕에서 오는 길에 덴버에 들렀다.

GRAMMAR AND NOTES

In this lesson we will study
1. Use of the particle -이 for personal names
2. Indefinite pronouns and indefinite modifiers:
   "someone," "some-," "certain"
3. Verbs 희망하다 and 원하다 "to wish," "to want," "to hope for"
   a. V. STEM + 기를 희망하다/기를 원하다
   b. N. + 을/를 원하다
4. Expressions for
   a. "on the way (going to)" 가는 길에
   b. "on the way (coming to)" 오는 길에
5. Construction of V. STEM + (으)려고 하다
   a. "to plan to," "to intend to"
   b. "is about to"
6. Chinese characters 交, 本, 京, 生, 先, 政, 治

1. Use of the particle -이 for personal names

When only the first name is used and the name ends in a consonant, the particle -이 is attached after the name and before other postpositions such as -가, -는, -를, or -와.

영식이는 오늘 편지를 쓰기로 했다.	Young-shik decided to write a letter today.
정순이와 같이 고등학교를 졸업했다.	I graduated from high school with Chung-soon.
일본에 가는 길에 영식이를 봤다.	I saw Young-shik on my way to Japan.
현숙이가 정치학을 전공했다.	Hyun-sook majored in political science.

When calling someone by his or her first name, -아 or -야 follows the name.

-야 comes after names that end in a vowel.

-아 comes after names that end in a consonant.

영희야!	Young-hie!
철수야!	Chul-soo!
영식아!	Young-shik!
정순아!	Chung-soon!

2. Indefinite pronouns and indefinite modifiers: "someone," "some-," "certain"

Question words such as 누구, 무엇, 언제, 얼마, and 몇 are also indefinite pronouns and indefinite modifiers when they are used in a statement:

Indefinite pronoun		*Indefinite modifier*	
누구	someone	어느	some-, certain
어디	somewhere	얼마	some (amount)
몇	a few	무슨	some kind of
무엇	something	어떤	some kind of
언제	sometime	몇	a few

Compare the following pairs of sentences :

그는 어느 대학에 다닌다. — He attends a certain college.
그는 어느 대학에 다녀요? — Which college does he attend?

그분은 어디에 가셨다. — He went somewhere.
그분은 어디에 가셨어요? — Where did he go?

그분은 얼마 동안 주무셨다. — She slept for a while.
그분은 얼마 동안 주무셨어요? — How long did she sleep?

나는 책을 몇 권 읽었다. — I read a few books.
책을 몇 권이나 읽었어요? — How many books did you read?

그는 무슨 일로 시내에 들어갔다. — He went to the city for (some) business.
무슨 일로 시내에 들어갔어요? — For what reason did he go to the city?

그는 무엇을 샀다. — He bought something.
그는 무엇을 샀어요? — What did he buy?

언제 한번 오세요. — Come to see us sometime.
언제 오세요? — When are you coming?

그는 어떤 집에 산다. — He lives in a certain house.
어떤 집에 사세요? — Which house do you live in?

저는 어디 좀 가요. — I am going somewhere.
어디에 가세요? — Where are you going?

누가 온다. — Someone is coming.
누구에게 편지를 쓰세요? — Who are you writing a letter to?

돈이 얼마(쯤) 있다. — I have some money.
돈이 얼마(쯤) 있어요? — How much money do you have?

3. Verbs 희망하다 and 원하다 "to wish," "to want," "to hope for"

The verbs 희망하다 and 원하다 are almost interchangeable, but 원하다 is used more broadly than 희망하다.

a. V. STEM + 기를 희망하다/원하다 "to wish," "to hope for"

동경에서 너를 만나기를 희망한다.	I hope to meet you in Tokyo.
그는 내년에 대학교에 가기를 희망한다.	He hopes to attend college next year.
나는 엔지니어가 되기를 원한다.	I want to become an engineer.

b. N. + 을/를 원하다 "to want"

부모님은 아들을 원하셨다.	The parents wished for a son.
어느 것을 원하세요?	Which one would you like?

4. Expressions for "on the way (going to)" 가는 길에, "on the way (coming to)" 오는 길에

These expressions always use the *present-tense* form even if the events happened in the past or will happen in the future.

a. 가는 길에

일본에 가는 길에 하와이에 들렀어요.	On the way to Japan, I stopped over in Hawaii.
상점에 가는 길에 편지를 부치겠어요.	On my way to the store I will mail the letter.

b. 오는 길에

학교에서 오는 길에 영희를 만났어요.	On my way here from school, I met Young-hie.
뉴욕에 오는 길에 우리는 덴버에 있는 친구를 찾아 봤어요.	On our way to New York, we visited a friend in Denver.

When used in the past tense, 간 길에 or 온 길에 means "when" or "while."

도쿄에 간 길에 사진기를 샀다.	When I went to Tokyo (as I was there) I bought a camera.

학교에 <u>간 길에</u> 도서관에 들렀다.	While I was at school, I stopped at (by) the library.
샌프란시스코에 <u>간 길에</u> 아세아 미술관을 보러 갔다.	While I was in San Francisco, I went to see the Asian Art Museum.
미국에 <u>온 길에</u> 영어를 배우기로 했다.	We decided to learn English while we are in the U.S.

5. Construction of v. STEM + (으)려고 하다 "to plan to," "to intend to," "is about to"

-(으)려고 하다 is an idiomatic use of the purposive connective -(으)려고 (see L16, GN6) with the verb 하다 "to do." The differences in meaning are understood in the context of the sentence. The construction can, however, be ambiguous and may mean either "intention" or "is about to."

a. "to plan to," "to intend to"

나는 내년 여름에 일본에서 친구를 <u>만나려고</u> 한다.	I plan to meet my friend in Japan next summer.
나는 한국어 책을 <u>읽으려고</u> 한다.	I intend/plan to read a Korean book.
우리는 부모님께 긴 편지를 <u>쓰려고</u> 한다.	We intend to write a long letter to our parents.

b. "is about to"

| 선생님께 일본에 대하여 <u>여쭈어</u> 보려고 한다. | We are about to ask our teacher about Japan. |

Time words such as 지금 "now" or 지금 막 "just now" are often used with -(으)려고 하다 to mean "is just about to."

| 나는 지금 밖에 <u>나가려고</u> 한다. | I am about to step outside now. |
| 나는 지금 막 밖에 <u>나가려고 한다</u>. | I am just about to step outside (now). |

6. Chinese characters

交	사귈 교 exchange	丶	亠	广	六	夯	交		
本	책 본 book	一	十	才	木	本			
京	서울 경 capital	丶	亠	亠	吉	古	京	京	京
生	날 생 born alive	丿	丿	仁	牛	生			
先	먼저 선 ahead	丿	仁	屮	生	步	先		
政	정치 정 (정사) politics	一	丁	下	正	正	政	政	政
治	다스릴 치 rule govern	氵	汁	沪	沪	治	治		

연습

A. 다음 질문에 대답하십시오.

　　1. 영식이는 오늘 무엇을 하기로 했습니까?

　　2. 영식이는 창호와 어떻게 아는 사이입니까?

　　3. 창호는 어디에서 무엇을 하고 있습니까?

　　4. 창호는 장래 무엇이 되기를 희망하고 있습니까?

　　5. 영식이는 올 여름에 무엇을 하려고 합니까?

　　6. 학생은 장래 무엇이 되기를 희망합니까?

　　7. 학생은 대학교를 졸업한 후 무엇을 하려고 합니까?

B. 다음 문장을 끝마치십시오.

　　8. 집에 가는 길에 ＿＿＿＿＿＿＿＿＿＿＿＿

　　9. 학교에 오는 길에 ＿＿＿＿＿＿＿＿＿＿＿＿

　　10. 기숙사로 가는 길에 ＿＿＿＿＿＿＿＿＿＿＿

　　11. 도서관으로 가는 길에 ＿＿＿＿＿＿＿＿＿＿

　　12. 식당으로 가는 길에 ＿＿＿＿＿＿＿＿＿＿＿

13. 미국으로 오는 길에 _____ _____
14. 외교관이 되기를 희망하며 _____
15. 의사가 되기를 희망하며 _____
16. _____ 여행을 안 가기로 했다.
17. _____ 예술가가 안 되기로 했다.

C. 다음 문장을 한국어로 번역하십시오.

18. I *decided to* write a letter to my teacher who is in Canada. (Use the honorific form.)
19. *After* my brother went to college, there was no letter from him.
20. What did you *decide to do* this (coming) summer?
21. Will you *stop by* Japan and Korea *on your way* to China?
22. Yes, I *plan to (intend to) stop by* Tokyo and Seoul.
23. What *will you do* if you go to China?
24. I *intend to* study the Chinese language at Beijing University. (Beijing University: 북경 대학)
25. Do you *intend to* teach Chinese?
26. Yes, I *hope to* teach at *some* high school.
27. He's gone *somewhere.* (Use 어디.)
28. There are *a few students* in the classroom. (Use 몇.)
29. Please come and visit us *sometime.* (Use 언제.)
30. I have *something to do* at home. (Use 할일.)
31. I waited *for a while.* (Use 얼마.) (to wait: 기다리다)

Lesson 18

제 십팔과 편지

창호에게
그동안 잘 있었는지 궁금하다.[1] 작년 가을에 보내 준
편지는 참 반갑게[2] 읽었다. 곧 회답을 못 해서
미안해.[3] 하루하루 미루다가[4] 이제껏 못 썼구나.[5]
나는 여전히 학교에 잘 다니고 있다. 요즘은 한국어를
택하는데 좀 어렵지만 재미있다. 한자도 좀 배우고
있다. 공부에 바쁠 너의 생활이 눈에 보이[6]는 것
같다.[7] 아무쪼록 건강하기를 빈다.
올 여름 한국에 여행을 가려고 하는데 가는 길에
일본에 들러서 너를 만나 보고 싶다.[8]
너의 계획은 어떤지 편지 연락하여 꼭 만나 보기로[9]
하자.

1990년 3월 10일
영식 씀

Patterns

1. <u>그동안 잘 있는지 궁금하다.</u>
   _____ 어떻게 지내_____
   _____ 잘 지냈_____
   _____ 학교에 잘 다니_____

2. <u>작년 가을에 보내 준 편지</u>
   ____ 여름_____
   ____ 봄_____
   ____ 겨울_____

3. 편지를 참 <u>반갑게 읽었다.</u>
   _____ 기쁘_____
   _____ 즐겁_____
   _____ 슬프_____

4. 곧 회답을 못 해서 <u>미안해</u>.
   __ 편지를 못 써서 _____
   __ 전화를 못 해서 _____
   __ 답장을 못 써서 _____

5. 이제껏 <u>못 썼구나.</u>
   _____ 했구나.
   _____ 갔구나.
   _____ 만났구나.

6. <u>너의 생활이</u> 눈에 <u>보이는 것 같다.</u>
   ____ 모습이 _____
   ____ 학교 생활이 _____

7. 보이는 <u>것 같다</u>.
   들리는 _____
   바쁜 _____
   보내는 _____

8. 나는 너를 만나 <u>보고 싶다.</u>
   나는 너와 같이 이야기하_____
   나는 편지를 쓰_____
   나는 한국에 가_____

   영희는 <u>너를 만나보고 싶어한다.</u>
   철수는 _____
   동생은 _____
   친구는 _____

9. 만나 <u>보기로 하자.</u>
   연락하_____
   편지를 쓰_____
   회답을 보내_____

10. <u>아무쪼록</u> 재미있게 <u>지내기를 빈다.</u>
    _____ 공부 잘 하_____
    _____ 건강 하_____
    _____ 사업이 잘 되_____

낱말

제 십팔과 (第十八課)	Lesson 18
그동안	during the period, meanwhile
궁금하다	to wonder about
작년 (昨年)	last year
편지 (便紙)	letter
보내 주다	to send (something for someone)
미안 (未安) 하다	to be sorry
반갑게 (반갑다)	gladly (to be glad)
회답 (回答)	response, reply
하루	one day (as a duration)
미루다가 (미루다)	while postponing it (to postpone, to delay)
이제	now
-껏	up until (emphatic)
여전히 (여전하다)	as usual (to be as usual)
택하다	to choose, to take (a course)
생활 (生活)	everyday life, living, livelihood
아무쪼록	by all means
건강하다	to be healthy
빈다. (빌다)	(I) pray. (to pray, to beg)
올 여름	this coming summer (this summer)
계획	plan
연락하다	to get in touch, to communicate
눈	eye; snow
보이다	to be seen, to be visible
기쁘게 (기쁘다)	happily (to be happy)
즐겁게 (즐겁다)	enjoyably (to be enjoyable, to be fun, to be cheerful)
답장	a reply (letter)
전화	telephone
받다	to receive
자주	often

낱말 연습 Vocabulary Exercise

1. 미국에 있는 <u>동안</u> 영어를 배웠다.
   삼 년 <u>동안</u> 한국어를 가르쳤다.
   석 달 <u>동안</u> 놀았다.

2. 동생에게서 전화가 없어서 <u>궁금하다</u>.
   집에서 소식이 없어서 <u>궁금하다</u>.

3. 작년에 책을 친구에게 <u>보내 주었다</u>.
   소식을 자주 <u>보내 주세요</u>.

4. 오랫동안 못 본 친구를 만나서 <u>반갑다</u>.
   편지를 <u>반갑게</u> 받았다.

5. <u>회답</u>이 없어서 궁금하다.
   <u>회답</u>을 쓰기가 싫다.

6. 숙제를 <u>미루고</u> 안 했다.
   회답을 <u>미루지</u> 마세요.

7. 대학 <u>생활</u>은 바쁘지 않다.
   미국 <u>생활</u>이 재미있다.

8. 장래의 <u>계획</u>을 말해 보세요.
   한국을 여행할 <u>계획</u>을 하고 있다.

9. 전화로 <u>연락해 주십시요</u>.
   편지로도 <u>연락하겠습니다</u>.
   <u>연락</u>이 없어서 궁금하다.

10. 상항에 가는 길에 백화점에 <u>들르겠다</u>.
    우리 집에 <u>들르세요</u>.

11. <u>이제껏</u> 소식이 없다.
    <u>지금껏</u> 한국에 못 가 봤다.

12. 아름다운 경치를 <u>눈으로 봤다</u>.
    너의 외국 생활을 <u>눈으로 보는 것</u> 같다.

GRAMMAR AND NOTES

In this lesson we will study

1. Verbs of "knowing":

    V. MOD. + 지 ⎰ 알다 "to know"
    ⎨ 모르다 "not to know"
    ⎱ 궁금하다 "to wonder"

2. Adverb -게 "-ly"
3. Sentence ending: intimate style -어/아
4. Interruptive connective -다가 "while doing"
5. Sentence ending -구나!/ -군! "Oh, I see that," "Oh, I realize that" (plain), -군요! (polite)
6. Passive constructions using -이, -리, -기, and -히
7. Construction of -ㄴ/은/는 것 같다 "It seems that," "It appears that"
8. Verbs of "wish": -고 싶다, -고 싶어하다
9. Sentence ending -기로 하자 "Let's plan to..." (plain)
    -기로 하십시다 (polite formal)
10. Chinese characters 活, 昨, 便, 紙, 回, 答, 未, 安

1. Verbs of "knowing":

V. MOD. + 지 ⎰ 알다   "to know"
⎨ 모르다   "not to know"
⎱ 궁금하다   "to wonder"

For expressions of uncertainty or for confirming questions, 는/은/을지 is used. It is usually followed by a "mental verb" such as 알다 "to know," 모르다 "not to know," and 궁금하다 "to be concerned, worried," "to wonder."

V. STEM + ⎰ 은/ㄴ ⎱   ⎰ 모르다
         ⎨ 는 ⎬ 지 ⎨ 알다
         ⎱ 을/ㄹ ⎰   ⎱ 궁금하다

Note the difference between descriptive verbs and action verbs in *present*-tense verbal modifiers.

a. Descriptive verbs

은/ㄴ지 *(present)*

뉴욕이 추운지 모르겠다. (춥 + 은 → 추운)	I wonder if it is cold in New York.
그분이 바쁜지 모르겠다. (바쁘 + ㄴ → 바쁜)	I wonder if he is busy.
그곳에 학생이 많은지 아세요? (많 + 은 → 많은)	Do you know if there are many students there?

을/ㄹ지 *(future)*

올 겨울이 추울지 궁금하다. (춥 + 을 → 추울)	I wonder if this coming winter will be cold.
시험이 어려울지 모르겠다. (어렵 + 을 → 어려울)	I wonder if the exam will be difficult.

었/았는지 *(past)*

그동안 잘 있었는지 궁금하다 (있 + 었 → 있었)	I wonder if you have been well.
작년에 한국이 추웠는지 모르겠다. (춥 + 었 → 추웠)	I wonder if it was cold in Korea last year.
그분이 어제 바빴는지 모르겠다. (바쁘 + 았 → 바빴)	I wonder if he was busy yesterday.

b. Action verbs

는지 *(present)*

대답이 맞는지 궁금하다. (맞 + 는 → 맞는)	I wonder if the answer is correct.
동생이 학교에 잘 다니는지 알고 싶다. (다니 + 는 → 다니는)	I would like to know if my younger brother is doing well in (attending) school.

을/ㄹ지 *(future)*

선생님이 몇 시에 오실지 아세요? (오시 + ㄹ → 오실)	Do you know what time our teacher is coming?
내일 비가 올지 아세요? (오 + ㄹ → 올)	Do you know if it will rain tomorrow?

었/았는지 *(past)*

내 대답이 맞았는지 알고 싶다. (맞 + 았 → 맞았)	I would like to know whether my answer was correct.
친구가 시험을 잘 봤는지 모르겠다.(보 + 았 → 봤)	I wonder whether my friend did well on the exam.

2. Adverb -게 "-ly"

Attached to a descriptive verb stem, -게 makes an adverb from a verb. This adverb form, like all other adverbs, always precedes the main verb.

반갑다	to be glad	반갑게 읽었다.	I read it gladly.
크다	to be big	크게 보인다.	It looks big.
노랗다	to be yellow	노랗게 된다.	It becomes yellow.
어렵다	to be difficult	어렵게 산다.	He has a hard life.

3. Sentence ending: intimate style -어/아

The -어/아 ending is the most intimate and informal style of speech. This style is used among children, between friends, or by an adult to a child. The choice of -어 or -아 follows the rules of choosing the polite informal ending -어요 or -아요 explained in L8, GN2.

The intonation pattern changes the meaning of the sentences. Questions are spoken with a rising intonation; statements and commands are spoken with a level or falling intonation.

참 미안해.	I am very sorry.
너의 소식을 반갑게 들었어.	I was happy to hear your news.
친구소식 들었어?	Did you hear about your friend?
너를 만나 보고 싶어.	I'd like to see you.
서울에 가 보고 싶어?	Do you want to go see Seoul?
빨리 와.	Come quickly.

4. Interruptive connective -다가 "while doing"

When -다가 is attached to a verb, it indicates an interrupted action by another action that follows. This connective form is used only when the subject is the same for both actions.

a. V. STEM. + 다가: interrupted action "while doing..."

숙제를 하다가 친구가 와서 밖에 나갔다.	While I was doing my homework, my friend came, and we went outside.
라디오를 듣다가 잠이 들었다.	While I was listening to the radio, I fell asleep.
동경에 가다가 대학 친구를 만났다.	On my way to Tokyo, I met my college friend.

b. V. STEM. + (었/았) + 다가: causal effect "because"

Sometimes -다가 indicates a causal effect similar to -어/아 서 or -기 때문에. For this effect the past tense 었/았 can be used.

하루하루 미루다가 이제껏 너에게 편지를 못 썼다.	Because I was putting it off day after day, I didn't write you until now.
늦게 나갔다가 숙제를 못 했다.	I didn't do the homework because I was out late.
늦잠을 자다가 뻐스를 놓쳤다.	I missed the bus because I slept late.

5. Sentence ending -구나!/ -군! "Oh, I see that," "Oh, I realize that" (plain), -군요! (polite)

This plain or polite ending expresses the speaker's new awareness of a fact or an event.

이제껏 너에게 편지를 못 썼구나!	(Oh, I realize that) I haven't been able to write you until now!
내 동생이 오는구나!	(Oh, I see that) my brother is coming!

아버지께서 오셨구나!	(Oh, I see that) my father came!
어머니께서 곧 오시겠구나!	(Oh, I see that) my mother will be coming soon!

Adding -요 to -군, an alternate form of -구나, makes the polite ending -군요.

벌써 봄이구나.	(plain)	
벌써 봄이군.	(plain)	It's already spring.
벌써 봄이군요.	(polite)	

6. Passive constructions using -이, -리, -기, and -히

Most transitive action verbs become intransitive passive verbs when one of the four suffixes -이, -리, -기, or -히 is added. The choice of a proper suffix for a given verb follows the general rules stated below, although there are exceptions.

For these passive constructions, the "actor" or an "agent" of the sentence is marked by postpositions as follows:

-에게/한테 *"by"* (*for persons and animate nouns*)

아이가 어머니에게 안겼다.	The child is being held by the mother.
쥐가 고양이한테 먹혔다.	The mouse was eaten by the cat.

-에 *"by"* (*for inanimate things*)

문이 바람에 닫혔다.	The door was shut by the wind.
산이 눈에 덮였다.	The mountain is covered with snow.

-(으)로 *"by"* (*for abstract nouns as a cause or an instrument*)

사고로 길이 막혔다.	The road is blocked because of an accident.
산이 눈으로 덮였다.	The mountain is covered with snow.

a. Use -이 when the verb stem ends in a vowel.

보다	보이다	너의 바쁜 생활이 (눈에) <u>보인</u>다.
to see	to be seen	I can see how busy your life is.
쓰다	쓰이다	글씨가 안 <u>쓰인</u> 종이
to write	to be written	a paper with no letters written on it (blank paper)
쓰다	쓰이다	그 책들은 잘 안 <u>쓰인</u>다.
to use	to be used	Those books are not widely used.
부르다*	불리다	링컨 대통령은 정직한 에이브라고 <u>불렸</u>다.
to call	to be called	President Lincoln was called "Honest Abe."

* 르 irregular verb (see L8, GN1).

b. Use -기 when the verb stem ends in ㄴ, ㅁ, or ㅅ.

안다	안기다	아이가 어머니에게 안겼다.
to hold	to be held	The child is held by his mother.
씻다	씻기다	길이 비에 씻기었다
to wash	to be washed	The road was washed (away) by rain.
담다	담기다	독에는 쌀이 담겼다.
to fill	to be filled	The jar is filled with rice.

c. Use -리 when the verb stem ends in ㄷ, ㄹ, or ㄽ.

듣다	들리다	좋은 소식이 <u>들렸</u>다.
to hear	to be heard	Good news was heard.
팔다	팔리다	옆 집이 <u>팔렸</u>다.
to sell	to be sold	The house next door was sold.
뚫다	뚫리다	산에 굴이 <u>뚫렸</u>다.
to bore (a hole)	to be bored	A tunnel was bored into the mountain.

d. Use -히 when the verb stem ends in ㄱ, ㄷ, ㅂ, ㅈ, or ㄼ.

먹다	먹히다	쥐가 고양이에게 <u>먹혔</u>다.
to eat	to be eaten	A mouse was eaten by a cat.
막다	막히다	길이 <u>막혔</u>다.
to block	to be blocked	The street is blocked.

닫다	닫히다	문이 바람에 <u>닫혔다</u>.
to close	to be closed	The door is closed by the wind.
잡다	잡히다	도둑이 순경에게 <u>잡혔다</u>.
to catch	to be caught	The thief was caught by a policeman.
밟다	밟히다	개미가 내 발에 <u>밟혔다</u>.
to step on	to be stepped on	The ants were stepped on by my foot.

   e. Use -이 when the verb stem ends in ㄲ, ㅌ, ㅍ, or ㅎ.

닦다	닦이다	신이 잘 <u>닦였다</u>.
to polish	to be polished	The shoes were polished nicely.
덮다	덮이다	시내가 눈에 <u>덮였다</u>.
to cover	to be covered	The city is covered with snow.
쌓다	쌓이다	책상 위에 책이 많이 <u>쌓였다</u>.
to pile	to be piled	Many books are piled up on the desk.
놓다	놓이다	접시에 오이가 <u>놓였다</u>.
to put, to place	to be put down, to be placed	A cucumber is placed on a plate.

   Remember that not all sentences can be expressed in passive form by transforming an action verb into a passive verb. In many cases, different verbs are used to express passive meaning, and in some cases it is not possible to express sentences in passive at all.

그는 나를 <u>쳤다</u>.	He hit me.
나는 그에게 <u>맞았다</u>.	I was hit by him.
	(맞다: to be hit; 치다: hit)

7. Construction of -ㄴ/은/는 것 같다 "It seems that," "It appears that"

   Always preceded by a verbal modifier, -것 같다 indicates an opinion of the speaker rather than a definitive statement. It often carries the meaning of "I think" in English. (See L22, GN5 for the construction v. MOD. + 것.)
   Note the difference between descriptive verbs and action verbs in the use of verbal modifiers for *present* tense.

a. A. V. + V. MOD. + 것 같다

는 (present)	바쁜 너의 생활이 눈에 <u>보이는 것</u> 같다. Your busy life seems almost visible to my eyes. (I can almost see your busy life.) 동생은 공부를 잘 <u>하는 것</u> 같다. My younger brother seems to do well in his studies.
을/ㄹ (future)	동생은 공부를 잘 <u>할 것</u> 같다. My younger sister looks as if she will do well in her studies.
은/ㄴ (past)	동생은 숙제를 다 <u>한 것</u> 같다. My younger sister seems to have finished her homework.

b. D. V. + V. MOD. + 것 같다

은/ㄴ (present)	한자는 <u>어려운 것</u> 같다. (어렵 + 은 → 어려운) Chinese characters seem difficult.
을/ㄹ (future)	한자는 <u>어려울 것</u> 같다. (어렵 + 을 → 어려울) It seems that Chinese characters would be difficult.

-것 같다 can be used in the past tense to mean "it seemed that," "it looked as if."

그는 북경에 <u>들를 것</u> 같았다.	It seemed that he would be stopping by Beijing.
그는 대만에 <u>들르는 것</u> 같았다.	It looked as if he was stopping in Taiwan.

8. Verbs of "wish": -고 싶다, -고 싶어하다

To express a wish, desire, or longing, use either -고 싶다 or -고 싶어하다, depending on the subject of the sentence.

a. -고 싶다 is used for a statement with the first-person subject "I" or "we" or for a question with the second-person subject "you."

(나는) 너를 만나 보고 싶다.	I would like to see you.
우리는 고향에 가고 싶었다.	We wanted to go visit our hometown.
무엇을 읽고 싶으세요?	What would you like to read?
어디에 들르고 싶으세요?	Where would you like to stop by?

b. -고 싶어하다 is used for all other subjects: for statements with the third-person subject "he," "she," "it," or "they" or the second-person "you."

그는 너를 보고 싶어한다.	He wants to see you.
그들은 집에 가고 싶어한다.	They want to go home.
그들은 한국 음악을 듣고 싶어한다.	They want to listen to Korean music.
그분은 무엇을 보고 싶어하세요?	What would she like to see?
그분들은 누구에게 연락을 하고 싶어하세요?	To whom do they wish to send a message?
너도 외교관이 되고 싶어한다.	You also want to become a diplomat.

9. Sentence ending -기로 하자 "Let's plan to..."

The polite formal form -기로 하십시다 means "Let's plan to... (if you please)," and the polite informal form -기로 해요 means "Let's plan to... (please)." -기로 하자 is the plain ending for "Let's plan to..."

Polite formal
빨리 계획하기로 하십시다.	(If you please) let us plan it quickly.

Polite informal
빨리 계획하기로 해요.	Please, let's plan it quickly.

Plain
빨리 계획하기로 하자.	Let's plan it quickly.

Do not use this expression to a social superior who is not a close relative or friend. Instead, use the question form:

빨리 가기로 하시겠어요?   Would you mind planning to leave quickly?

내일 만나기로 하시겠어요?   Would you like to plan on meeting (someone) tomorrow?

10. Chinese characters

活	살 활 life live	氵	氵	氵	汗	汗	活	活	
昨	어제 작 yesterday past	日	昨	昨					
便	편할 편 conve- nient	亻	亻	亻	佰	佰	佰	便	便
紙	종이 지 paper	乚	糸	糸	糸	紅	紅	紙	紙
回	돌 회 turn	丨	冂	冂	回	回	回		
答	대답 답 answer reply	丿	𠂉	竹	竹	竻	竻	竺	答
未	아닐 미 not	一	二	丰	未	未			
安	편안 안 peace quiet	丶	丷	宀	宀	安	安		

연습

A. 다음 질문에 대답하십시오.

1. 영식이는 언제 창호의 편지를 받았어요?
2. 영식이는 왜 창호에게 미안하다고 했어요?
3. 영식이는 왜 이제껏 창호에게 회답을 못 했어요?
4. 영식이는 이번 여름에 어디에 가려고 해요?
5. 영식이는 왜 일본에 들르려고 합니까?

B. 다음 문장을 끝마치십시오.

6. 하루하루 미루다가 _____
7. 비행기가 멀리서 보이다가 _____
8. 음악 소리가 들리다가 _____
9. 경제학을 전공하다가 _____
10. 일본에서 여행을 하다가 _____

C. 다음 문장을 주어에 따라 "-고 싶다" 또는 "-고 싶어하다"로 끝마치십시오. (주어: subject)

11. 한국에 간다: 나는 _____
　　　　　　　　　영희는 _____

12. 대학생활을 재미있게 보낸다:
　　　　　　　　　나는 _____
　　　　　　　　　철수는 _____

13. 친구를 만나본다:
　　　　　　　　　나는 _____
　　　　　　　　　동생은 _____

14. 백화점에 들른다:
　　　　　　　　　나는 _____
　　　　　　　　　친구는 _____

D. 다음 문장을 한국어로 번역하십시오.

15. I *wonder if* you are getting along well. I *wonder if* your parents are well, too. (Use hon.)

16. I *wonder if* you received the letter that I sent you last September.

17. I *was glad to* receive your letter. (I gladly received your letter.)

18. I *am sorry* I could not come to your party.

19. I *am sorry* I could not finish the homework. (I could not do all the homework.)

20. A year has gone by *while (I've been) putting it off day after day.*

21. *It seemed as though* all of (the city of) Tokyo *could be seen* from the airplane.

22. *It seems as though* the music *is being heard* from afar.

23. I want to meet you *on my way to* Korea.

24. *Let's make sure* that we keep in touch.

25. My friend *would like (wishes)* to visit China.

26. We *would like to see* your (everyday) life.

27. *Would you like to stop by* Seoul on your way to China?

28. *My parents would like to* meet my friends.

29. Chul-soo *would like to* become a diplomat, while Young-hie *would like to* become an engineer.

Lesson 19

제 십구과   한국에 대하여

대화

영희: 한국은 동남아세아의 나라들 중의 하나[1] 인가요?

철수: 아니요. 한국은 극동에 있어요. 한국, 일본, 그리고 중국을 보통 극동이라고 하지요.

영희: 한국은 중국의 일부분이었나요?

철수: 아니요. 중국과 경계를 같이 하고[2] 있으나[3] 중국의 일부분이었던[4] 일은 없어요.[5] 한국은 사천년이 넘는 고유한 역사와 문화를 가지고 있어요.

영희: 옛날에 한국은 왕국이었어요?

철수: 네, 삼국시대부터[6] 시작하여 고려 시대를 거쳐, 조선시대까지,[6] 약 2,000 여년 동안 왕국 이었습니다.

영희: 그럼 민주주의 정부는 언제부터 시작됐어요?

철수: 1945년 제이차 세계대전이 끝난 후부터 이지요. 1945년 8월 15일 독립이 된 후, 남한에는 대한민국을 세우고, 북한에는 조선 인민 공화국을 세웠어요. 그래서 한국은 둘로[7] 나누어져 있으나 곧 통일이 되[8]기를 바라지요.[9]

Patterns

1. 중국은 아세아의 나라들 중의 하나이다.
   일본은 극동 아세아 나라들 _____
   영국은 유럽에 있는 왕국 _____

2. 한국, 일본, 중국을 극동<u>이라고 하지요</u>.
   신라, 고구려, 백제를 삼국 _____
   왕이 있는 나라를 왕국 _____

3. 한국은 중국의 일부분이었던 <u>일이 없다</u>.
   죤은 한국에 가 본 _____
   알라스카를 거쳐 간 _____

4. 한국에 삼국이 있었던 <u>일이 있다</u>.
   한국어로 편지를 써본 _____
   나는 일본에 들러 본 _____

5. 중국과 국경을 같이 하고 있<u>으나</u> 중국의 일부분
   이었던 일은 없다.
   날씨는 더우____ 비가 온다.
   중국어는 하____ 일본어는 못 한다.
   겨울철은 시작됐____ 눈이 안 온다.
   학기가 끝났____ 기숙사에 남아 있겠다.

6. 약 **2,000**여년 <u>동안</u> 왕국이었다.
   방학 _____(에) 한국에 갔다.
   다섯 시간 _____ 비행기를 탔다.
   여름 _____(에) 일을 했다.
   내년 일년 _____ 여행을 하겠다.

7. 민주주의 정부가 <u>언제부터</u> 시작됐어요?
   제이차 세계대전이 _____
   삼국 시대가 _____
   가을 학기가 _____

8. 제이차 세계대전이 <u>끝난 후부터</u> 한국은 둘로
   나누어졌다.
   고려시대가 _____ 조선시대가 시작되었다.
   공부 시간이 _____ 일을 시작했다.

9. 제일차 세계대전이 <u>끝나기 전부터</u> 미국은 유럽을
   도와주었다.
   조선시대가 _____ 기독교가 한국에 들어왔다.
   공부 시간이 _____ 집에 갈 생각을 했다.

10. 통일 되기를 바란다.
꼭 들르_____
곧 오_____
독립이 되_____

낱말

제 십구과 (第十九課)	Lesson 19
동남 아세아	Southeast Asia
극동	Far East
보통	in general, usually
일부분 (一部分)	a part
경계	boundary, border
넘다	to exceed, to go over
고유한 (고유하다)	unique (to be unique)
역사	history
문화 (文化)	culture
가지다	to have, to possess
옛날	old days
왕국	kingdom
삼국 시대	Three Kingdoms period
-부터 ... 까지	from...to/until
시작 (始作)하다	to begin, to start
고려 시대	Koryŏ period
거치어 (거치다)	passing through (to pass through, to go by)
조선	Chosun (dynasty)
-여	about, odd (e.g., "There are thirty-odd houses.")
민주주의	democracy
정부	government
시작되다	to be started
제이차	second round
세계 (世界)	world
대전	great war, world war

끝난 (끝나다)	finished, ended (to end)
독립 (되다)	independence (to become independent)
남한	South Korea
북한	North Korea
대한민국	Republic of Korea
조선 인민 공화국	Democratic People's Republic of Korea
세우다	to establish, to erect
그래서	so, therefore
나누다	to divide
나누어지다	to become divided
통일이 되다	to be united
바라다	to hope for
곧	soon, right away
신라	Shilla (dynasty), Kingdom of Shilla
고구려	Koguryŏ (dynasty), Kingdom of Koguryŏ
백제	Paekche (dynasty), Kingdom of Paekche
유럽	Europe
국경	national border, national boundary
제일차 세계 대전	First World War
학기	school term
기독교	Christianity
들어오다	to enter, to come in

GRAMMAR AND NOTES

In this lesson we will study
1. Expression for "one (out) of ... ," "one of ..." ...중의 하나
2. Expression for "to share ... ": -을/를 같이 하다
   (... 하고 있다)
3. Concessive connective -(으)나 "although," "even though,"
   "but"
4. Verbal modifier -던
   a. v. STEM + 던 habitual or repetitive past "used to,"
      "had been," "had done"
   b. v. STEM + 었/았+던 factual past "had been,"
      "had done"
5. Constructions for
   a. v. MOD. + 일이 있다 "there has been," "I have been"
   b. v. MOD. + 일이 없다 "there has never been,"
      "I have never been"
6. Postposition -부터 ... 까지 "from ... to," "from ... until"
7. Postposition -(으)로 "by/in" (as in "divided by/in")
8. Passive construction N. + 되다
9. Constructions for
   a. v. STEM + 기를 바라다 "to wish," "to long for"
   b. v. MOD. + 것을 바라다 "to wish that"
10. Chinese characters 文, 化, 始, 作, 部, 世, 界

1. Expression for "one out of ... ," "one of ... " ... 중의 하나

... 중의 하나 means literally "one among."

한국은 극동에 있는 나라들 중의 하나이다.	Korea is one of the countries in the Far East.
둘 중의 하나를 주세요.	Please give me one of the two.
한국, 일본, 중국 중의 한 나라만 가 보겠어요.	I will visit only one of the countries, Korea, Japan, or China.
소련은 (우리가) 경계를 같이 하고 있는 나라 중의 하나이다.	Russia is one of the countries we share a border with.

2. Expression for "to share ... :" -을/를 같이 하다 (... 하고있다.)

Literally this expression means "to do (something) together," but it extends to the meaning "to share (something) with," as in "share a border with" or "share a meal with."

한국은 중국과 경계를 같이 하고 있다.	Korea shares a border with China.
우리는 수요일마다 점심을 같이 한다.	We share (have) lunch together every Wednesday.
뜻을 같이 하는 사람들이 모였다.	People who share the same purpose are gathered together.

3. Concessive connective -(으)나 "although," "even though," "but"

-(으)나 has a meaning close to -지만, and the two can be used interchangeably. -(으)나 is used more in written language than in spoken language.

그리스와 터키는 경계를 같이 하고 있으나 사이가 좋지 않다.	Greece and Turkey share a border, but they are not friendly to each other.
스페인은 다시 왕국이 되었으나 민주주의 정부를 갖고 있다.	Although Spain became a kingdom, it has a democratic government.
제이차 세계대전이 오래 전에 끝났으나 아직도 평화가 없다.	Even though World War II ended long ago, there is no peace. (평화: peace)

4. Verbal modifier -던

a. V. STEM + 던 habitual or repetitive past "used to," "had been," "had done"

When -던 is attached directly to a verb stem, it indicates the habitual aspect of the verb. (See L11, GN1, and L15, GN1 for other modifier forms.)

놀다	놀던	아이들이 놀던 곳
to play	used to play	the place where children used to play
다니다	다니던	우리가 다니던 학교
to attend	used to attend	the school we used to attend
듣다	듣던	우리가 듣던 음악
to listen to	used to listen to	the music we used to listen to
읽다	읽던	우리가 읽던 책
to read	used to read	the book we used to read (or, the book we had been reading)

b. v. STEM + 었/았 + 던 factual past "had been," "had done"

When -던 is used with the tense marker -었 or -았, it indicates a fact or an event that occurred in the past. It can be translated into English in the past perfect tense, as in:

이다	이었던	일부분이었던 일
to be	had been	the fact that ... had been a part
가다	갔던	우리가 갔던 백화점
to go	had gone	the department store that we had gone to
나누어지다	나누어졌던	나누어졌던 두 독일
to be divided	had been divided	the two Germanys, which had been divided
빌리다	빌렸던	내가 도서관에서 빌렸던 책
to borrow	had borrowed	the book I had borrowed from the library

5. Constructions for "there has been," "there has never been"

일 has a wide range of meaning besides "work," such as "event," "business," "matter," and "problem." It is often used with 있다 (e.g., 일이 있다) or 없다 (e.g., 일이 없다) to indicate an experience, as in "there has been" or "there has never been."

a. V. MOD. + 일이 있다 "there has been," "I have been"

캘리포니아는 멕시코의 일부분이었던 일이 있다.	California had once been a part of Mexico. (It is the case that California was once a part of Mexico.)
나는 남부에 가본 일이 있다.	I have been to the south.

b. V. MOD. + 일이 없다 "there has never been," "I have never been"

미국은 왕국이었던 일이 없다.	The U.S. has never been a kingdom.
그 나라는 민주주의 정부를 가져 본 일이 없다.	That country never had a democratic government.
나는 아프리카에 가 본 일이 없다.	I have never been to Africa.

6. Postposition -부터 ... -까지 "from ... to," "from ... until"

This expression is used for both time and space. -에서부터 may be used in three ways: 에서, 부터, and 에서부터. They are usually interchangeable, as in the following examples:

a. Time

오늘부터 내일까지	from today until tomorrow
1910년 {부터 / 에서* / 에서부터} 1986년까지	from 1910 to 1986
1월부터 12월까지	from January to December
세시부터 일곱시까지	from three to seven o'clock

* -부터 and -에서부터 can be used without the ...까지 phrase to mean "from" or "since." But -에서 cannot be used for the same meaning without the ...까지 phrase. For example, one can say 1960년(에서)부터 미국에 살았어요 (I have lived in the U.S. since 1960), but not 1960년에서 미국에 살았어요.

b. Space

여기 $\begin{Bmatrix} 부터 \\ 에서 \\ 에서부터 \end{Bmatrix}$ 저기까지 from here to there

중국 $\begin{Bmatrix} 부터 \\ 에서 \\ 에서부터 \end{Bmatrix}$ 일본까지 from China to Japan

하나 $\begin{Bmatrix} 부터 \\ 에서 \\ 에서부터 \end{Bmatrix}$ 열까지 from one to ten
(idiomatically, "everything")

아이 $\begin{Bmatrix} 부터 \\ 에서 \\ 에서부터 \end{Bmatrix}$ 어른까지 from children to adults

7. Postposition - (으)로 "by/in" (as in "divided by/in")

In addition to the meanings "as" and "in the role of" (L7, GN7), -(으)로 can mean "by/in," as in "divided by/in."

한국은 둘로 나누어졌다.	Korea was divided in two.
여섯을 셋으로 나누면 둘이 된다.	If you divide six by three, you will get two.
반으로 나누어 주십시오.	Please divide it in half (for me).

8. Passive construction: N. + 되다

Some action verbs that are derived from Sino-Korean nouns by adding the word 하다 "to do" become passives when 하다 is replaced by 되다 "to become."

준비 preparation

준비하다 to prepare	약을 준비했다. I prepared the medicine.
준비되다 to be prepared, to be ready	약이 준비 됐다. The medicine is ready.

시작 beginning/start

시작하다	학기가 9월에 시작했다.
to begin/start	The semester started in September.
시작되다	학기가 9월에 시작됐다.
to be begun/started	The semester was begun in September.

통일 unification

통일하다	나라가 통일하기를 바란다.
to unify	I hope the country will unify.
통일되다	나라가 통일되기를 바란다.
to be unified.	I hope the country will be unified.

9. Constructions for -기를 바라다 "to wish," "to long for"

Like 원하다 and 희망하다 (L17, GN3), 바라다 is preceded by -기를 or in some cases -것을 to express "wish," "desire," or "longing."

a. V. STEM + 기를 바라다 "to wish," "to long for"

한국이 통일되기를 바란다.	We wish Korea to be unified.
누구나 민주주의가 되기를 바란다.	Everybody wishes the country to be democratic.

b. V. MOD. + 것을 바라다 "to wish that"

한국이 통일되는 것을 바란다.	(We) wish that Korea would be unified.
누구나 민주주의가 되는 것을 바란다.	Everybody would like to see (it) become democratic. (Everybody would like to see democracy.)

10. Chinese characters

文	글 문 letters culture	丶	二	ナ	文			
化	될 화 change transform	ノ	イ	仁	化			
始	시작 시 begin	く	女	女	女	妒	妒	始	始
作	지을 작 make	ノ	イ	什	作			
部	조각 부 piece part	二	ㅗ	立	咅	咅	咅	部	
世	세상 세 (인간) world	一	十	卅	世	世		
界	경계 제 world boundary	丶	冂	曰	田	田	界	界	界

연습

A. 제19과를 읽고 다음 질문에 대답하십시오.

1. 극동에 있는 나라는 어느 나라들입니까?

2. 한국과 경계를 같이 하고 있는 나라는 어느 나라들입니까?

3. 인도도 극동에 있는 나라입니까? (인도: India)

4. 옛날에 일본은 중국의 일부분이었던 일이 있나요?

5. 한국은 언제부터 민주주의 정부가 시작되었습니까?

6. 한국은 얼마 동안 왕국이었습니까?

7. 한국의 역사는 얼마나 되었습니까?
미국의 역사는요?

8. 극동에 가 본 일이 있어요?

9. 미국은 언제 독립했나요?

10. 미국은 어느 나라들과 경계를 같이 하고 있지요?

B. 다음 어구를 사용하여 짧은 글을 지으십시오.
   (Write short sentences using the following expressions.)
   11. 일부분
   12. ___ 부터 ___ 까지
   13. ___ 동안
   14. ___ ㄴ/은 후부터
   15. 가지고 있다
   16. 끝나다
   17. 거치다
   18. 통일하다
   19. 세우다
   20. 바라다
   21. 나누어지다

C. 다음 문장을 보기와 같이 바꾸고 그 뜻을 영어로 써 보십시오. (Change the present-tense modifiers into habitual modifiers and translate into English.)
   보기: 아이들이 노는 운동장 → 아이들이 놀던 운동장
        the sports field where the children used to play
   22. 우리가 다니는 학교 →
   23. 친구가 일하는 백화점 →
   24. 부모님이 사시는 집 →
   25. 어머니가 보고 싶어하는 아들 →
   26. 아버님이 하시는 사업 →

D. 다음 문장을 한국어로 번역하십시오.
   27. Although Korea is a small country, it has a long history of *over 4,000 years.*
   28. The U.S. *shares a border with* Canada on the north and Mexico on the south.
   29. Korea *became independent* on August 15, 1945, but it *was divided in* two.
   30. When were East and West Germany united?
   31. Since I am *usually* busy from 8 A.M. to 5 P.M., please come around 6 P.M.
   32. What would you say is *the unique history and culture* of the U.S.?

33. *(From) when* will school begin?
34. *We hope that* North and South Korea will *become united* soon.
35. I came to San Francisco *through (via)* Honolulu.
36. I *have never been (gone)* to Southeast Asia.
37. *Has* California *ever been a part of* Mexico?

E. "미국에 대하여" 작문을 지으십시오. (Write a short composition about America.)

Lesson 20

제 이십과 전화

따르릉, 따르릉 ...

간호원 : 여보세요? 김 내과입니다.
영식 : 의사 선생님[1]을 좀 뵈려고 하는데요.[2]
간호원 : 성함이 어떻게 되시지요?
영식 : 이영식인데요.
간호원 : 네, 잠깐만 기다려 주세요. 어디가
아프세요?
영식 : 열이 나고 온 몸이 아파요.
간호원 : 아주 몹시 아프십니까?
영식 : 네, 의사 선생님을 곧 좀[3] 뵈었으면
좋겠습니다.[4]
간호원 : 오늘 오후 한 시 반에 오실 수[5] 있습니까?
영식 : 네, 그러지요.
간호원 : 전화번호 좀 주시겠어요?
영식 : 네, 칠오이의 팔육사구 입니다.
간호원 : 그럼 이따 오세요. 오실 때[6] 진찰권을
가지고 오세요.
영식 : 네.

Patterns

1. 좀 뵈려고 하는데요.
   기다리려고 하는____
   몹시 아픈____
   의사 선생님이 안 계신____
   어디 가셨는____

2. 좀 뵈었으면 좋겠습니다.
   __ 놀러 오십시요.
   __ 기다리십시요.
   __ 주십시요.

3. 뵈었으면 좋겠습니다.
   오셨으면 _____
   전화해 주시면 _____
   기다려 주시면 _____
   오실 수 있으면 _____

4. 내일 오실 수 있습니까?
   전화해 주실 _____
   다시 (전화) 걸어 주실 _____
   의사 선생님을 뵐 _____

5. 내일 갈 수 없는데요.
   전화할 _____
   내일부터 시작할 _____
   오후에는 뵐 _____

6. 잠깐만 기다려 주세요.
   _____ 와 _____
   _____ 도와 _____
   _____ (전화를) 바꿔 _____

7. 진찰권을 가지고 오세요.
   연필_____
   꽃_____
   점심_____

8. 전화 번호 좀 주시겠어요?
   진찰권 _____
   성함 _____
   주소 _____

낱말

제 이십과 (第 二十課)	Lesson 20
따르릉	ringing sound
전화 (電話)	telephone
간호원	nurse
여보세요.	Hello! (when answering the phone)
내과 (內科)	internal medicine (physician)
의사	medical doctor
뵈려고 (뵙다)	in order to see (to see a person—hon.)
성함	name (hon.)
열	fever, temperature
열이 나다	to have a fever
온	entire
몸	body
몹시	severely
기다리다	to wait
걸다	to telephone, to hang up
전화를 걸다	to telephone
울리다	to ring, to resonate
놓다	to put down, to install
바꾸다	to change
바꿔 드리다	to put someone on the phone (hon.)
끊다	to cut, to sever, to hang up
통화	getting through (on a phone)
통화중이다	phone is busy
외과 (外科)	surgical medicine, surgery
소아과	pediatric medicine
치과	dentistry
안과	ophthalmology
가지고 가다	to take along (something)
가지고 오다	to bring along (something)

교환(수)	operator
진찰권	medical card
오전 (午前)	morning, A.M.
오후 (午後)	afternoon, P.M.
주소	address

전화할 때 필요한 말 Useful expressions on the telephone

전화(가) 왔어요.	A phone call came. (There's a phone call.)
전화(를) 받으세요.	Please answer the phone.
전화(를) 걸어요.	I am telephoning.
전화가 울려요.	The phone is ringing.
전화를 끊겠어요.	I will hang up the phone.
전화로 전했어요.	I communicated by phone.
전화를 잘못 걸었어요.	I got the wrong number.
전화가 통화중이에요.	The phone is busy.
전화번호를 바꿨어요.	I changed the phone number.
전화를 바꿔 드리겠어요.	I will hand (change) the phone to someone else.
전화가 안 걸려요.	The phone call is not getting through.
전화가 끊어져요.	The phone call gets disconnected.
(전화)번호를 돌려요.	I dial a number.
전화를 놓아요.	I have a phone installed.

GRAMMAR AND NOTES

In this lesson we will study
1. Honorific form of address: TITLE + (선생)님
2. Sentence ending -ㄴ/은/는데요 (polite informal)
3. Uses of 좀 "a little," "please"
4. Expression for "I wish ...": -(으)면 좋겠다
5. Constructions for
   a. -ㄹ/을 수 있다 "can," "to be possible"
   b. -ㄹ/을 수 없다 "cannot," "to be impossible"
6. Expression for "when," "while," "at the time when":
   -ㄹ/을때
7. Chinese characters 午, 後, 前, 內, 科, 電, 話

1. Honorific form of address: TITLE + (선생)님

To address someone respectfully, 선생님 is added after a person's title or name. Some titles take only -님.

Educational or institutional titles

김 선생님	Mr. Kim
교장 선생님	principal
의사 선생님	doctor (M.D.)
이 박사님	Dr. Lee (Ph.D.)
총장님	university president
학장님	dean (college)

Business, trade, or government titles

사장님	president (of a company)
과장님	manager, head of a department
장관님	minister/secretary (in government)

2. Sentence ending -ㄴ/은/는 데(요) (polite informal)

-ㄴ/은/는데(요) is an ending derived from the connective ending -ㄴ/은/는데, which means "and," "but," "by the way," or "and then." Building on the connective meaning, -ㄴ/은/는 데(요) is most frequently used in colloquial speech as an opener to a question or a request or to solicit a response without specifically asking a question. This ending is also used to imply that there is something left unsaid. What is left unsaid has to be understood from the context of the dialogue, but in general -ㄴ/은/는데(요) has three main functions:

a. Soliciting a response by implying "I say," "Don't you think so?" "Is it true?" "Is it possible?"

선생님을 뵈려고 <u>하는데요</u>.	Well, I would like to see the teacher. (Is it possible? Is she in?)
비가 올 것 <u>같은데요</u>.	(I say,) it looks like it's going to rain.
야구를 하면 <u>좋겠는데요</u>.	It would be nice to play baseball. (Don't you agree?)
올림픽이 서울에서 열린 다고 <u>들었는데요</u>.	I heard that the Olympics will be held in Seoul. (Is it true?)

b. A mild protest, as in "but (I think)..."

{ 빨리 구경 가자! { 벌써 <u>늦었는데</u>!	Let's hurry and go to the show! (But) it's already late!
그분이 다섯시까지 오신 다고 <u>했는데요</u>.	But he said he'd be here by 5.

c. A mildly apologetic expression, as in "I am afraid" or "I am sorry but ..."

잘 <u>모르겠는데요</u>.	(Well, I am afraid) I don't know.
제가 어떻게 할 수 <u>없겠는데요</u>.	(Well, I am sorry but) I cannot do anything (about it).

3. Uses of 좀 "a little," "please"

좀 has several meanings, depending on the context. It is commonly used to mildly urge someone to do something or to express "a little" or "a bit."

좀 놀러 와요.	Please come and visit me.
좀 기다리세요.	Please wait.
좀 읽어 주세요.	Would you please read it for me?
한국어를 좀 해요.	I can speak a little Korean.
한국어를 좀 알아요.	I know a little Korean.

4. Expression for "I wish": -(으)면 좋겠다

-(으)면 좋겠다 is a combination of the conditional connective -(으)면 and the verb 좋다 "to be good." -(으)면 좋다 means literally "It would be nice if ... ," but when used with -겠, it conveys the meaning "I wish ..."

의사 선생님을 <u>뵈었으면</u> <u>좋겠다</u>.	I wish I could see the doctor. (뵙다 is the humble form of 보다 "to see.")
친구가 책을 가지고 <u>왔으면 좋겠다</u>.	I wish that my friend would bring the book.
간호원이 전화를 걸어 <u>주면 좋겠다</u>.	I wish that the nurse would call me.

5. Constructions for -ㄹ/을 수 있다 "can," "to be possible" -ㄹ/을 수 없다 "cannot," "to be impossible"

These constructions express strong possibilities or impossibilities of an event or action. Changing the tense of 있다/없다 gives various shades of meaning.

a. V. STEM + ㄹ/을 수 있다 "can," "to be possible"

내일 <u>오실 수 있습니까</u>?	Can you come tomorrow?
어제 <u>올 수 있었는데요</u>.	I could have come yesterday.
그분은 내일 <u>오실 수 있으시다</u>.	(He/She) can come tomorrow. (hon.)

내일 <u>올 수 있어요</u>.	(He/She/I) can come tomorrow. (polite informal)
내일 <u>올 수 있겠다</u>.	(I think) he can come tomorrow.
빨리 <u>할 수 있다</u>.	We can do it quickly.
빨리 <u>할 수 있었겠다</u>.	(I think) he could have done it quickly.

b. V. STEM + ㄹ/을 수 없다 "cannot," "to be impossible"

내일 <u>갈 수 없다</u>.	I cannot go tomorrow.
어제 <u>갈 수 없었다</u>.	I could not go yesterday.
영식이는 한글을 <u>읽을 수 없었다</u>.	Young-shik could not read Korean.
어떻게 <u>할 수 없다</u>.	(We) can't do anything.
어떻게 <u>할 수 없었다</u>.	(We) could not have done anything.
<u>할 수 없다</u>.	It can't be helped.
<u>할 수 없겠다</u>.	I may not be able to do it.

6. Expression for "when," "while," "at the time when" -ㄹ/을 때

We have seen that -때 is a dependent noun that is used with another noun, e.g., 점심 때, 세살 때, 방학 때 (see L10, GN4). -때 is also used with the -ㄹ/을 modifier to mean "when," "while," or "at the time when."

<u>오실 때</u> 진찰권을 가지고 오세요.	When you come, please bring your medical card.
의사를 <u>기다릴 때</u> 전화가 왔다.	While (I was) waiting for the doctor, the phone rang.
병원에 <u>갔을 때</u> 의사가 없었다.	When I went to the hospital, the doctor was not there.
병원에 <u>갈 때</u> 약방에도 들르겠어요.	When I go to the hospital, I'll stop by the pharmacy.
<u>아플 때는</u> 병원에 가 보세요.	Go see a doctor when you are sick.

7. Chinese characters

午	낮 오 noon	ノ	／	二	午			
後	뒤 후 after	ノ	彳	华	华	华	後	後
前	앞 전 before	﹨	﹀	产	广	前	前	前
內	안 내 inside	｜	冂	內	內			
科	과목 과 class science	ノ	二	千	千	禾	禾	科	科
電	번개 전 (전기) (electricity)	一	厂	雨	雨	雩	雩	雷	電
話	말씀 화 talk	二	言	言	言	言	許	許	話

연습

A. 다음 질문에 대답하십시오.

　　1. 영식이는 누구에게 전화를 했습니까?

　　2. 누가 전화를 받았습니까?

　　3. 전화할 때 Hello! 를 한국말로 어떻게 합니까?

　　4. 영식이는 왜 전화를 했어요?

　　5. 간호원은 영식이에게 몇 시에 오라고 했어요?

　　6. 전화할 때 The line is busy 를 무엇이라고 해요?

　　7. 전화를 잘못 걸면 무엇이라고 하겠어요?

　　8. 전화를 끊을 때 무엇이라고 해요?

B. 다음 문장을 끝마치십시오.

　　9. 선생님을 뵈려고 하는데 ＿＿＿＿＿＿＿＿＿＿＿＿

　　10. 비가 올 것 같은데 ＿＿＿＿＿＿＿＿＿＿＿＿＿＿

　　11. 야구를 하면 좋겠는데 ＿＿＿＿＿＿＿＿＿＿＿＿

　　12. 친구가 온다고 했는데 ＿＿＿＿＿＿＿＿＿＿＿＿

　　13. 잘 모르겠는데 ＿＿＿＿＿＿＿＿＿＿＿＿＿＿＿

14. 진찰권이 없으면 _____
15. 전화번호를 모르면 _____
16. 몸이 아프면 _____
17. 김 선생을 뵈려고 하면 _____

C. 다음 문장을 한국어로 번역하십시오.

18. *Is it possible* to see Dr. Lee at 3:30?
19. *Can* you speak Korean well? (*Is it possible* for you to speak ....)
20. Where *can* I buy the *medical card?*
21. Even though it is after 10 P.M., *is it possible to* go to a restaurant?
22. Because I don't have time, I *can't go see* an eye doctor until next week.
23. *I wish (it would be nice if)* I could call my friend in Seoul.
24. *I wish* my friend would call me this afternoon.
25. *I wish* I knew her phone number.
26. Please *do not disconnect the phone* until next Tuesday.
27. Would you wait for *a moment?*
28. What is your *phone number?* your *address?*
29. When (one) is sick, (one) *cannot* study.
30. How do you *make a long-distance call?* (long-distance call: 장거리 전화)
31. I *wish* the phone would *be installed* today.

Lesson 21

제 이십일과   병원

대화 A

의사 : 어디가 편찮으세요?

영식 : 열이 나고 목이 아픈데요.[1]

의사 : 속은 괜찮으세요?

영식 : 배는 아프지 않아요. 그런데 목이 아파서 삼키지 못하겠어요.

의사 : 어디 좀 봅시다. 목이 잔뜩 부었군요. 기침은 안 합니까?

영식 : 좀 해요. 그리고 온 몸이 아파요.

의사 : 독감이 드신 것 같은데, 약을 좀 지어 드릴테[2]니 잡수시고 푹 쉬십시오. 방을 따뜻하게 하고[3] 한 며칠 꼭 쉬어야 됩니다.[4] 그리고 한 사흘[5] 후에도 낫지 않으면 다시 오세요.

영식 : 네. 그럼 안녕히 계십시오.

대화 B

약제사 : 이영식 씨.

영식 : 네.

약제사 : 약이 다 준비됐습니다. 알약은 네 시간마다 하나씩 잡수시고 물약은 주무시기 전에 잡수십시오. 잊으시면 안 됩니다.[6]

영식 : 네, 알겠습니다.

Patterns

1. 목이 아파요.
   머리_____
   손_____
   다리_____
   팔_____

2. 독감이 들었다.
   감기_____
   병_____

3. 약을 지어 드릴 테니 잡수세요.
   추우면 감기가 들 ____ 옷을 따뜻하게 입으세요.
   피곤하실 ____ 푹 쉬십시오.
   열이 날 ____ 아스피린을 잡수십시오.

4. 며칠 꼭 쉬어야 됩니다.
   약을 꼭 잡수셔_____
   방을 따뜻하게 해_____
   병원에 가_____
   의사 선생님을 뵈어_____

5. 열이 날 때는 밖에 나가면 안 됩니다.
   약을 먹고 맥주를 마시_____
   약 먹는 것을 잊으시_____
   배가 아플 때 많이 먹으_____

6. 네 시간마다 하나씩 잡수십시오.
   하루에 두 개__ 잡수십시오.
   한 달에 두 번__ 오십시오.
   일 년에 세 번__ 집에 갑니다.
   이틀에 한 번__ 학교에 나갑니다.
   일 주일에 세 번__ 수영을 갑니다.

낱말

제 이십일과 (第二十一課)	Lesson 21
병원 (病院)	hospital
편찮다	to be sick, ill (hon.)
의사 (醫師)	medical doctor
목	throat, neck
속	inside, interior; stomach
괜찮다	to be all right
배	stomach, tummy
삼키다	to swallow, to gulp
독감	flu
독감이 들다	to catch the flu
약 (藥)	medicine
약방 (藥房)	pharmacy
짓다	to make, to concoct
지어 드리다	to make for someone
푹	fully
방	room
따뜻하다	to be warm
한	about (estimate)
며칠	a few days, how many days
사흘	three days
낫다	to get well, to get better
주무시다	to sleep (hon.)
준비	preparation
준비하다	to prepare
준비되다	to be prepared, to be ready
알약	tablet, pill (알: egg, a little round object)
물	water, liquid
물약	liquid medicine
약제사	pharmacist
잊다	to forget
감기	cold

병	disease
병이 들다	to become sick
옷	clothes
피곤하다	to be tired
입다	to wear, to put on clothing
맥주	beer
붓다	to swell
잔뜩	much, a lot, fully

몸의 부분　Body parts

머리	head, hair, brain
머리카락 (머리칼)	hair
얼굴	face
이마	forehead
눈	eye
눈썹	eyebrow
코	nose
입	mouth
입술	lip
이	tooth, teeth
볼/뺨	cheek
턱	chin
귀	ear
목	neck, throat
어깨	shoulder
등	back
허리	waist
가슴	chest
배	stomach, abdomen
팔	arm
팔목	wrist
다리	leg
발	foot
발목	ankle

손	hand
왼손	left hand
오른손	right hand
손가락	finger
손톱	fingernail
발가락	toe
무릎	knee

증세 Physical symptoms

기침을 하다 (기침)	to cough (cough)
재채기를 하다 (재채기)	to sneeze (sneeze)
하품을 하다 (하품)	to yawn (yawning)
딸꾹질을 하다 (딸꾹질)	to hiccup (hiccup)
토하다	to vomit
설사를 하다 (설사)	to have diarrhea (diarrhea)
손/발이 저리다 (손, 발)	to be numb in the hands and feet (hand, foot)
어지럽다	to be dizzy
기운이 없다 (기운)	to be weak (energy, strength)
밥맛이 없다 (밥맛)	to have no appetite (appetite)
피가 나다 (피)	to bleed (blood)
정신이 있다/없다 (정신)	to be alert/to be absent-minded (mind, spirit)
정신을 잃다	to become unconscious
숨을 쉬다 (숨)	to breathe (breath, life)
땀이 나다/땀을 흘리다 (땀)	to sweat, to perspire (sweat)
(발을) 다치다	to get hurt, injured
(발을) 삐다	to sprain

GRAMMAR AND NOTES

In this lesson we will study
1. Verbs with multiple meanings: 아프다, 보다, 하다, 듣다, 자다, 짓다
2. Construction of V. STEM + ㄹ/을 터이다 "to be expected of"
3. Causative D.V. + 게 하다 "to cause or make someone or something be ..."
4. Construction of
   V. STEM + TENSE + 어/아야 하다 ⎫ "must," "have to,"
   V. STEM + TENSE + 어/아야 되다 ⎭ "should"
5. Counting days
6. Construction of
   a. -(으)면 안 되다 "must not"
   b. 안 ... 어/아야 되다 "ought not," "must not," "should not"
7. Chinese characters 病, 院, 藥, 房, 醫, 師

1. Some verbs have multiple meanings when translated into English:

아프다
a. hurt, ache	발이 아프다.	My feet hurt.
	배가 아프다.	I have a stomachache.
b. be sick	그는 오늘 아프다.	He is sick today.

보다
a. see	금문교를 보았다.	We saw the Golden Gate Bridge.
b. look	저 다리를 보세요!	Look at the bridge!
c. watch	두 주일 동안 그의 집을 봤다.	I watched her house (house-sat) for two weeks.
	어제 밤 동생을 봤다.	I watched (baby-sat) my younger sister last night.
d. read	나는 아침 신문을 봤다.	I read the morning paper.

말하다

a. speak	그는 말을 잘 한다.	He is a good speaker. (He speaks well.)
b. talk	말하지 마!	Don't talk!
c. say	지금 말 할 수 없다.	I can't say it now.
d. tell	누구에게도 말하지 마세요.	Please don't tell anyone.

이야기하다

a. talk	이야기를 잘 한다.	He talks well.
b. tell	좀 이야기 해주세요.	Please tell us.

듣다

a. hear	그 소식을 들었다.	I heard the news.
b. listen	우리는 음악을 들었다.	We listened to the music.

자다

a. go to bed	나는 열두시에 잤다.	I went to bed at 12:00.
b. sleep	나는 열두시간 잤다.	I slept twelve hours.

짓다

a. cook	오늘 아침에 밥을 지었다.	I cooked rice this morning.
b. build	산 위에 집을 지었다.	We built a house on the mountain.
c. compose	짧은 글을 지으십시오.	Write a short composition.
d. sew	어머니가 새옷을 지어 주셨다.	Mother sewed me a new dress.

2. Construction of v. STEM + ㄹ/을 터이다 "to be expected of"

When the dependent noun -터 is used with the -ㄹ/을 modifier, it indicates that a situation or an event is expected to occur. This expression is usually used with a clause connective such as -이니 "since," -이지만 "although," -이고 "and," or -인데 "so."

a. -ㄹ/을 터 + 이니(까) "since," "since/as (it) is expected to," "so"

Note that -테 is a contracted form of -터이, and 까 may be dropped.

약을 좀 지어 드릴테니 잡수십시오.	I will prepare some medicine for you, so please take it.
옷을 따뜻이 안 입으면 감기가 들테니 쟈켓을 입어요.	If you don't dress warmly, you'll catch a cold, so put on a jacket.
비가 올테니 우산을 가지고 가라.	Since it is expected to rain, take an umbrella.

b. -ㄹ/을 터 + 이지만 (→ 테지만) "but," "even though," "although"

열이 날 테지만 걱정하지 마십시오.	Even though you will have a fever, do not worry.
일이 많으실 테지만 푹 쉬십시오.	Although you may have lots of work (to do), please rest fully.

c. -ㄹ/을 터 + 인데 (→ 텐데) "since/as (it) is expected to..."

아플 텐데 오늘 집에서 쉬어라.	(I expect) you will be sick, so rest at home today.
학교에 아무도 없을 텐데 뭣 하러 가니?	Since nobody will be at school, why are you going there?

d. -ㄹ/을 터 + 이고 (→ 테고) "and," "so"

기차는 늦었을 테고 어떻게 하나?	(I am sure) I am late for the train, so what shall I do?
도서관에 가도 닫혔을 테고 어떻게 하지요?	Even if I go to the library, it will be closed, so what can I do?

3. Causative D.V. + 게 하다 "to cause or make someone or something be ... "

When a descriptive verb is used with -게 하다, it expresses "to make something be ... "

따뜻하다	따뜻하게 하다	방을 따뜻하게 해요.
to be warm	to make ... warm	Make the room warm.
싸다	싸게 하다	값을 싸게 해요.
to be cheap	to make ... cheap	Make the price cheap.
차다	차게 하다	방을 차게 하지 마세요.
to be cold	to make ... cold	Don't make the room cold.

4. Construction of
V. STEM + TENSE + 어/아야 하다 ⎱ "must," "have to,"
V. STEM + TENSE + 어/아야 되다 ⎰ "should"

Both -어/아야 되다 and -어/아야 하다 indicate an obligation or the necessity of an action. However, -어/아야 하다 is a little stronger than -어/아야 되다.

한 며칠 <u>쉬어야 한다</u>.	You must rest a few days.
한 며칠 <u>쉬었어야 한다</u>.	You should have rested a few days.
다음 주에는 집에 <u>있어야 한다</u>.	You must stay home next week.
우리는 일을 <u>끝마쳐야 한다</u>.	We must finish our task.
이 약을 <u>먹어야 된다</u>.	You must take this medicine.
이 알약을 <u>먹었어야 한다</u>.	You should have taken this pill.

For emphasis, 꼭 "for sure" is added to -어/아야 되다 or 어/아야 하다.

이 약을 꼭 <u>먹어야 돼요</u>.	You must take this medicine (for sure).
이 책을 꼭 <u>읽어야 해요</u>.	I must read this book (for sure).

Notice that the negative counterpart of -어/아야 하다 and -어/야야 되다 is -(으)면 안되다 "must not." (See GN6 below.)

5. Counting days

For small numbers, usually up to ten days, the following words are used, especially in spoken language. They are equivalent to the Sino-Korean words 일일(一日), 이일(二日), 삼 일(三日), and so on,

하루	one day	엿새	six days
이틀	two days	이레	seven days
사흘	three days	여드레	eight days
나흘	four days	아흐레	nine days
닷새	five days	열흘	ten days

6. Construction of -(으)면 안 되다 "must not," 안 ..어/아야 되다 "ought not," "must not," "should not"

The expression for "must not" uses the conditional form of -(으)면 and 안 된다 rather than -어/아야 as in "must" -어/아야 되다.

a. V. STEM + (으)면 안 되다 "must not," "should not" (literally, "If (you) do ... it wouldn't do.")

한국어 시간에 영어를 하면 안 된다.	One must not speak English in Korean class.
오랫동안 기침을 하면 안 된다.	One must not cough too long.
감기가 들면 안 된다.	One must not catch a cold.

b. 안 + V. STEM + TENSE + 어/아야 하다/되다 "ought not"

기침을 오래 안 해야 된다.	One ought not cough too long.
감기가 안 들어야 한다.	One ought not catch a cold.
한국어 시간에 영어를 안 해야 한다.	One ought not speak English in Korean class.
약을 먹기 전에 아침을 안 먹어야 된다.	One ought not eat breakfast before taking the medicine.

7. Chinese characters

病	병 병 disease	丶	亠	广	疒	疒	疒	病	病
院	집 원 center	阝	阝	阝'	阝'	阝宀	阝宁	阝完	院
藥	약 약 medicine	丶	艹	艹	艹	苩	蒩	藥	藥
房	방 방 room	丶	亠	彐	户	户	庐	房	房
醫	병고칠의 cure	一	匚	医	医	医殳	殹	醫	醫
師	스승 사 teacher	丿	𠂤	𠂤	𠂤	𠂤	帥	師	師

연습

A. 다음 질문에 대답하십시오.
  1. 영식이는 어떻게 아픕니까? (어디가 아픕니까?)
  2. 의사는 영식이가 왜 아프다고 하셨습니까?
  3. 의사는 영식이에게 어떻게 하고 쉬라고 하셨습니까?
  4. 알약은 언제 먹고 물약은 언제 먹어야 됩니까?
  5. 한 사흘 후에도 낫지 않으면 어떻게 하라고 하셨
     습니까?
  6. 학생은 머리가 아프면 보통 무슨 약을 먹어요?
  7. 눈이 아픈데 무슨 의사에게 가야 됩니까?
  8. 감기가 들었을 때는 어떻게 합니까?
  9. 애기가 열이 있는데 무슨 의사에게 가야 됩니까?

B. 다음 문장을 영어로 번역하십시오.
  10. 발이 부었는데 왜 부었는지 아세요?
  11. 독감인 것 같으니 이 약을 닷새 동안 잡수시고 푹
      쉬세요.
  12. 하루 이틀만 지나면 열이 내릴 것입니다.
  13. 학교를 사흘이나 안 가면 안 됩니다.

14. 이 약을 잡수시면 곧 나을테니 걱정하지 마십시오.
(걱정하다: to worry)

15. 오늘은 치과에 전화를 걸 수 없었어요.

16. 그러나 내일은 전화를 할 수 있겠는데요.

17. 감기가 들어서 열이 많이 있을 테니 집에서 쉬세요.

C. 다음 낱말을 사용하여 짧은글을 지으십시오.

18. 편찮다

19. 주무시다

20. 잡수시다

D. 다음 문장을 한국어로 번역하십시오.

21. When you have a cold, you *should* rest well.

22. If you have a fever, you *should* take some medicine.

23. You *must* come to the hospital by 8 o'clock.

24. If you have a stomachache, you *should not* eat a lot.

25. You *should not* forget the appointment with the doctor.

26. Please rest about two days, since your body *will be aching*.

27. Since your fever *will come down* when you take this medicine, don't worry.

28. One should drink lots of water *every day*.

29. *Is* the medicine *ready*?

30. Please *get ready* quickly.

Lesson 22

제 이십이과 운동

대화 A

데이빗 : 한국에서는 어떤[1] 운동을 많이 합니까?

영식 : 야구, 축구, 농구 등을 매우 좋아해요.[2]
그리고 배구와 정구도 많이 합니다.

데이빗 : 미식 축구는 어떻습니까?

영식 : 대학생들이 좀 하지만 그렇게 잘 알려져[3]
있지 않습니다. 요즘 미국에서는 태권도가
인기가 있다는 말을 들었는데요?

데이빗 : 네. 태권도 뿐만 아니라[4] 중국무술도 인기가
있어요. 저도 태권도를 조금 배우다가 그만
두었습니다.

Patterns

1. 어떤 운동을 많이 합니까?
   어떤 일_____
   어떤 공부_____
   어떤 사업_____

2. 저는 농구가 좋아요.   친구는 농구를 좋아해요.
   ____ 수영_____   ____ 수영_____
   ____ 씨름_____   ____ 씨름_____
   ____ 체조_____   ____ 체조_____

3. <u>저는</u> 탁구<u>가</u> 싫어요.   친구는 탁구<u>를</u> 싫어해요.
  __ 농구_____   __ 농구_____
  __ 야구_____   __ 야구_____
  __ 수구_____   __ 수구_____

4. 태권도<u>는</u> 잘 알려져 있다.   태권도<u>는</u> 잘 알려져 있지 않다.
  야구_____   야구_____
  배구_____   배구_____
  미식 축구_____   미식 축구_____

5. 태권도 뿐만 아니라 중국무술도 인기가 있어요.
  그 학생은 운동 _____ 음악__ 잘 한다.
  축구 _____ 야구__ 잘 알려져 있다.
  철수는 한국어 _____ 일본어__ 잘 한다.

6. 정구를 배우다가 그만 두었다.
  대학교에 다니_____
  영어를 가르치_____
  운동을 하_____

대화 B

영희: 1988년 올림픽이 서울에서 성대하게 열렸다는 기사를 신문에서 보았는데, 한국에서는 여기에 대해서 어떻게 생각합니까?[5]

김 선생: 매우 기쁘게 생각하지요. 한국 사람들은 운동도 물론 좋아하지만 올림픽 같은 세계적인 행사를 서울에서 갖은 것[6]을 무엇보다도[7] 자랑스럽게 여겨요.[8]

영희: 올림픽을 위해서[9] 특별한 준비를 많이 했습니까?

김 선생: 그래요. 이미 여러가지 시설이 되어 있었지만, 세계 각국에서 오는 선수들, 그리고 관광객, 또 신문, 텔레비젼 기자들의 편리를 위해 많은 준비가 필요했지요.

Patterns

1. 올림픽에 대하여 어떻게 생각해요?
   미식 축구_____
   무술_____
   그 신문 기사_____

2. 행사를 서울에서 갖은 <u>것을 자랑스럽게 여겨요</u>.
   운동을 잘 한 _____
   무술을 배운 _____
   올림픽에 나가는 _____
   테니스를 잘 치는 _____

3. <u>무엇보다도</u> 자랑스럽다.
   _____ 어렵다.
   _____ 인기가 있다.
   _____ 좋아한다.

4. 자랑스럽게 <u>여긴다</u>.
   기쁘_____
   특별하_____
   어렵_____

5. 올림픽을 위해서 무슨 준비가 필요하지요?
   관광객_____
   기자들의 편리_____
   선수들_____

낱말

제 이십이과 (第二十二課)	Lesson 22
운동 (運動)	sports, exercise
어떤	what kind of, a certain
야구	baseball
축구	soccer
농구	basketball
-등	etcetera
좋아하다	to like
배구	volleyball
미식 (美式)	American-style

미식 축구	football
알리다	to announce (to let it be known)
알려지다	to be known
태권도	tae-kwon-do
인기 (人氣)	popularity
인기가 있다	to be popular
텔레비젼/테레비	television
올림픽	Olympic games
무술	martial arts
모두	all, entirely
그만두다	to quit
수영	swimming
수영하다/헤엄치다	to swim
씨름	wrestling
씨름하다	to wrestle
체조	gymnastics
체조하다	to exercise, to do gymnastics
탁구	table tennis (ping-pong)
탁구치다	to play ping-pong
수구	water polo
수구하다	to play water polo
싫어하다	to dislike
성대하다	to be grand
열리다	to be opened, (meetings) to be held
기사 (記事)	(newspaper) article
-에 대해서 (대하여)	concerning, about
생각하다	to think, to consider, to regard
물론	of course
세계적	international, world-scale
세계적으로	internationally, worldwide
행사 (行事)	event, happening

갖다 (가지다)	to have, to own—contracted form (to own)
자랑 (자랑스럽다)	pride (to be proud, to be boastful)
여기다	to consider, to regard
특별한 (특별하다)	special (to be special)
그래요.	Yes, that is so.
이미	already
시설	facility
각국	each country, various nations
선수	athlete, player, champion
입장	procession, entrance
관광객	sightseer, tourist, spectator
위하다	to support
위해 (위하여, 위해서)	for the sake of—contracted form
필요하다	to be necessary, to be needed
문제	problem, question
손기정	Sohn Ki-jung (marathon winner of the 1936 Olympics)
마라톤	marathon
역사	history
역사적	historical
지다	to lose
이기다	to win
메달	medal
메달을 따다	to win a medal
훈련 (훈련하다)	training, discipline (to train)
패스	pass
상점	store
유엔	U.N.
대표	representative
국기	national flag

레스링	wrestling
권투	boxing
맛이 있다	to be tasty
날리다	to fly (in the wind)

낱말 연습

1. 열리다
   문이 바람에 열린다.
   올림픽이 서울에서 열렸다.
   이 창문이 열리지 않는다.

2. 기사
   그 신문에 난 기사를 봤어요?
   학교 신문에 기사를 썼다.

3. -에 대해서
   그 문제에 대해서 생각하는 것을 쓰십시오.
   그 신문 기사에 대해서 어떻게 생각해요?

4. 기쁘다/기뻐하다
   오랫동안 못본 친구를 만나서 참 기뻤다.
   금메달을 딴 선수들은 매우 기뻐했다.

5. 좋다/좋아하다
   저는 수영이 좋아요.
   형은 레스링을 좋아하고 동생은 권투를 좋아해요.

6. 세계적/세계적으로
   세계적 문제
   세계적으로 유명하다.
   세계적으로 인기가 있다.

7. 갖다 (가지다)
   돈 가진 것이 없는데요.
   가지신 물건을 잊지 마십시오.
   점심을 가지고 오십시오.

8. 자랑스럽다

    동생이 올림픽에 나가게 되어서 참 자랑스럽다.

    나는 이 학교에 다니는 것이 자랑스럽게 생각된다.

9. 무엇보다도

    무엇보다도 중요한 것은 도서관 시설입니다.

    나는 그 영화가 무엇보다도 재미있어요.

10. 특별히

    요즈음 특별히 하는 일이 없어요.

    어제는 시험준비를 특별히 많이 했다.

    특별히 맛있는 것이 무엇이에요?

11. 여러가지

    시장에 가면 여러가지 상점이 있다.

    백화점에 가서 여러가지 물건을 샀다.

12. 시설

    체육관의 시설이 많이 좋아졌다.

    그 병원은 시설이 좋지 않다.

13. 각국

    유엔에 가면 각국의 국기들이 날리고 있다.

    세계 각국의 대표들이 나와 있다.

14. 선수

    손기정 씨는 한국의 유명한 마라톤 선수이었다.

    "선수 입장"

15. 관광객

    가을에는 날씨가 좋아서 관광객이 많다.

    관광객들은 경치가 좋은 곳 뿐만 아니라 역사적인 곳도 구경하고 싶어한다.

16. 기자

    신문 기자들은 특별한 패스를 가지고 다닌다.

    기자 생활을 해 봤어요?

17. 편리

    차가 있으면 편리하다.

    기숙사에 살면 편리하지요?

18. 준비
준비가 다 됐어요?
오늘 저녁에는 시험 준비를 해야 된다.

19. 필요하다
학생은 책이 필요하다.
나는 무엇보다도 잠이 필요해요.

GRAMMAR AND NOTES

In this lesson we will study
1. Question word and indefinite modifier 어떤-
   a. "what kind of," "which"
   b. "some," "a certain"
2. Verbs
   a. 좋다 or 좋아하다 "to like"
   b. 싫다 or 싫어하다 "to dislike"
3. Construction of continuous stative: v. + 어/아 있다
   "to be in the state of ——ing ..."
4. "not only ... but also" connective
   a. V. STEM + TENSE + ㄹ/을 뿐만 아니라
   b. N. PHRASE + 뿐만 아니라
5. Verb "to think" or "to believe"
   a. -라/다고 생각하다
   b. -게 생각하다
6. Expression for "the fact that": V. MOD. + 것
7. Postposition: comparative -보다 ... (더) "more than"
8. Verb -게 여기다 "to consider," "to feel"
9. Expressions for "for," "for the sake of" 위해서
10. Chinese characters 運, 動, 美, 式, 行, 事, 記

1. Question word and indefinite modifier 어떤-

As we saw in L17, GN2, 어떤 means "what kind of" or
"which" when it is used for a question, but when it is used for a
statement it means "some," an indefinite modifier.

a. 어떤 "what kind of," "which"

한국에서는 어떤 운동을 많이 합니까?	What kinds of sports do they play a lot of in Korea?

그분은 <u>어떤</u> 사람이에요?	What kind of person is he?
<u>어떤</u> 뻐스를 타세요?	Which bus do you take?

b. 어떤 "some," "a certain"

<u>어떤</u> 사람이 찾아 왔었어요.	Someone came to see you.
<u>어떤</u> 나라에서는 눈을 못 봐요.	In some countries, they never see snow.
<u>어떤</u> 선수들은 한국어를 잘 해요.	Some athletes speak Korean well.

Let us review other question words used as indefinite pronouns and modifiers.

누구	who?	저분이 <u>누구</u>세요?	Who is he?
	someone	<u>누가</u> 오셨는데요.	Someone came.
어느	which?	<u>어느</u> 것이 좋으세요?	Which do you like?
	some/any	<u>어느</u> 것이나 괜찮아요.	Whichever is all right.
무엇	what?	<u>무엇</u>을 잡수시겠어요?	What would you like to eat?
	something	<u>무엇</u>이나 좋습니다.	Anything is OK.
어디	where?	<u>어디</u>에 여행을 하셨습니까?	Where did you travel?
	somewhere	<u>어디</u> 좀 가야겠습니다.	I must go somewhere.
몇	how much/ many?	책을 <u>몇</u> 권 사셨지요?	How many books did you buy?
	some amount	방안에 사람이 <u>몇</u>이 있었다.	There were a few people in the room.

2. Verbs 좋다 or 좋아하다 "to like," 싫다 or 싫어하다 "to dislike"

The feeling verbs such as "like," "dislike," "happy," and "sad" can be expressed in two ways, depending on the subject of the sentence.

a. -이/가 좋다 (싫다, 기쁘다, 슬프다) is used with a first-person subject, 나 or 우리. -이/가 좋다 is also used for a question whose subject is a second person, 너 or 너희들.

나는 운동이 좋다.	I like sports.
우리는 한국말 공부가 좋다.	We like to study the Korean language.
편지 쓰는 것이 좋아요?	Do (you) like to write letters?

b. -을/를 좋아하다 (싫어하다, 기뻐하다, 슬퍼하다) is used for all other cases.

한국 사람들은 운동을 좋아한다.	Koreans enjoy sports.
학생들은 숙제를 싫어한다.	Students dislike homework.
그는 친구가 온 것을 기뻐한다.	He is glad that his friend came.
그는 동생이 떠난 것을 슬퍼했다.	He was sad that his younger brother left.
너는 나를 싫어한다.	You dislike me.

3. Construction of continuous stative: v. + 어/아 있다 "to be in the state of being ..."

While continuous action is expressed by v. + 고 있다 "to be ——ing," a continuous state is expressed by v. + 어/아 있다 "to be in the state of (being...)." Often this construction is used with passive verbs.

미식 축구는 잘 알려져* 있지 않다.	American football is (in the state of being) not well known.
한국은 둘로 나누어져* 있다.	Korea is divided into two (and it is in the state of division).

* See L16, GN2 for passive verbs v. + 어/아지다.

값이 적혀* 있다.	The price is written.
물고기가 그물에 잡혀* 있다.	The fish is caught in the net.
그릇에 물이 담겨* 있다.	The water is (contained) in the bowl.

* See L18, GN6 for deriving passives by adding the suffixes 이, 리, 기, or 히.

| 책이 책상위에 <u>놓여 있다</u>. | The books are (put) on the desk (and they are lying there). |
| 학생들은 <u>앉아 있고</u> 선생은 <u>서 있다</u>. | The students are (in the state of) sitting and the teacher is (in the state of) standing. |

4. "Not only ... but also" connective -뿐만 아니라 ... 도

To connect two clauses with the meaning "not only ... but also," use -ㄹ/을 뿐만 아니라 after a verb and 뿐만 아니라 after a noun phrase.

a. V. STEM + (TENSE) + ㄹ/을 뿐만 아니라

그는 정구를 잘 칠 뿐만 아니라 음악도 잘 한다.	He not only plays tennis well but also does well in music.
그는 일을 <u>할 뿐만 아니라</u> 학교에도 다닌다.	He not only works but also goes to school.
그는 일을 <u>했을 뿐만 아니라</u> 학교도 다녔다.	He not only worked but also went to school.

b. N. PHRASE + 뿐만 아니라

한국 뿐만 아니라 일본과 중국도 극동에 있다.	Not only Korea but also Japan and China are in the Far East.
남자들 뿐만 아니라 여자들도 무술을 잘 한다.	Not only men but women also do well in martial arts.
태권도 뿐만 아니라 씨름도 인기가 있다.	Not only tae-kwon-do but also wrestling is popular.

5. Verb "to think" or "to believe" 생각하다

생각하다 is a verb derived from the noun 생각. It has a wide range of meaning from "thoughts" and "consideration" to "idea" and "concept" and can be made into verbs such as 생각 나다 "to get an idea" and 생각하다 "to think."

a. 이다 V. STEM + 라고 생각하다 (only for present tense of 이다); all other V. STEM + 다고 생각하다 "to think that," "to believe that"

As in reported speech (L12, GN2), -다고 or -라고 is used with 생각하다; -라고 is used only for the verb 이다 "to be" in the present tense.

오늘 저녁 비가 올 것 이라고 생각해요.	I think it will rain tonight.
그렇다고 생각해요.	I believe it (to be) so.

b. D.V. + 게 생각하다 "to think (it is)," "to consider (it to be)"

-게 changes the descriptive verb into an adverbial phrase for 생각하다. (See L18, GN2 for -게 adverbs.)

여기에 대해서 어떻게 생각합니까?	What do they think about this?
좋게 생각해요.	I consider it favorably.
아버지는 영식이를 자랑 스럽게 생각한다.	Father is proud of Young-shik.

6. Expression for "the fact that": V. MOD. + 것

As we saw in Lesson 11, a relative clause is made from a verbal modifier plus a noun. Similarly, V. MOD. + 것 means "the fact that" or functions like a gerund in English, as in "having" or "becoming" in the examples.

경기를 서울에서 갖게 된 것에 대해서 어떻게 생각하십니까? (past tense)	What do you think about the fact that the game was held in Seoul?
그는 여름에 관광객이 많은 것을 기뻐한다. (pres. tense)	She is happy about having lots of tourists in summer.
그는 아버지가 되는 것을 자랑스럽게 여긴다. (pres. tense)	He is proud of becoming a father.

Note that the tense may change in the verbal modifier.

큰 행사가 있을 것 (future)	the fact that there will be a big event

큰 행사가 <u>있는 것</u> (present)   the fact that there is a big
event

큰 행사가 <u>있었던 것</u> (past)   the fact that there was a big
event (See L19, GN4b.)

7. Postposition: comparative -보다 ... (더) "more than"

-보다 ... (더) is attached to the thing compared to and
usually precedes the subject of comparison. For example, "A is
bigger than B," B + 보다 precedes A. 더 "more" may be used
for emphasis.

미국에서는 야구<u>보다</u> 축구가 <u>더</u> 인기가 있다.	Football is more popular than baseball in the U.S.
한국사람들은 오랜 <u>역사보다</u> 한글을 <u>더</u> 자랑스럽게 여긴다.	Koreans are more proud of *hangŭl* than their long history.
그는 <u>무엇보다도</u> 운동을 좋아한다.	He likes sports more than anything.

8. Verb -게 여기다 "to consider," "to feel"

-게 is used here to change a descriptive verb into an
adverbial phrase, as in -게 생각하다 (see GN5b above). The verb
여기다 is used only with descriptive verbs of feeling such as "to
be sad," "to be happy," "to be proud," or "to be annoyed." 여기다
may substitute for 생각하다 but not vice versa.

자랑스럽<u>게</u> 여긴다. 자랑스럽<u>게</u> 생각한다.	to be/feel proud
반갑<u>게</u> 여긴다. 반갑<u>게</u> 생각한다.	to feel/be glad
귀찮<u>게</u> 여긴다. 귀찮<u>게</u> 생각한다.	to feel annoyed
슬프<u>게</u> 여긴다. 슬프<u>게</u> 생각한다.	to feel sad
그는 아들이 트럼펫을 잘 부는 것을 자랑스럽<u>게</u> 생각했다.	He is proud that his son plays the trumpet well.

| 전화가 하루 종일 울리는 것을 <u>귀찮게 생각했다</u>. | I was annoyed by the phone ringing all day. |
| 나를 보러 오는 것을 <u>반갑게 여긴다</u>. | I am glad that he comes to see me. |

9. Expressions for "for," "for the sake of" 위해서

-을/를 위해서 derives from the verb 위하다 (meaning "to be supportive of," "to be devoted to," or "to respect"), which is used in a limited context, such as 나라를 위하다 "to be patriotic" or 남편을 위하다 "to be devoted to her husband." The much more commonly used form -을/를 위해서 means "for (someone, some objective, or something)" or "for the sake of."

a. -을/를 위하다 "to do for (the sake of)," "to be supportive of"

| 부모는 자식을 <u>위한다</u>. | Parents are supportive of their children. |

b. -을/를 위해서 "for (the sake of)"

<u>올림픽을 위해서</u> 준비를 많이 한다.	They are making a lot of preparations for the Olympics.
<u>선수들을 위해서</u> 호텔을 짓는다.	They are building hotels for the athletes.
신문 기자들의 편리를 <u>위해서</u> 준비가 필요하다.	Preparations are necessary for the convenience of newspaper reporters.

10. Chinese characters

運	움직일운 carry	′	⌐	⌐	冖	骨	亘	軍	運
動	움직일동 move	一	二	仁	台	盲	盲	動	動
美	아름다울 미 beauty	`	` ̈	⅄	⅄	¥	羊	兰	美
式	법 식 style	一	二	厂	工	式	式		
行	갈 행 go	′	⼃	彳	彳	㣔	行		
事	일 사 work	一	⼁	冖	马	写	写	事	事
記	기록할기 record	`	⼆	⼆	⾔	⾔	言	言	記

연습

A. 다음 질문에 대답하십시오.
  1. 한국에서는 무슨 운동을 많이 합니까?
  2. 미국의 대학생들은 어떤 운동을 많이 합니까?
  3. 미국에서는 왜 무술이 인기가 있습니까?
  4. 세계적으로 인기가 있는 운동은 무엇입니까?
  5. 축구와 미식 축구는 어떻게 다릅니까?
  6. 올림픽을 위해서는 왜 많은 준비가 필요합니까?
  7. 다음 올림픽에 나갈 선수를 아세요?
  8. 학생은 무슨 운동을 좋아해요?
  9. 이 대학교에서는 무술을 가르칩니까?
  10. 학생은 무술을 배워 본 일이 있어요?

B. 다음 낱말을 써서 짧은 글을 지으십시오. ("보다 ... 더"를 보기와 같이 사용할 것)

보기: (운동, 음악, 좋아하다) 저는 운동<u>보다</u> 음악을 <u>더</u> 좋아해요.

11. (야구, 농구, 재미 있다)
12. (배구, 축구, 인기가 있다)
13. (관광시설, 운동시설, 필요하다)
14. (공기가 맑은 것, 관광시설이 많은 것, 자랑스럽다)
15. (미식축구, 축구, 잘 알려져 있다)

C. 다음 문장을 한국어로 번역하십시오.

16. The 1984 Olympic games *were held* in Los Angeles.
17. Although soccer *is well known* in Korea, football *is not*.
18. *What kinds of sports* do college students in Korea *play*?
19. Do you *consider* sports *important*? (중요하다: to be important)
20. I think sports *are necessary*.
21. Young-shik does well *not only* in his studies *but also* in many sports.
22. *Not only* Koreans *but also* all those who study Korean can speak Korean well.
23. Who do you think is *the most popular* athlete in the U.S.?
24. Why is football *not so popular* in Korea?
25. *What kinds of sports* do you *enjoy (playing)*?
26. What kinds of *sports facilities* are available at your school?
27. Who *won* the football (game)? We *did*.

D. "대학생과 운동"에 대하여 작문을 지으십시오.
(Write a short composition about "대학생과 운동.")

Lesson 23

제 이십삼과   음식에 대하여

　　각 나라마다 문화와 풍속이 다르듯이[1] 음식도 다르다.
동양을 잘 모르는 사람들은 한국, 중국, 일본 음식을
혼동하기 쉽다. 세 나라는 다 쌀을 주식으로 먹고 간장을
쓰지만 각각 다른 특성을 가지고[2] 있다.

　　보통 한국 음식은 맵고 양념이 많이 들고, 소고기와
채소를 많이 쓴다. 중국 음식은 돼지고기와 닭고기를
많이 쓰고 음식 종류가 어느 나라보다도 많다.
그 반면에,[3] 일본 사람들은 생선을 많이 먹으며, 맛이
달고 기름에 튀긴 것을 좋아한다.

　　물론 동양의 음식 뿐만 아니라 서양 음식도 나라에
따라 특성이 있다. 예를 들어 마시는 것을 보더라도,[4]
영국은 위스키로 유명하고 독일은 맥주, 그리고 불란서는
포도주로 잘 알려져 있다.

Patterns

1. 풍속이 다르듯이 음식도 다르다.
     말_____ 풍속_____
     옷_____ 집_____

2. 특성을 가지고 있다.
     긴 역사_____
     고유한 문화_____

3. 한국인은 소고기를 많이 쓴다. <u>그 반면에</u> 중국인은
   돼지고기를 많이 쓴다.
   한국음식은 맵고 양념이 많이 들었다. _____ 일본
   음식은 달다.
   유럽에서는 축구가 인기가 있다. _____ 미국에서는
   야구가 인기가 있다.
   불란서는 포도주로 유명하다. _____ 독일은 맥주로
   유명하다.

4. 동양 음식 <u>뿐만 아니라</u> 서양 음식<u>도</u> 있다.
   마실 것 _____ 먹을 것_ 있다.
   매운 것 _____ 신 것_ 있다.

5. <u>예를 들어</u> 마시는 것을 <u>보더라도</u> 나라마다 다르다.
   _____ 입는 것_____
   _____ 먹는 것_____

대화

영식이와 창호는 어느날 저녁, 명동에 있는 한식집에
식사를 하러 갔다.

종업원: 어서 오십시오. 몇 분이십니까?
 영식: 두 사람이에요.
종업원: 이리 오십시오.
 영식: 메뉴 좀 보여주세요.
 창호: 나는 여기 처음 와 보는데 참 크고 사람도
       많군!⁵ 뭘⁶ 먹을까?⁷
 영식: 글쎄... 나는 불고기 정식으로 할래.⁸
 창호: 정식에는 무엇이 나오니?⁹
 영식: 밥, 국, 나물, 김치, 그런 반찬들이 나오나 봐.¹⁰
 창호: 그거 너무 많지 않을까? 나는 좀 간단한 것을
       먹을래. (좀 생각한 후) 비빔밥을 먹어야겠다.¹¹
종업원: 주문하시겠어요?
 영식: 네, 불고기 정식 하나 하고, 비빔밥 하나
       주세요.
 창호: 냉수도 좀 가져 오세요.

Pattern

1. 식당이 참 크고 사람도 <u>많군</u>!
   경치도 좋고 날씨도 <u>좋군</u>!
   음식이 맛도 있고 보기도 <u>좋군</u>!
   밥도 많이 주고 반찬도 여러가지가 나오<u>는군</u>!

2. 뭘 먹을까?
   __ 할래?
   __ 살래?
   __ 하니?
   __ 주문하니?
   __ 마시니?

3. <u>무엇이/뭐가</u> 나오니?
   _____ 있니?
   _____ 좋을까?

4. 그런 반찬들이 나오<u>나 봐</u>.
   맛이 있_____
   국도 주_____
   정식을 주문했_____

5. 비빔밥을 먹어야겠다.
   차를 좀 마셔_____
   새우를 튀겨_____
   닭을 구어_____

6. <u>가지고</u> 오세요.
   _____ 가세요.
   _____ 다니세요.

낱말

제 이십삼과 (第二十三課)	Lesson 23
각 (각각) (各各)	each
문화 (文化)	culture
풍속 (風俗)	custom
음식 (飲食)	food
혼동	confusion
혼동하다	to confuse

-기 쉽다	to be easy to ...
주식 (主食)	main food, staple
간장	soy sauce
특성	special characteristic
맵다	to be hot, spicy
양념	spice
들다	to take, to hold, to lift up
소	cow
고기	meat
채소	vegetables
닭	chicken
종류	kind, type, sort
반면	the opposite side
반면에	on the other hand, in contrast
생선	fish
맛	flavor, taste
달다	to be sweet
기름	oil
튀기다	to deep fry
-뿐만 아니라	not only
동양 음식 (東洋飲食)	Oriental dish
서양 음식 (西洋飲食)	Western dish
-에 따라	according to, following
예	example
예를 들다	to show an example
마시다	to drink
-더라도	even if
위스키	whisky
맥주	beer
포도	grape
포도주	wine
부엌	kitchen
옷	clothes
저녁	dinner, evening

명동	Myung-dong, a street in Seoul
한식집	Korean restaurant
식사	meal
식사(를)하다	to have a meal
종업원	employee
어서	please, quickly (as an urging adverb)
몇 분	how many persons (hon.)
메뉴	menu
처음	the first time, beginning
뭘 (무엇을 →무얼 →뭘)	what (contracted form)
글쎄	well ...
불고기	broiled beef
정식	a full-course meal
밥	cooked rice, meal
국	soup
나물	vegetable dish
김치	kimchi, pickled (Napa) cabbage
그런 (그렇다)	such (to be so)
반찬	side dishes
그거 (그것)	that, it
너무	too (much)
간단하다	to be simple
비빔밥	rice mixed with vegetables
주문하다	to order
보리차	barley tea
냉수	cold water

음식 Food

갈비	short ribs
소고기	beef
돼지고기	pork

닭고기	chicken
생선구이	broiled fish
굽다	to broil
갈비찜	short-rib stew
찌다	to steam, to stew
나물	seasoned vegetables
무치다	to add seasoning (to vegetables)
김치를 담(그)다	to make kimchi
튀김	deep-fried food
볶음	pan-fried food
볶다	to pan fry
국	soup
끓이다	to boil
만두국	wonton soup
떡국	soup with rice cake
찌개	stewlike soup
냉면	a cold noodle soup
온면	a hot noodle soup

양념 Spices

고추가루	red pepper powder
마늘	garlic
파	green onion
생(강)	ginger
고추장 (고치장)	hot pepper paste
된장	soybean paste
소금	salt
깨소금	sesame salt
설탕	sugar
후추 (가루)	black pepper (powder)
(식)초	vinegar
참기름	sesame oil
콩기름	soybean oil

마실 것 Beverages

물	water
차	tea
사이다	soft drink, soda
콜라	cola
맥주	beer
정종	rice wine, sake
소주	hard liquor similar to vodka
막걸리	undistilled rice wine
술	liquor, alcoholic beverage

맛 Flavor

맛이 있다	to be tasty
맛이 없다	to be not tasty
맵다	to be hot (spicy)
짜다	to be salty
달다	to be sweet
시다	to be sour
싱겁다	to be bland
쓰다	to be bitter

온도 Temperature

뜨겁다 (뜨거운)	to be intensely hot (hot)
차다 (찬)	to be cold (cold)
덥다 (더운)	to be hot (hot)
따뜻하다 (따뜻한)	to be warm (warm)
식다 (식은)	to get cold (cold)

불고기 만드는 법 (조리법) Recipe for bulgogi

소고기	1 근 (얇게 썬 것)
간장	2 큰 숟갈 (테이블 스푼)
설탕	1 큰숟갈
깨소금	1 찻숟갈

참기름	1 찻숟갈 (티스푼)
파	2 개 (가늘게 썬 것)
마늘	1 쪽 (다진 것)
후추가루	$\frac{1}{4}$ 찻숟갈

1 근 = 1.3 lb.

1 쪽 = 1 clove, 1 piece

양념들을 잘 섞어서 놓고 소고기 썬 것을 한 조각씩 넣었다가 다같이 큰 그릇에 담는다. 약 두 시간쯤 냉장고에 넣어 둔다. 양념이 잘 된 후에 냉장고에서 꺼내서 숯불에 구워 접시에 담는다.

얇다	to be thin (flat object)
숟갈	spoon
가늘다	to be thin (long object)
다지다	to mince
섞다	to mix
썰다	to slice
조각	piece (flat piece)
그릇	dish
담다	to place in
냉장고	refrigerator
넣어두다	to keep in, to place in
꺼내다	to take out
숯불	charcoal fire
접시	plate

GRAMMAR AND NOTES

In this lesson we will study
1. Expressions for "just as," "like" -듯이, "It seems as if" -듯 하다
2. Two-word verb 가지고 + v. "having," "possessing"
3. Contrastive connective
   a. 그 반면에 "In contrast,"
   b. 반면에 ". . . in contrast"
4. "Even-if" connective: -더라도
5. Sentence ending -군(요) "Oh, I see that ..."
6. Colloquial contractions 뭘, 그거, 그게, 그런
7. Sentence ending -ㄹ/을까(요)? "Will it?" "Shall (I, we)?" "I wonder if ..."
8. Sentence ending -ㄹ/을래 "will," "shall"
9. Question ending -니? intimate or plain style
10. Construction of -나 봐(요) "I think," "It seems that," "It appears that"
11. Construction of -(어/아)야 겠다 "must," "should," "have to"
12. Chinese characters 飮, 食, 風, 俗, 主, 英, 各

1. Expressions for "just as," "like" -듯이, "it seems as if" -듯하다

-듯이, a connective that precedes the main clause, means "just as," "like," or "as if."

-듯하다, a sentence ending, means "it seems as if" or "it seems somewhat."

a. V. STEM + 듯이 "just as," "like"

말이 다르듯이 풍속도 다르다.	The custom is different just as the language is different.
옷이 비슷하듯이 음식도 비슷하다.	Their food is similar just as their clothes are similar.

b. V. MOD. + 듯하다 "it seems as if," "it seems somewhat"

해가 날 듯하다.	It seems as if the sun will come out.

영어가 독일어보다 쉬운 듯하다.	It seems that English is somewhat easier than German.
중국 음식보다 한국 음식이 양념을 더 쓰는 듯하다.	It seems that Korean food uses more spice than Chinese food.

2. Two-word verb 가지고 + v. "having," "possessing"

The use of 가지다 "to have" or "in possession of" with another verb is very productive in Korean. 가지고 can be used with most action verbs.

가지고 오다	to bring	가지고 돌아오다	to bring back
가지고 가다	to carry away	가지고 돌아가다	to take back
가지고 있다	to possess	가지고 말하다	to speak with
가지고 산다	to live with (responsibility, guilt, etc.)	가지고 다니다	to carry with

각 나라의 음식은 특성을 가지고 있다.	Every nation's food has special characteristics.
그는 언제나 우산을 가지고 다닌다.	He always carries an umbrella.
영식이는 신념을 가지고 말했다.	Young-shik spoke with conviction.
사람은 빵만 가지고 살 수는 없다.	Man does not live by bread alone.

3. Contrastive connective 그 반면에 "In contrast," 반면에 "... in contrast"

Like all other connectives, 반면에 has two forms, 그 반면에 for the sentence-initial position and -ㄴ/은/는 반면에 for the clause-medial position connecting two clauses. However, for stylistic variation, 그 may be omitted as well and simply 반면에 used at the beginning of a sentence.

a. 그 반면에 "In contrast"

중국 사람들은 돼지고기를   Chinese use a lot of pork.
많이 쓴다. <u>그 반면에</u> 일본   In contrast, Japanese use
사람들은 생선을 많이 쓴다.   fish a lot.

b. V. MOD. + 반면에 "... in contrast"

중국 사람들은 돼지 고기를   Chinese use a lot of pork,
많이 <u>쓰는 반면에</u>, 일본   but (in contrast) Japanese
사람들은 생선을 많이 쓴다.   use fish a lot.

4. "Even - if" connective: -더라도

Attached to a verb stem or the past tense, -더라도 conveys supposition, as in "Suppose you're right." It can be translated as "even if," "if," or "even if it's the case."

V. STEM + 더라도   present or future supposition
V. STEM + 었/았 더라도   past supposition

마시는 것을 <u>보더라도</u>   If we take a look at the
나라마다 다른 특성을   (world's) beverages, every
가지고 있다.   country's has different
                             characteristics.

<u>외국에 가더라도</u>   Even if you go to a foreign
한국어를 잊지 말아라!   country, do not forget
                             Korean!

할 일이 <u>많았더라도</u>   Even if you had a lot of work
왔어야 한다.   to do, you should have come.

<u>어려웠더라도</u> 너는   Even if it was difficult, you
그일을 했어야 된다.   should have done the work.

5. Sentence ending -(는)군(요) "Oh, I see that ..."

This ending expresses a mild exclamation or a rhetorical statement; it does not necessarily address anyone. In this and other endings with -(요) such as -ㄹ/을까(요), -ㄹ/을래(요), and -ㄴ/은/는데(요), the -요 forms mark the polite informal style while the forms without -요 mark the plain style.

a. Present tense

When used with an action verb, -는 precedes 군(요). When used with a descriptive verb, just a verb stem precedes -군(요).

> A. V. + 는군(요)
>
> 음식을 많이 <u>주는군</u>.   Oh, I see they serve lots of food.
>
> 비빔밥을 <u>주문하는군</u>.   Oh, I see you're ordering *bibimbap.*
>
> 냉수를 <u>마시는군</u>.   I see you're drinking cold water.
>
> D. V. STEM + 군(요)
>
> 음식이 <u>간단하군</u>.   I see that the food is simple.
>
> 사람이 <u>많군</u>.   Oh, there are lots of people.
>
> 반찬이 <u>짜군</u>·   Oh, the side dishes are salty.

b. Past tense

Both action and descriptive verbs take -군(요) with the past-tense marker -었 or -았.

> A. V. + 었/았군(요)
>
> 음식을 <u>혼동했군(요)</u>.   Oh, I was confused about the food.
>
> 김치는 참 잘 <u>알려졌군(요)</u>.   (Oh, I see that) kimchi is indeed well known.
>
> 생선을 기름에 <u>튀겼군(요)</u>.   (Oh, I see that) the fish is deep-fried.
>
> D. V. + 었/았군(요)
>
> 돼지고기가 너무 <u>매웠군(요)</u>.   (I see that) the pork was too spicy.
>
> 불고기가 너무 <u>달았군(요)</u>.   (I see that) the *bulgogi* was too sweet.
>
> 음식종류가 <u>많았군(요)</u>.   (Oh, I see that) there were many kinds of food.

6. Colloquial contractions 뭘, 그거, 그게, 그런

In spoken language, frequently used words, phrases, and endings are often contracted or omitted, resulting in short forms:

뭐	from 무엇	"what"
뭘	from 무엇을	"what-DIR. OBJ."
그거	from 그것	"that-thing"
그게	from 그것이	"that-SUBJ."
그런	from 그러한	"such a"
어서옵쇼	from 어서 오십시오	"Welcome."

Shortening also occurs in borrowed foreign words:

아파트	apartment
데모	demonstration
슈퍼	supermarket
파인쥬스	pineapple juice

7. Sentence ending -ㄹ/을까(요)? "Will it?" "Shall (I, we)?" "I wonder if ..."

This ending expresses guessing, seeking permission, or approval of a proposed action by asking.

-ㄹ까(요) is used with verb stems that end in a vowel.

-을까(요) is used with verb stems that end in any consonant except ㄹ.

For verb stems that end in ㄹ, only 까(요) is used. This rule also applies to the -ㄹ/을래 ending in GN8 below.

뭘 먹을까요?	What shall I eat?
김치가 매울까요?	(I wonder if) kimchi is hot?
정식에 무엇이 나올까?	What (do you suppose) will they serve for a full-course meal?
지금 주문할까?	Shall we order now?
뭘 살까?	What shall I buy?
그 사람이 알까?	Would he know?

8. Sentence ending -ㄹ/을래 "will," "shall"

This intimate, informal future ending follows a verb stem and can be a statement or a question, depending on the intonation. In general, the intonation rises at the end of a question and falls in a statement. (See GN7 above for the formation.)

Statement	Question
불고기 정식으로 할래.	불고기 정식으로 할래?
I will take *bulgogi jŏngsik*.	Will you have *bulgogi jŏngsik*?
학교에서 공부할래.	학교에서 공부할래?
I am going to study at school.	Will you study at school?
한국 음식을 먹을래.	한국 음식을 먹을래?
I will have Korean food.	Will you have Korean food?

9. Question ending -니? intimate or plain style

Attached directly to the verb stem or STEM + TENSE (었/았 or 겠), this intimate or plain question ending goes with the intimate-style sentence ending -어/아.

정식에는 무엇이 나오니?	What does *jŏngsik* include?
(잘 모르겠어.)	(I am not sure.)
영국은 마시는 것이 무엇으로 유명하니?	What kind of drink is famous in England?
(위스키로 유명해.)	([It] is famous for whisky.)
음식이 맛 있었니?	Was the food tasty?
(그저 그랬어.)	(It was so-so.)

10. Construction of -나 봐(요) "I think," "It seems that," "It appears that"

The informal -나봐 or polite informal -나봐요 expression is used in spoken language to indicate uncertainty.

V. STEM + (TENSE) + 나 봐(요)

그런 반찬들이 나오나 봐요.	I think such (those kinds of) side dishes accompany (the meal).
누가 오나 봐요.	It seems that someone is coming (approaching).
맛이 없나 봐요.	It seems it *is* not tasty.
맛이 없었나 봐요.	It seems it *was* not tasty.
매웠나 봐요.	It seems it *was* hot (spicy).

11. Construction of -(어/아)야 겠다

V. STEM + (어/아)야 겠다, which expresses future intention, is less strong than -(어/아)야 하다 or -(어/아)야 되다 "must," "should," "have to" (see L21, GN4) and has the underlying meaning of "I think" or "I guess."

비빔밥을 먹어야 겠다.	(I think) I should have *bibimbap*.
정식을 주문해야 겠다.	(I guess) I should order *jŏngsik*.
맥주를 좀 마셔야 겠다.	(I think) I will drink some beer.

Compare the following statements:

중국 음식에 대해서 알아야 한다/된다.	One must know something about Chinese food.
중국 음식에 대해서 좀 알아야 겠다.	(I think) I'd better know something about Chinese food.

12. Chinese characters

飲
마실 음
drink
食
먹을 식
eat
風
바람 풍
wind
俗
풍속 속
custom
主
주인 주
master
英
꽃부리 영
flower
brave
各
각 각
each

연습

A. 다음 질문에 대답하십시오.
1. 영식이와 창호는 어디로 식사를 하러 갔어요?
2. 영식이는 무엇을 먹기로 했어요?
3. 창호는 무엇을 주문했어요?
4. 학생은 식당에 가면 보통 무엇을 주문해요?
5. 동양 음식의 주식은 무엇입니까?
6. 일본 음식과 중국 음식은 어떻게 다릅니까?
7. 동양 음식 중에서는 어느 나라 음식이 가장 종류가 많습니까? (가장: the most)
8. 집에서는 주로 어떤 음식을 많이 해요?
9. 학생은 양념이 많이 든 음식을 좋아해요?
10. 미국 음식의 특성은 무엇입니까?

B. 다음 문장을 끝마치십시오.
11. 각 나라의 말이 다르듯이 _____
12. 불란서는 포도주로 유명하듯이 _____
13. 한국에서는 보리차를 많이 마시는 반면에 _____
14. 맛이 없더라도 _____
15. 음식이 간단하더라도 _____

C. 다음 문장을 한국어로 번역하십시오.
16. He *brought back* various kinds of spices from India. (India: 인도)
17. Please *take* this *back* to your house.
18. *Have* you *ever tasted* (eaten) Korean food? Chinese food? Thai food? (Thai: 태국)
19. What *will* you have/eat? I *should* have something simple.
20. *Will* you order? (intimate style)
21. *Would* you *please* bring some hot tea? (polite informal)
22. *In general*, spicy foods taste good.

23. *Just as* there are many kinds of wine, there are also many kinds of beer.

24. Mexican food is, of course, spicy (hot), but Korean food is *spicier*.

25. It is *easy to confuse* Korean food with Chinese food.

D. 간단한 조리법을 써 보십시오. (Write your favorite recipe.)

Lesson 24

제 이십사과   백화점

1층

점원 : 어서 오십시오. 무엇을 찾으십니까?

죤 : 남자들 셔츠와 내복이 어디에 있습니까?

점원 : 삼층에 있습니다. 저기 있는 에레베타를 타고 가셔서 삼층에서 내려 오른쪽으로 보십시오.

죤 : 참, 한국 자개품들은 어디에 있지요?

점원 : 칠층에 가구들 파는 데¹ 같이 있습니다.

죤 : 고맙습니다.

3층

죤 : 남자 셔츠는 어디에 있습니까?

점원 : 저쪽에 있어요.

죤 : 제가 입으려고 하는데 중 (中) 싸이즈가 맞을까요?

점원 : 맞을 것 같은데요. 소매가 짧을지 모르니까 한번 입어 보시겠어요?

죤 : 대 (大) 중 (中) 소 (小) 세 싸이즈 밖에² 없습니까?

점원 : 네. 그런데요 ...

죤 : 혹시 노란색³은 없나요?

점원 : 잠깐만 ... 찾아 보지요. 네, 있습니다. 그런데 짧은 소매군요.

존 : 긴 소매라야만 되⁴겠는데요. 그냥 이것으로
　　 하지요.
점원 : 네, 그것은 4,500원입니다. 감사합니다. 또
　　 오십시오.

7층

점원 : 무엇을 찾으시지요?
　존 : 한국 자개품을 찾는데요.
점원 : 이리로 오십시오. 여기는 화병, 보석 상자,
　　 쟁반들이 있고 저기는 좀 큰 가구들이
　　 있습니다.
　존 : 미국에 선물로 가지고 갈 것이라⁵ 너무 큰
　　 것은 안 되고 자그마한 것이 좋겠습니다.
점원 : 쟁반이나 꽃병이 어떻습니까? 그리 크지도
　　 않고 값도 좋고요.
　존 : 이 꽃병은 얼마나 하지요? 이 네모 쟁반은요?
점원 : 꽃병이 정가는 5,000원인데, 요즘 쎄일이라
　　 10퍼센트를 싸게 해 드립니다. 네모 쟁반은
　　 3,500원이고, 이 둥근 쟁반은 4,000원입니다
　존 : 그럼 이 둥근 쟁반 두 개 하고 그 꽃병
　　 하나만 주십시오.
점원 : 네, 그러십시오. 선물용이니⁶ 상자에 따로 따로
　　 넣어 드릴까요?
　존 : 네, 그렇게⁷ 해 주세요. 여기 어디에 공중전화가
　　 있습니까? 그동안 잠깐 갔다 오게요.⁸
점원 : 그렇게 하십시오. 바로 에레베타 옆에 있습니다.

Patterns

1. 오른쪽으로 보십시오.
　 왼쪽____ 들어가십시오.
　 반____ 나누세요.
　 둘____ 나누세요.
　 학생____ 왔어요.
　 신문 기자____ 일해요.

영어____ 무엇이라고 해요?
한국어____ 말하세요.

2. 가구 파는 데가 어디지요?
  생선 파는 _____
  운동하는 _____
  에레베타 타는 _____
  물건을 찾는 _____

3. 짧을지 모른다.
  내복이 맞을지 _____
  긴 소매인지 _____
  입을 수 있을지 _____

4. 소(小) 싸이즈 밖에 없습니까?
  이것 _____
  긴 소매 _____
  노란색 _____

5. 무엇을 찾으시지요?
  어디에 가시_____
  무슨 쟁반이_____
  무엇을 넣으시___

6. 가지고 갈 것이라 작아야 돼요.
  가지고 다닐 것_____
  상자에 넣을 것_____
  선물로 줄 것_____

7. 싸게 해 드립니다.
  좋게 _____
  자그마하게 _____
  빨리 _____

8. 선물용이니 상자에 넣어 주세요.
  학생용이니 싸게 해 _____
  곤색셔츠를 찾아 _____

9. 따로 넣어 드릴까요?
  같이 _____
  많이 _____
  조금 _____

10. <u>그렇게</u> 해 <u>주세요</u>.
    _____ 하세요.
    _____ 바쁘세요?
    _____ 됐어요?

11. <u>잠깐 갔다</u> <u>오게요</u>.
    ___ 다녀 _____
    ___ 있다 _____
    ___ 보고 _____

12. <u>잠깐 갔다</u> <u>오게</u> 기다리세요.
    ___ 다녀 _____
    ___ 있다 _____
    ___ 보고 _____

13. (셔츠를) <u>얼마 주고</u> 샀습니까?
    (영화를) _____ 봤습니까?
    (전시회를) _____ 들어갔습니까?
    (뻐스를) _____ 탔어요?
    (저녁을) _____ 먹었어요?

낱말

제 이십사과 (第二十四課)	Lesson 24
백화점 (百貨店)	department store
일층 (1층)	first floor, ground floor
점원	sales clerk, salesperson
남자	man, male
셔츠	shirt
내복	underwear
삼층 (3층)	third floor
에레베타	elevator
내리다	to get off
오른쪽	right side
입다	to wear, to put on (clothes)
맞다	to fit
소매	sleeve
짧다	short

한번	once, one time
대, 중, 소 (大, 中, 小)	large, medium, small
혹시	by any chance, if
노란색 (노랑)	yellow
잠깐	a short while, a moment
긴 (길다)	long (to be long)
그냥	as is
칠층 (7층)	seventh floor
화병 (꽃병)	vase
자개품	mother-of-pearl inlaid item
가구	furniture
보석	precious stone, jewelry
상자	box
쟁반	tray
선물	gift, a present
선물용	to be used as a gift
작다	to be small
자그마하다	to be smallish
네모	four-sided, square or rectangle
정가	regular price
싸다	to be cheap, inexpensive
둥근 (둥글다)	round (to be round)
따로 (따로따로)	separately, apart
넣다	to put in
공중전화	public phone
값	price
바로	right, just
빨간색 (빨강)	red color (red)
파란색 (파랑)	blue color (blue)
흰색 (하양)	white color (white)
곤색	navy blue color
까만색 (까망)	black color (black)
색 (色)	color

Verbs "to wear" and "to take off"

쓰다 *"to wear"*	벗다 *"to take off"*
모자를 쓴다.	모자를 벗는다.
안경을 썼다.	안경을 벗었다.
수건을 쓰겠다.	수건을 벗겠다.
입다 *"to wear"*	벗다 *"to take off"*
옷을 입는다.	옷을 벗는다.
코트를 입었다.	코트를 벗었다.
치마를 입어요.	치마를 벗어요.
신다 *"to wear," "to put on"*	벗다 *"to take off"*
신을 신었다.	신을 벗었다.
양말을 신는다.	양말을 벗는다.
장화를 신겠어요.	장화를 벗겠어요.
운동화를 신었어요.	운동화를 벗었어요.
끼다 *"to insert"*	빼다 *"to remove"*
반지를 끼다.	반지를 뺀다.
장갑을 꼈다(끼었다).	장갑을 벗었다.
걸다/하다 *"to hang"*	
목걸이를 건다.	목걸이를 뺐다.
귀걸이를 건다.	귀걸이를 뺐다.
차다 *"to dangle," "to wear"*	풀다 *"to untie"*
시계를 찼다.	시계를 푼다.
칼을 찬다.	칼을 풀다.
매다 *"to tie"*	풀다 *"to untie"*
넥타이를 맨다.	넥타이를 푼다.
벨트를 맸다.	벨트를 풀었다.

Note that while "to wear" has different verbs for different parts of the body, "to take off " has 벗다 for most parts of the body except 반지를 빼다, 시계를 풀다, and 넥타이를 풀다.

모자	hat	귀걸이	earrings
안경	glasses	신	shoes
반지	ring	양말	stockings, socks

장갑	gloves	장화	boots
코트	coat, overcoat	구두	shoes (leather)
치마	skirt	운동화	sneakers
바지	pants, trousers	시계	watch
저고리	Korean blouse	수건	towel, kerchief
목걸이	necklace	칼	knife

GRAMMAR AND NOTES

In this lesson we will study
1. Dependent noun -데 "place," "spot," "location"
2. Expression for "only": N.P. 밖에 + NEG. V.
3. Irregular ㅎ verbs
4. Construction of N. + 이라야(만) 되다/하다 "it has to be"
5. Causal connective -(이)라 "because it is," "since it is," "as it is"
6. Causal connective -(으)니(까) "because," "since"
7. Expression for "so," "in that way": 그렇게
8. "So-that" connective: V. STEM + 게요 "so," "so that," "in order that"
9. Chinese characters 小, 色, 貨, 店, 個

1. Dependent noun -데 "place," "spot," "location"

-데, like -곳, is always used with a verbal modifier :

가구를 파는 데가 많다.	There are many places where they sell furniture.
사람들이 잘 데가 없다.	There is no place for people to sleep.
밝은 데로 가세요.	Please go where it's light.
나는 방학동안에 간 데가 없다.	I didn't go anywhere during the vacation.

2. Expression for "only": N. PHRASE 밖에 + NEG. V.

밖에 means literally "outside of" but is generally translated as "only" when it is used with a negative 안 or 못 or with negative verbs like 없다 or 모르다.

a. 밖에 + 없다 "there is only," "I have only"

세 싸이즈밖에 없어요.	There are only three sizes.
오불밖에 없다.	I have only five dollars
내복은 흰색밖에 없다.	There is only white underwear.

b. 밖에 + 안 되다 "it is only," "it amounts to only"

이 꽃병은 저것의 반밖에 안된다.	This vase is only half that size.
지금 두시밖에 안 됐다.	It is only two o'clock now.

c. 밖에 + 모르다 "to know only"

나는 독일어 밖에 모른다.	I know only German.
그는 공부 밖에 모른다.	He is interested only in his studies.

d. 밖에 + 못 + v. "can do only"

나는 서울에 석달 밖에 못 있었다.	I could stay in Seoul only three months.
그는 뉴욕밖에 못 갔다.	He could go only to New York.
그는 두장밖에 못 읽었다.	He could read only two pages.

e. 밖에 + 안 + v. "to do only"

나는 피아노 연습을 한 시간 밖에 안 한다.	I practice piano only for an hour.
죤은 쟁반 밖에 안 샀다.	John bought only trays.
거기서는 가구 밖에 안 판다.	They sell only furniture there.

3. Irregular ㅎ verbs

Some verb stems ending in ㅎ drop the ㅎ before a vowel suffix.

		-은	(으)면	(으)세요
노랗다	to be yellow	노란	노라면	노라세요
빨갛다	to be red	빨간	빨가면	빨가세요
까맣다	to be black	까만	까마면	까마세요
하얗다	to be white	하얀	하야면	하야세요
파랗다	to be blue	파란	파라면	파라세요
그렇다	to be in that way	그런	그러면	그러세요
어떻다	to be in a certain manner	어떤	어떠면	어떠세요

Some ㅎ verbs do not change.

좋다	to be good	좋은	좋으면	좋으세요
넣다	to put in	넣은	넣으면	넣으세요
놓다	to place	놓은	놓으면	놓으세요
많다	to be many	많은	많으면	많으세요
낳다	to give birth	낳은	낳으면	낳으세요

4. Construction of N. + 이라야(만) 되다/하다 "It has to be"

Originally from the verb 이다 "to be" followed by 야(만)되다/하다 "it must," -이라야(만)되다/하다 means "It has to be (such and such a thing or person)." It conveys a stronger sense of "must" than -(어/아)야 되다/하다. 만 may be added for emphasis. Please note that 라야(만)되다/하다 is used only for the verb 이다 and cannot be used for any other verb. -(어/아)야(만)되다/하다 is used for all other verbs. (See L21, GN4.)

한국어 책이라야(만) 된다.   It has to be a Korean book.
알약이라야(만) 된다.   It has to be pills (not liquid).
높은 의자라야만 한다.*   It has to be a tall chair.

* 이 of 이라야 is usually dropped after a noun ending in a vowel.

5. Causal connective -(이)라 "because it is," "since it is," "as it is"

-(이)라, the short form of -(이)라서, conveys the meaning "because it is ..." and is similar to -(어/아)서, -기 때문에, and -(으)니까 in GN6 below. -(이)라 is used only after a noun phrase; 이 is dropped after a noun ending in a vowel.

선물용이라 작아야 한다.	Since it is for a gift, it has to be small. (condition)
이것은 형님의 편지라 제가 읽을 수 없습니다.	Because this is a letter for my brother, I cannot read it. (cause)
이것은 당신의 책임이 아니고 내 책임이라 내가 끝내야 된다.	As this is my responsibility, not yours, I must finish it.
외국에 가지고 갈 것이라 작아야 됩니다.	Since it is something that I will be taking abroad, it should be small.
동생에게 줄 것이라 그에게 맞을 셔츠를 찾았다.	Because it is for my brother (something I will give to my brother), I looked for a shirt that would fit him.

6. Causal connective -(으)니(까) "because," "since"

This connective has a meaning close to -(어/아)서 and is often used without 까.

선물용이니(까) 좋아야 된다.	Since it is for a gift, it must be nice.
둥근 쟁반이 없으니 네모를 사겠다.	Since there are no round trays, I will buy a square one.
중 싸이즈가 너무 크니 사지 말아요.	Because medium is too big, do not buy it.

7. Expression for "so," "in that way": 그렇게

Aside from the literal meaning of "so" or "in that way," 그렇게 also means "as you wish," or "all right." It can also be a euphemistic way of saying "yes" when used with 하다, as in 그렇게 하지요.

따로 따로 넣어 드릴까요?	Shall I put them separately?
네, 그렇게 해 주세요.	Yes, please (do it that way).
좀 싸게 해 주시겠어요?	Would you please make it cheaper (for us)?
그렇게 해 드리지요.	I will do so (as you wish).

8. "So-that" connective: V. STEM + 게(요) "so," "so that," "in order that"

When used after an action verb, -게 is a clause connective, but it may appear as a sentence ending when the clauses are inverted or one of the clauses is not fully said but understood.

공중전화가 어디 있는지 좀 말씀해 주시겠어요?	Please tell me where the public phone is.
전화 좀 하게요.	So I can make a call.
잠깐만 기다려 주세요.	Please wait a moment.
곧 갔다 오게요.	So I can make a short visit.
공부하게 좀 조용히 하세요.	Please be quiet so we can study.

9. Chinese characters

小
작을 소
small
色
색 색
color
貨
재물 화
goods
店
가게 점
store
個
낱 개
item

연습

A. 다음 질문에 대답하십시오.

1. 존은 백화점에서 무엇을 사려고 했습니까?
2. 삼층에서는 무엇을 샀습니까? 얼마에 샀습니까?
3. 칠층에서는 무엇을 샀어요? 얼마 주고 샀어요?
4. 존은 왜 작은 것을 달라고 했습니까?
5. "Welcome." 또는 "Come in, please." 를 무엇이라고 합니까?
6. 백화점은 무엇을 하는 데입니까?
7. 학생은 무슨 싸이즈의 신을 신어요?
8. 정가가 1,000원인데 15%를 싸게 하면 얼마지요?

B. 영어로 번역하십시오.

9. 선물을 <u>반으로</u> 나누었다.
10. 저는 지금 집<u>으로</u> 가고 있습니다.
11. 저쪽<u>으로</u> 가 보십시오.
12. 미국에서 신문 기자<u>로</u> 일했습니다.
13. 선물용<u>으로</u> 쟁반을 샀습니다.
14. 한국에 비행기<u>로</u> 가려고 합니다.
15. "무슨 색<u>으로</u> 드릴까요?" "곤색<u>으로</u> 주십시오."

C. "밖에"를 사용하여 다음 질문에 대답하십시오.

16. 무슨 싸이즈가 있습니까?
    <u>(中)</u> 중 싸이즈밖에 없습니다.
17. 돈이 얼마나 있으십니까?
    <u>($10)</u>
18. 며칠 동안 유럽에 계셨습니까? <u>(일 주일)</u>
19. 어제 무엇을 사셨습니까? <u>(선물)</u>
20. 이층에서는 무엇을 팝니까? <u>(가구)</u>
21. 무슨 외국어를 하십니까? <u>(불어)</u>
22. 무슨 색 셔츠가 있습니까? <u>(파란색)</u>

D. 다음 문장을 한국어로 번역하십시오.

23. The shirt size *ought to be* medium.
24. The salesperson *ought to be* courteous. (courteous: 친절하다)

25. The gift *must not be* expensive.

26. The pants *must not be* too short.

27. One *must not* bargain in department stores.

28. Please wrap it nicely *so that* we can give it to our parents.

29. *Do you know if* the dress *will fit* her?

30. *Do you know whether* John *bought* the mother-of-pearl inlaid vase?

31. I would like to know *where they sell* postage stamps. (postage stamps: 우표)

32. I would like to know *whether they sell* white shoes in that store.

33. I *don't know if* there is a public phone on the second floor.

34. I *don't know how much* the jewelry box is.

35. It *seems that* the sleeves are too long.

36. Since the price *seems* reasonable (cheap), why don't you (please) buy a lot.

37. This round tray *seems* good for a present.

Lesson 25

제 이십오과　시장

　　오늘 아침에는 먹을 것이 다 떨어져서 시장에 갔다.
바다에서 곧 잡아 온 듯한 가지각색의 생선과 밭에서
캐온 것 같은 채소가 보기 좋았다.
　　식품의 값이 적혀[1] 있지 않아서 하나 하나 값을 물어
봐야 했다.

대화 A

　　　　　존 : 이 생선은 얼마나 해요?
　생선장수 : 두 마리에 500원만 주십시오.
　　　　　존 : 좀 싸게 해[2] 주지 않으시겠어요?
　생선장수 : 싼 값인데요. 자, 그럼 세 마리에 600원만
　　　　　　　내세요.

대화　B

　야채장수 : 싱싱한 오이 사 가[3]세요.
　　　　　존 : 한 묶음에 얼마에요?
　야채장수 : 1,000원인데 900원에 해 드릴께요.[4]
　　　　　존 : 800원만 합시다.[5]

　　아침 거리[6]를 사러 온 많은 사람들 틈에 끼어, 이같이
재미있게 흥정을 하며, 두 시간이나 장을 보러 다녔다.[7]

Patterns

1. 바다에서 곧 잡아온 <u>듯한</u> 생선이 많았다.
   밭에서 캐온 _____ 채소가 보기 좋았다.
   어디에서 본 _____ 사람이었다.
   나에게 맞을 _____ 옷이 없었다.
   비가 올 _____ 날씨였다.

2. 밭에서 캐온 <u>것 같은</u> 채소가 보기 좋았다.
   바다에서 잡아온 _____ 생선이 많았다.
   어디에서 들어 본 ____ 음악이었다.
   나에게 맞을 _____ 옷이 없었다.
   맛이 있을 _____ 음식이 많이 있었다.

3. 채소들이 <u>보기 좋았다.</u>
   음악이 듣_____
   그 옷이 입_____
   그 펜이 쓰_____
   그 생선이 먹_____

4. 값이 <u>적혀 있지 않았다.</u>
   한자_____
   날짜_____
   이름_____
   번호_____

5. 값을 <u>물어 봐야 했다.</u>
   길_____
   한자_____
   이름_____
   방법_____

6. 값을 <u>물어 봐야 한다.</u>
   옷을 입어 _____
   흥정을 해 _____
   한자를 써 _____
   지하철을 타 _____

7. 500원만 <u>주십시오.</u>
   생선 두 마리_____
   오이 한 무더기_____
   과자 한 봉지_____
   커피 두 잔_____

8. <u>싱싱한</u> 오이 <u>사 가세요</u>.
   _____ 배추 _____
   _____ 생선 _____
   _____ 무 _____

9. <u>한</u> 무더기에 얼마에요?
   __ 봉지_____
   __ 파운드_____
   __ 꾸러미_____
   __ 상자_____

10. 900원에 해 <u>드릴께요</u>.
    1,000원에 _____
    싸게 _____
    잘 _____

11. 아침 거리를 사<u>러</u> 왔어요.
    장을 보__ 다녔다.
    극장에 구경을 하__ 갔다.
    저녁을 먹__ 식당에 갔다.

12. <u>재미있게</u> 홍정을 했다.
    _____ 장을 봤다.
    _____ 놀았다.
    _____ 읽었다.
    _____ 지냈다.

낱말

제 이십오과 (第二十五課)	Lesson 25
시장 (市場)	market, grocery store
먹을 것	food, things to eat
바다	sea, ocean
잡아 오다	to catch and bring
가지각색	every color, all kinds
밭	garden, (growing) field
캐(어) 오다	to dig up and bring
식품 (食品)	groceries, food

적히다	to be written (passive form of 적다: to write, to record)
생선장수	fish merchant
-마리	head of (counter for animate objects)
싸다	to be cheap; to wrap
야채(野菜)장수	vegetable merchant
싱싱하다	to be fresh
묶음	bundle
드리다	to give (to an honorific person)
아침거리	things for breakfast
틈	in between; among
끼다	to be wedged in, to be in the midst, to be included
흥정을 하다	to bargain
장을 보다	to go grocery shopping
내다	to pay
돈을 내다	to pay money
방법	method
지하철	subway
봉지	bag
잔	cup
파운드	pound
꾸러미	bundle, packet

Noun counters

1. 단 : bunch, bundle

파	green onion (파 한 단)
시금치	spinach
무(우)	daikon radish
당근	carrot

2. 근: unit of weight (1.3 pounds)

설탕	sugar (설탕 한 근)
밀가루	flour
쌀가루	rice flour
고기	meat

3. 마리: head

개	dog (개 한 마리)
강아지	puppy
고양이	cat
쥐	mouse, rat
꿩	pheasant

4. 채: building unit

집	house (집 한 채)
빌딩	building

5. 대: vehicle counter

차, 자동차	car, automobile
뻐스	bus (뻐스 한 대)
기차	train
비행기	airplane

6. 척: counter for ship or boat

배	boat, ship (배 한 척)
기선	steamship

7. 모: cube

두부	tofu (두부 한 모)

GRAMMAR AND NOTES

In this lesson we will study
1. More on passive -히
2. More on causative V. STEM + 게 하다
3. Two-word verbs 어/아 오다 and 어/아 가다: direction modal
4. Sentence ending -ㄹ/을께(요) "will do"
5. Sentence ending -(만) 합시다 "Let's make it (just) ..."
6. Dependent noun -거리 "material," "stuff," "things"
7. Expressions for
   a. "to go around (in order) to do" -(으)러 다니다
   b. "to go around doing" -(으)며 다니다
8. Chinese characters 場, 品, 野, 茱

1. More on passive -히

The verb 적히다 "to be written," "to be recorded" is a passive form of 적다 "to write," "to record." (For the derivation of passive forms from active verbs, see L18, GN6. See also L22, GN3, for continuous state.)

식품의 값이 <u>적혀</u> 있지 않았다.	The prices for food items were not written (on them).
오늘은 생선이 많이 <u>잡혔다</u>.	A lot of fish were caught today.

Not all verbs can be made passive. For example, 팔다 "to sell" becomes passive by adding -리, thus 팔리다 "to be sold," but 사다 "to buy" cannot be made passive by using a suffix.

오이가 다 <u>팔렸다</u>.	The cucumbers were all sold out.
우리가 오이를 다 <u>샀다</u>.	We bought all the cucumbers. (It is not possible to say "All the cucumbers were bought by us.")

2. More on causative V. STEM + 게 하다

This construction means "to make (someone or something) do something" or "to cause (someone or something) to do something." When used with descriptive verbs, -게 하다 means to "cause or make (someone or something) be . . ." (see L21, GN3).

그는 생선값을 <u>싸게 해</u> <u>주었다.</u>	He sold the fish cheaper (to me). (He made the price of fish cheap for me.)
어머니가 그에게 야채값을 <u>쓰게 했다.</u>	Mother made him write the prices of the vegetables.
그 약이 나를 <u>졸리게 한다.</u>	The medicine makes me sleepy.
우리 선생님은 우리에게 책을 <u>읽게 하신다.</u>	Our teacher makes us read books.

3. Two-word verbs -어/아 오다 and -어/아 가다: direction modal

Many verbs are used with -어/아 오다 and -어/아 가다 to convey the directional aspect of the verb. The directional reference point is always the speaker and 오다 "come" always means toward the speaker.

사 가세요	Please buy (and take it with you).
사 오세요	Please buy (and bring it).
잡아 가다	to catch and take away
잡아 오다	to catch and bring
찾아 가다	to go and visit
찾아 오다	to come and visit
빌려 가다	to borrow and take away
빌려 오다	to borrow and bring

4. Sentence ending -ㄹ/을께(요) "will do"

This ending is used with an action verb (and 있다) to indicate an intention or a plan of a first-person subject. (See L23, GN7 and 8, for the choice of -ㄹ or -을.)

900원에 해 <u>드릴께요</u>.   *I will* make it 900 won for you.
싸게 해 <u>드릴께요</u>.   *I will* make it cheap for you.
다섯시까지 <u>있을께요</u>.   *I will* be here until five o'clock.
300원만 <u>낼께요</u>.   *I will* pay only 300 won.

5. Sentence ending -(만) 합시다 "Let's make it (just) ..."

This idiomatic expression is often used in bargaining.

800원만 <u>합시다</u>.   Let's make it just 800 won.
싸게 <u>합시다</u>.   Make it cheap. (Give me a good price.)
100원에 <u>합시다</u>.   Let's make it 100 won.

6. Dependent noun -거리 "material," "stuff," "things"

-거리 must follow a noun. It is usually used with food nouns like 아침 "breakfast," 저녁 "dinner," 반찬 "side dish," and 국 "soup."

국 <u>거리</u>   ingredients for soup
아침 <u>거리</u>   things for breakfast
김치 <u>거리</u>   ingredients for kimchi
반찬 <u>거리</u>   ingredients for side dishes

It is also used with 이야기 (얘기) "story" or 일 "work."

이야기 <u>거리</u>가 없다.   There is nothing to talk about.

날마다 일 <u>거리</u>가 많다.   There is a lot of work to do every day.

7. Expressions for "to go around (in order) to do" -(으)러 다니다, "to go around doing" -(으)며 다니다

a. -(으)러 다니다 means literally "to go around (in order) to do something."

일을 보러 <u>다녔다</u>.   (He) went around to take care of his business.

일을 <u>하러 다녔다</u>.	(He) commuted to (do) his work.
아침 거리를 <u>사러 다녔다</u>.	(He) went around to buy groceries for breakfast.
물고기를 <u>잡으러 다녔다</u>.	(He) went (fishing) trying to catch fish.

b. -(으)며 다니다 means literally "to go around while doing (something)."

그는 저녁 거리를 <u>사며</u> 다녔다.	He went around buying groceries for dinner.
그는 돈을 <u>쓰며 다녔다</u>.	He went around spending money.
그는 은행에서 <u>일하며</u> 대학을 <u>다녔다</u>.	He attended college while working at a bank.
그 아이는 라디오를 <u>들으며 다닌다</u>.	That child goes around listening to the radio.

8. Chinese characters

場	마당 장 place	一	十	圵	圵	坍	场	場	場
品	물건 품 things	丶	口	口	口	呂	品	品	品
野	풀 야 field	丶	口	日	旦	甲	野	野	野
菜	나물 채 vegetable	一	十	艹	艹	苂	苂	菜	菜

연습

A. 다음 질문에 대답하십시오.
    1. 존은 오늘 아침 어디에 갔어요?
    2. 시장에는 무엇들이 보기 좋았어요?
    3. 존은 왜 식품값을 물어 봐야 했어요?
    4. 생선은 한 마리에 얼마나 해요?
    5. 생선 세 마리에 얼마를 내라고 했어요?
    6. 오이는 한 무더기에 얼마였어요?
    7. 야채장수는 오이를 얼마나 싸게 해 주었어요?
    8. 존은 얼마 동안 장을 보러 다녔어요?

B. 다음 어구를 사용하여 짧은 글을 지으십시오.
    9. 가지각색
  10. 싱싱하다
  11. 하나하나
  12. 얼마나
  13. 흥정(을) 하다
  14. 장(을) 보다

C. 다음 낱말을 이용하여 문장을 만드십시오.
  15. (시장, 생선, 사다, 가다, 두 마리)
  16. (쥐, 고양이, -게 하다, 보다, 뛰다)
  17. (집, 한 채, 자동차, 두 대, 짓다, 사다)
  18. (시금치, 당근, 한 단, 무겁다)
  19. (비행기, 한 척, 배, 한 대, 비싸다)

D. 다음 문장을 한국어로 번역하십시오.
  20. It seems that I *am out of* sugar.
  21. The price of food *seems expensive* these days.
  22. *While shopping* for groceries, we had to bargain.
  23. I *will make* it ₩500 *less (for you)*.
  24. Please pay (me) *just* ₩10,000.
  25. Please *buy (and take)* some fresh vegetables.
  26. *Let's* go grocery shopping. (hon. polite)
  27. *Are* many fish *caught* in this river?
     No, not many *are caught* here.

28. What is the price *for a (head of)* fish?
29. Because the prices *are not written,* I don't know how much it is.
30. How much is *a bag of* flour?
31. *Make him come* quickly!
32. She *made her sister write* a letter once a week.

Lesson 26

제 이십육과 속담

　어느 나라 말에나 속담이 있다. 속담은 누가
만들었는지 또는 언제 만들어졌는지는 모른다. 그러나
속담은 옛 조상으로부터 내려 오면서 경험에 의하여[1]
만들어진 지혜의 말이라고 하겠다.[2]
　그러므로 우리가 흔히 쓰고 있는 속담들에는 국민의
특성과 재질, 그리고 정신 등이 반영되어 있다. 그뿐만
아니라 인류의 공통적인 진리가 나타나 있기도 하다.
　다음의 몇 가지 속담을 통하여[3] 그 예를 찾아 보기로
하자.

1. 구슬이 서 말이라도 꿰어야 보배다.
2. 등잔 밑이 어둡다.
3. 아니 땐 굴뚝에 연기 나랴.[4]
4. 고래 싸움에 새우등 터진다.
5. 세살 버릇 여든까지 간다.
6. 바늘 도둑이 소도둑 된다.
7. 떡 줄 사람은 생각도 안 하는데 김치국부터 마신다.
8. 하늘이 무너져도[5] 솟아날 구멍이 있다.
9. 아는 길도 물어 가라.[6]
10. 소 잃고 외양간 고친다.
11. 아무리 급해도 바늘 허리 매어서는 못 쓴다.
12. 발 없는 말이 천리 간다.
13. 밤 말은 쥐가 듣고 낮 말은 새가 듣는다.

14. 호랑이도 제말 하면 온다.
15. 시작이 반이다.
16. 중이 염불에는 마음[7]이 없고 잿밥에만 마음이 있다.

짧은 속담

1. 금강산도 식후경
2. 하늘의 별 따기
3. 누워서 떡 먹기
4. 우물 안 개구리
5. 울며 겨자 먹기
6. 수박 겉 핥기
7. 쇠귀에 경 읽기
8. 이웃 사촌
9. 제 눈에 안경
10. 안 되면 조상의 탓

Patterns

1. 경험에 의하여 만들어졌다.
   지혜_____
   특성_____
   재질_____

2. 지혜의 말이라고 하겠다.
   경험_____
   진리_____

3. 정신이 반영되어 있다.
   특성_____
   재질_____
   경험_____

4. 공통적인 진리가 나타나 있다.
   국민의 특성_____
   조상의 지혜_____
   인류의 경험_____

5. 나타나 있기도 하다.
   반영되어 _____
   표현되어 _____

6. 속담을 통하여 그 예를 찾아 보기로 하자.
   경험_____
   특성_____
   진리_____

낱말

제 이십육과 (第二十六課)	Lesson 26
속담 (俗談)	proverb
옛	old, ancient
조상	ancestor
-(으)로부터	from (postposition)
내려 오다	to come down, to be handed down
경험	experience
-에 의하여 (의하다)	by, according to (to be based on)
지혜	wisdom
그러므로	therefore
흔히	frequently, often
국민 (國民)	people (of a nation)
특성	unique characteristics
재질	talent, potential
정신 (精神)	spirit, mind
반영	reflection
반영되다	to be reflected
인류 (人類)	human being
공통적 (共通的)	common
진리	truth
나타나다	to appear, to come out
통하여 (통하다)	through, by (to pass through)
구슬	beads
서 (세)	three (adj. form used with counters)
말	a unit of measure (equals about 4.8 gallons)
꿰다	to string (beads)
보배	treasure, jewel
등잔	lamp (usually old-fashioned lamp with oil and wick)

어둡다	to be dark
(불을) 때다	to build a fire
굴뚝	chimney
연기	smoke
연기 나다	to smoke
고래	whale
싸움	fight
새우	shrimp
터지다	to be broken, to be torn, to burst
버릇	habit
바늘	needle
도둑	thief
떡	rice cake
무너지다	to collapse, to crumble
솟아나다	to spring up, to rise
구멍	hole
잃다	to lose
외양간	stable
고치다	to fix, to correct
아무리	no matter how
급하다	to be urgent, to be in a hurry
매다	to tie
말	horse, word
리	measure of distance (about 2.4 miles)
밤	night, evening
쥐	mouse, rat
낮	daytime
새	bird
호랑이	tiger
제	one's own
금강산	Diamond Mountain (in Kangwon-Do province, part of which is in North Korea)

식후경	sightseeing after a meal
별	star
따다	to pick (a fruit off a tree, a flower, etc.), to win
누워 (눕다)	in repose (to lie down)
우물	a well
개구리	frog
울다	to cry, to weep
겨자	mustard
수박	watermelon
겉	outside, surface
핥다	to lick
쇠 (소의)	of a cow
경	sutra (Buddhist scriptures)
이웃	neighbor
사촌	cousin
안경	eyeglasses
탓	blame, fault
중	Buddhist monk
염불	Buddhist prayer
마음	heart, mind
재	offering, Buddhist ceremony
잿밥	food served at a Buddhist ceremony

GRAMMAR AND NOTES

In this lesson we will study
1. Expressions for "in accordance with," "by," "from"
   -에 의하여
2. Construction of -이라 + 고 하겠다, -다 + 고 하겠다
   "I could say that . . ." "It can be said that . . ."
3. Expression for "through," "by means of " -을/를 통하여
4. Sentence ending -(으)랴!: a rhetorical question or
   statement, plain style
5. "Even-if" connective -어/아도
6. Sentence ending -어/아라: plain or intimate command
7. Uses of 마음 "heart," "mind," "spirit," "personality," etc.
8. Chinese characters 談, 民, 精, 神, 共, 通, 的, 人, 類

1. Expressions for "in accordance with," "by," "from" -에 의하여

의하여 derives from the verb 의하다 "to be based upon,"
which is rarely used by itself. The postpositional phrase -에
의하여 is commonly used after a noun phrase.

경험에 의하여 만들어진 속담이다.	It is a proverb drawn from experience.
교통법에 의하여 10불을 냈다.	He paid $10 in accordance with the traffic law.
다수의 의견에 의하여 결정됐다.	It was decided in accordance with the majority opinion.
고조선은 단군에 의하여 세워졌다고 한다.	It is said that ancient Korea was founded by Tangun.

2. Construction of -이라 + 고 하겠다. -다 + 고 하겠다. "I could say that . . ." "It can/could be said that . . ."

As we learned earlier -이라고 하다 and -다고 하다 are used with reported speech (see L12, GN2). Inserting -겠- in the reported speech forms conveys the meaning "We/I could say that . . ." or "It could be said that . . ."

그것은 지혜의 말이라고 하겠다.	We can say that they are words of wisdom.
그는 진리를 위해서 사는 사람이라고 하겠다.	We could say that he lives for truth.
그는 소 잃고 외양간 고친다고 하겠다.	We can say that he is fixing the barn after his cows were stolen.
속담은 풍속의 특성을 반영한다고 하겠다.	It can be said that proverbs reflect special character-istics of customs.

3. Expressions for "through," "by means of" -을/를 통하여

N.P. + 을/를 통하여

속담을 통하여 그 예를 찾아 보자!	Let's try to find an example through proverbs.
신문을 통하여 그의 소식을 들었다.	I heard the news about him through a newspaper.

4. Sentence ending -(으)랴!: a rhetorical question or statement, plain style

This ending is used in a specific context, such as when a person is making a resolution or a rhetorical question or statement.

V. STEM + (으)랴!

아니 땐 굴뚝에 연기 나랴!	Could there be smoke from a chimney without a fire!

살 길이 <u>없으랴</u>!	Wouldn't there be a means for survival?
공든 탑이 <u>무너지랴</u>!	Would the pagoda built with much effort ever collapse?

5. "Even-if" connective -어/아도

Attached to a verb stem, -어/아도 has a sense of supposition and subjunctive. But when it is used with the past tense -었/았, it is factual, there is no supposition, and it is translated as "even though." (See also L23, GN4.)

V. STEM + 어/아도   present, future, or supposition/ subjunctive

V. STEM + 었/았 + 어도   past, factual

하늘이 <u>무너져도</u> 솟아날 구멍 있다.	Even if heaven falls down, there is a hole through which one can rise. (There is always hope.)
그 속담을 <u>들었어도</u> 알아 듣지 못하겠다.	Even though I heard the proverb, I do not understand (it).
그는 예의는 <u>없어도</u> 친절하다.	Even though he has no manners, he is very friendly.

6. Sentence ending -어/아라: plain or intimate command

-어/아라 is the plain or intimate command form that goes with the -어/아 ending (see L18, GN3). This command will be perceived as rude unless used among intimate friends or addressed to children.

아는 길도 물어 <u>가라</u>!	Make sure even if you know the directions!
여기에 나타나지 <u>말아라</u>!	Don't show up here!
이 담을 <u>무너뜨려라</u>!	Tear down this wall!
<u>조심해라</u>!	Be careful!

7. Uses of 마음 "heart," "mind," "spirit," "personality," etc.

마음 has a wide range of meaning and is used in various idiomatic expressions.

a. { -ㄹ/을 마음이 있다   "to be interested in"
{ -ㄹ/을 마음이 없다   "to be not interested in"

한국어를 공부할 마음이 있다.	I am interested in studying Korean.
그는 공부할 마음이 없다.	He is not interested in studying.

b. { 마음이 좋다   "to be kind-hearted"
{ 마음이 나쁘다   "to be mean-spirited"

영희는 마음이 좋은데 영식이는 마음이 나쁘다.	Young-hie is nice, but Young-shik is not.
마음이 좋은 사람은 좋은 친구가 될 수 있다.	A good-hearted person can be a good friend. (A nice person makes a good friend.)
마음이 나쁜 사람을 본 일이 없다.	I have never seen a mean person.

c. { 마음에 있다   "to like," "to favor"
{ 마음에 없다   "to be not interested in"

영희는 철수가 마음에 있는데 철수는 영희가 마음에 없다.	Young-hie likes Chŏl-su, but Chŏl-su is not interested in Young-hie.
누가 마음에 있어요?	Whom do you have in mind?

d. 마음대로 "as one wishes," "(do) one's own way"

마음대로 해라!	Do as you please! Have it your way!
마음대로 하면 안 된다.	You must not do as you please.
그는 언제나 마음대로 한다.	He always does as he pleases.
나는 마음대로 할 수 없다.	I can't do as I please.

그는 <u>마음대로</u> 돌아다닌다.　He goes around as he pleases.

e. 마음이 강/약하다　"to have a strong/weak will"

<u>마음이 강해서</u> 쉽게 포기하지 않을 것이다.　He will not give up easily because he has a strong will.

<u>마음이 약한</u> 사람은 성공하지 못한다.　A weak-minded person cannot succeed.

f. 마음을 합하다　"to put minds together," "to make a concerted effort"

<u>마음을 합하여</u> 독립을 얻었다.　Having made a concerted effort, they gained their independence.

<u>마음을 합하면</u> 못 할 일이 없다.　There is nothing that cannot be accomplished if we put our hearts into it.

g. 마음/양심에 걸리다　"to bother (one's conscience)," "to feel uncomfortable," "to feel guilty" (양심 = conscience)

선생님에게 거짓말을 해서 <u>마음/양심에 걸린다</u>.　It troubles my conscience that I lied to my teacher.

길에서 본 노인이 <u>마음에 걸린다</u>.　The old man I saw on the street bothers me.

h. 마음을 쓰다　"to be generous," "to be concerned," "to worry"

<u>마음을 써서</u> 소년단에게 100불을 주었다.　Being generous, I gave $100 to the Boy Scouts.

그런 일에 <u>마음을 쓰지</u> 말아라!　Don't worry about such things!

i. 마음에 들다　"to like," "to prefer"

그 구두가 <u>마음에 든다</u>.　I like those shoes.

나는 산 보다 바다가 <u>마음에 든다</u>.　I prefer the sea to the mountains.

8. Chinese characters

談	말씀 담 converse	言	訁	訁	訞	談	談	談	談
民	백성 민 people	フ	フ	尸	戸	民			
精	정할 정 spirit	丶	丷	丷	半	米	粐	粓	精
神	신 신 divine	丶	ラ	ネ	ネ	初	神	神	神
共	한가지 공 together	一	十	卄	世	共	共		
通	통할 통 go through	フ	マ	乛	乃	甬	甬	甬	通
的	과녁 적 adj. particle	ノ	亻	仢	白	白	白	的	的
人	사람 민 man	ノ	人						
類	같을 유 species	丷	丷	半	米	米	米	类	類

연습

A. 다음 질문에 대답하십시오.

1. 속담은 어떻게 만들어졌습니까?
2. 속담에는 무엇이 반영되어 있습니까?
3. 속담은 한국말에만 있습니까?
4. 한국 속담과 비슷한 영어의 예를 들어 보십시오.
   a.
   b.
   c.
5. 학생은 왜 흰색/빨간색/까만색이 마음에 듭니까?
6. 동양인들의 공통점은 무엇이라고 하겠습니까?
7. 서양인들의 공통점은요?

8. 경험이 많은 사람은 지혜도 많다고 생각합니까?

9. 우리는 속담을 통해서 무엇을 배울 수 있습니까?

10. 학생은 어떤 속담을 좋아해요?

B. 다음 문장을 끝마치십시오.

11. 영희는 운동에는 마음이 없고 _____

12. 철수는 영희에게 마음이 있으나 _____

13. 그분은 재질이 많을 뿐만 아니라 _____

14. 그 학생은 마음이 좋을 뿐만 아니라 _____

15. 그분은 한국어를 잘 할 뿐만 아니라 _____

16. 아무리 급해도 _____

17. 아무리 생각해도 _____

18. 아무리 흔해도 _____

19. 재질이 있어도 _____

20. 경험이 없어도 _____

C. 다음 문장을 한국어로 번역하십시오.

21. Although we do not know who made the proverbs (*by whom the proverbs were made*), they are words of wisdom.

22. He *not only* has much experience *but also* has much wisdom.

23. This is a treasure that *has been handed down* from the olden days.

24. What are some *frequently used* proverbs in English?

25. What *is reflected* in these examples?

26. What English saying is similar to "호랑이도 제 말 하면 온다"?

27. Since *they say that* habits acquired at age three last (go) until age eighty, we should teach children good habits.

28. Because I have only lived in Albany, I am like "*a frog in a well.*"

29. Since *they say that* "Beginning is getting halfway done," let's hurry and begin!

30. Even though I met him, I *can't recall* his name. (recall: 생각(이) 나다)

Glossary

가구	N. furniture
가는 길에	ADV. on one's way (going) to
가늘다	D.V. to be thin, to be wiry
가다	V. to go
가르치다	V. to teach
가르치십니다. (가르치다)	V. Someone (hon.) teaches.
가방	N. bag, briefcase, handbag
가셨습니까? (가다)	V. Did (you) go?
가십시오. (가다)	V. Please go.
가슴	N. chest, breast
가을	N. fall, autumn
가장	ADV. the most
가져오다	V. to bring
-가지	N. item, type, thing
가지각색	N. every color, all kinds
가지다	V. to have, to possess
각-	ADJ. each
각국	N. each country
간단하다	D.V. to be simple
간장	N. soy sauce
간호원	N. nurse
갈비	N. short ribs
감기 (들다)	N. cold (to catch cold)

감사하다	v. to be grateful, to thank
갑니다. (가다)	v. (I) am going. (to go)
값	n. price
갔습니다. (가다)	v. (I) went.
갖다 (가지다)	v. to have, to own
같은 (같다)	adj. like, same (to be like, to be the same)
같이	adv. together
-개	n. item, piece (noun counter)
개구리	n. frog
거울	n. mirror
거치어 (거치다)	adv. through (to pass through)
걱정하다	v. to worry
건축가	n. architect
걷다	v. to walk
걸다	v. to hang
-것	n. thing, item
겉	n. outside, surface
겨울	n. winter
겨자	n. mustard
경	n. sutra, Buddhist scripture
경계	n. boundary, border
경기	n. game, contest
경제학	n. economics
경치	n. scenery
경험	n. experience
계시다	d.v. to exist (hon.)
계십니다. (계시다)	d.v. (He/she) is (here).
계십니까? (계시다)	v. Is (he/she) here?
계십시오. (계시다)	v. Please stay.
계절	n. season
계획	n. plan
고구려	n. Koguryŏ (dynasty)
고기	n. meat

고등학교	N. high school
고래	N. whale
고려 시대	N. Koryŏ period
고맙습니다. (고맙다)	V. Thank you. (to thank)
-고 싶다	V. to wish for, to want to
고유한 (고유하다)	ADJ. unique (to be unique)
고추장/고치장	N. hot pepper paste
고치다	V. to fix, to correct
곤색	N. navy blue
곧	ADV. soon, right away
공기	N. air
공부	N. study
공부하십니까? (공부하다)	V. Are (you) studying? (to study)
공부합니다. (공부하다)	V. (I) am studying.
공원	N. park
공중전화	N. public phone
공책	N. notebook
공통적 (공통적이다)	ADJ. common (to be in common)
공학	N. engineering
공항	N. airport
과학자	N. scientist
관광객	N. tourist, spectator, sightseer
괜찮다	D.V. to be all right
괜찮아요.	D.V. It is all right.
교실	N. classroom
교회	N. church
구멍	N. hole
구슬	N. beads
구월	N. September
구이	N. broiled food
국	N. soup
국민	N. people (of a nation)
국민학교	N. elementary school

굴뚝	N. chimney
굽다	V. to broil
궁금하다	D.V. to be wondering about
귀	N. ear
그거/그것	PRON. that, it
그것	PRON. that, that thing
그냥	ADV. as is, as the condition is
그래서	CONJ. so, therefore
그래요.	V. Yes, that is so.
그러나	CONJ. but, however
그러므로	CONJ. therefore
그런	ADJ. such
그럼	CONJ. well then
그렇습니다. (그렇다)	V. That is so. (to be so)
그만	ADV. to that extent; enough
그만두다	V. to quit, to stop
그분	N. that person, he/she
극동	N. Far East
극장	N. theater
글쎄	ADV. well . . .
글자	N. letter, character
금강산	N. Diamond Mountain
금요일	N. Friday
급하다	D.V. to be urgent, to be in a hurry
기다리다	V. to wait
-기 때문에	CONJ. because of ——ing
-기로 되다	V. it turns out that . . .
기름	N. oil
기쁘다	D.V. to be glad, to be happy
기사	N. article
기숙사	N. dormitory
-기 쉽다	D.V. easy to ——ing
-기 시작하다	V. to begin to

기운	N. strength, energy
기자	N. reporter
기차	N. train
기침	N. cough
기후	N. weather, climate
긴 (길다)	ADJ. long (to be long)
김	N. Kim (surname)
김 선생	N. Mr. Kim
김치	N. kimchi, pickled cabbage
김치를 담(그)다	V. to make kimchi
까만색 (까망)	N. black color (black)
-까지	POST. until, up to
깨닫다	V. to realize, to understand
깨소금	N. sesame salt
-껏	POST. up until (emphatic)
꽃	N. flower
꽃이 피다	V. to bloom, to blossom
꾸레미	N. bundle, packet
꽤	ADV. quite, somewhat
꿰다	V. to string (beads)
끊다	V. to cut, to sever
끓이다	V. to boil
끝난 (끝나다)	ADJ. finished (to finish)
끼다	V. to put on (gloves), to be wedged in, to be included
나	PRON. I
나가시겠어요? (나가다)	V. Will (you) go out? (to go out)
나누다	V. to divide
나누어지다	V. to become divided
나다 (연기, 해)	V. come out, arise (sun, smoke)
나라	N. country, nation
나무	N. tree
나물	N. vegetable dish
나쁘다	D.V. to be bad

나성	N. Los Angeles
나오다	V. to come out, to appear
나온 (나오다)	ADJ. came out, originated (to come out)
나왔어요. (나오다)	V. (He/she) came out. (to come out)
나타나다	V. to appear
나흘	N. four days
날씨	N. weather
남대문	N. the Great South Gate
남자	N. man, male
남한	N. South Korea
낫다	V. to get well, to get better
낮	N. daytime
내다	V. to pay
내려오다	V. to come down, descend
내리다	V. to get off
내복	N. underwear
내일	N. tomorrow
냉면	N. a cold noodle soup
냉수	N. cold water
너	PRON. you (plain)
너무	ADV. too, overly
넘다	V. to exceed, to go over
네	ADV. yes; PRON. you, your (plain)
네	ADJ. four, e.g. 네개, 네살, 네시
네모	N. square, rectangle, four-sided
넷	N. four
-년	N. year, year of
노력하다	V. to make an effort, to try
논문	N. thesis, paper
놀다	V. to play, to rest
농구	N. basketball

높아지다 (높다)	v. to become high/tall (to be high/tall)
놓다	v. to put down
누구	PRON. who
누구의	PRON. whose
누구의 것	PRON. whose, whose item
눈	N. eye; snow
눈이 오다	v. to snow (the snow comes)
눕다	v. to lie down
늦겨울	N. late winter
늦다	D.V. to be late
다	ADV. all
다닙니다. (다니다)	v. (I) attend. (to attend)
다르다	D.V. to be different
다리	N. leg; bridge
다방	N. tearoom, coffee shop
다시	ADV. again
다음	ADJ. next, the following
다음 주일	N. next week
다지다	v. to pound, to chop
다치다	v. to be hurt, to be injured
단풍	N. fall color (leaves)
단풍이 들다	v. to turn to fall colors
달다	D.V. to be sweet
닭	N. chicken
답장	N. replying letter
닷새	N. five days
당수	N. karate
당신	PRON. you
대, 중, 소	N. large, medium, small
대륙	N. continent
대륙성	ADJ. continental
대왕	N. great king
대학교	N. college, university

대학생	N. college student
대한민국	N. Republic of Korea
대회	N. big meet, great contest
-더라도	CONJ. even if
더운	ADJ. hot
덥다	D.V. to be hot
도둑	N. thief
도서관	N. library
도쿄	N. Tokyo
독감	N. flu
독감이 들다	V. to catch the flu
독립	N. independence
독일 (독일어)	N. Germany (the German language)
돈	N. money
돋다	V. to sprout, to bud
돌아오다	V. to come back
돕다	V. to help
동경	N. Tokyo
동남 아시아	N. Southeast Asia
동대문	N. the Great East Gate
동사	N. verb
동생	N. younger brother or sister
동안	N. duration, period
동양 음식	N. Oriental dish
돼지 고기	N. pork
됐어요/되었어요. (되다)	V. (It) became. (to become)
되다	V. to become
된장	N. soybean paste
둥근 (둥글다)	ADJ. round (to be round)
뒤	N. back, behind
드리다	V. to give (to an hon. person)
듣다	V. to hear, to listen
-들	N. plural marker

들다	v. to take, to hold, to lift up
들르다	v. to stop by
등	n. back
-등	n. etc., and so on
등산하다	v. to mountain climb
등잔	n. lamp (usually old-fashioned)
따다	v. to pick; to win
따뜻한 (따뜻하다)	ADJ. warm (D.V. to be warm)
따라	ADV. according to, following
따로/따로 따로	ADV. separately, apart
따르릉	n. ringing sound
딸꾹질	n. hiccup
땀	n. sweat
때다	v. to build fire
때문에	ADV. because of
떡	n. rice cake
떡국	n. rice cake soup
떨어지다	v. to fall, to be out of; to be worn out
또는	CONJ. or
또한	CONJ. also
똑	ADV. exactly
뛰다	v. to run, to jump, to compete
뜨겁다	D.V. to be hot
뜻	n. meaning
로스앤젤레스	n. Los Angeles
-리	n. -li (measure of distance, about 2.4 miles)
-마리	n. head of (counter for animate objects)
마시다	v. to drink
마음	n. mind, heart
막걸리	n. undistilled rice wine

-만	POST. only
만나다	V. to meet
만두국	N. wonton soup
만들다	V. to make
많습니다. (많다)	D.V. (there) are many, a lot (to be plentiful)
말	N. word, language; horse
-말	N. unit of measure (about 4.8 gallons)
맑다	D.V. to be clear, to be transparent
맛	N. flavor, taste
맛이 없다	D.V. to be bland, not tasty
맛이 있다	D.V. to be tasty
맞는 (맞다)	ADJ. be fitting, fit (to fit)
매다	V. to tie
매우	ADV. very, extremely
맥주	N. beer
맥주집	N. beer house
맵다	D.V. to be hot, to be spicy
머리	N. head, hair, brain
먹으러 (먹다)	CONJ. (in order) to eat (to eat)
먹을것	N. food, things to eat
먼저	ADV. ahead
멀다	D.V. to be far
메뉴	N. menu
메달	N. medal
메달을 따다/얻다	V. to win a medal
멕시코	N. Mexico
며칠	N. a few days, how many days
명사	N. noun
명동	N. Myung-dong (a street in Seoul)
몇	PRON. how many
몇 분	N. how many persons

몇 시에	ADV. at what time
모두	ADV. all, entirely
모레	N. the day after tomorrow
모르겠어요. (모르다)	V. I would not know. (don't know)
목	N. neck, throat
목요일	N. Thursday
몸	N. body
몹시	ADV. severely
못	ADV. cannot
무너지다	V. to collapse
무더기	N. bundle
무릎	N. knee
무술	N. martial arts
무슨	ADJ. what kind of
무슨 일	N. what kind of work, matter, event
무엇	PRON. what
무치다	V. to mix
묶음	N. bunch, bundle
문	N. door
문방구	N. stationery store
문자	N. writing system, letter
문화	N. culture
물	N. water, liquid
물론	ADV. of course
물약	N. liquid medicine
미국	N. the United States of America
미루다가 (미루다)	CONJ. while postponing (to postpone)
미술	N. fine arts
미술관	N. art museum
미식	N. American style
미안하지만 (미안하다)	CONJ. I'm sorry but . . .(to be sorry)

미안해요. (미안하다)	v. (I) am sorry. (to be sorry)
미장원/미용실	N. beauty shop
민주주의	N. democracy
밑	N. underneath, below
바꾸다	v. to change, to exchange
바꿔 드리다	v. to make an exchange for someone(hon.)
바늘	N. needle
바다	N. sea, ocean
바라다	v. to hope for
바람	N. wind
바람이 불다	v. the wind blows (to be windy)
바로	ADJ. right, just
바빠요. (바쁘다)	D.V. (I) am busy. (to be busy)
바위	N. rock
박물관	N. museum
박 선생	N. Mr. Park
밖	N. outside
반	N. half
반갑게 (반갑다)	ADV. gladly (to be glad)
반대로	ADV. on the contrary
반면	N. the opposite side
반면에	ADV. on the other hand
반영되다	v. to be reflected
반찬	N. side dishes
받다	v. to receive
발	N. foot
밤	N. night, evening
밥	N. cooked rice, meal
방	N. room
방법	N. method
방학	N. school vacation
밭	N. garden, growing field

배	N. stomach, tummy; ship, boat
배구	N. volleyball
배우기 (배우다)	N. learning (to learn)
배우다	V. to learn
백성	N. common people
백제	N. Paekche (dynasty)
백화점	N. department store
버릇	N. habit
버리다	V. to throw away, to abandon, to discard
버클리	N. Berkeley
벌써	ADV. already
변호사	N. lawyer, attorney-at-law
별	N. star
병	N. disease
병원	N. hospital
보고 (보다)	CONJ. see and (to see, look)
보내 주다 (보내다)	V. to send to (to send)
보러 (보다)	CONJ. (in order) to see (to see)
보리차	N. roasted barley tea
보배	N. treasure, gem
보석	N. jewelry, precious stone
보이다	V. to be seen, to be visible
보통	ADV. in general
볶다	V. to panfry
볶음	N. panfried food
봄	N. spring
봅니다 (보다)	V. (I) am looking at (to see)
뵙다 (뵐려고)	V. to see an hon. person (in order to see)
부르겠어요. (부르다)	V. (I) will call. (to call)
부식	N. secondary foods
부인	N. wife (hon.)
부엌	N. kitchen
-부터	POST. from

북경	N. Beijing, Peking
북한	N. North Korea
분명하다	D.V. to be distinct; to be sure
불	N. fire, light
불고기	N. barbecued beef
불란서 (불어)	N. France (the French language)
붓다	V. to swell; to pour
브라운	N. Brown (surname)
비가 오다	V. the rain comes (to rain)
비빔밥	N. rice dish mixed with vegetables
비서	N. secretary
비슷하다	D.V. to be similar
비행기	N. airplane
비행장	N. airport
빌어 쓰다	V. to borrow and use
빌다	V. to borrow; to pray, to beg
빌리다	V. to borrow
빌려 주다	V. to lend
빨간색 (빨강)	N. red color (red)
빨리	ADV. rapidly, fast, early, soon
빨리 하세요 (빨리하다)	V. please do quickly (to do quickly)
뻐스 정류장	N. bus stop
-뿐만 아니라	CONJ. not only
삐다	V. to sprain
사다	V. to buy
사람	N. person, man
사무실	N. office
사십니까? (살다)	V. Does (he/she) live (somewhere)? (to live)
사업	N. business
사업가	N. businessman

사업을 하다	V. to do business, to be in business
사월	N. April
사이다	N. cider
사철	N. four seasons
사촌	N. cousin
사흘	N. three days
-살	N. years old
삼국 시대	N. Three Kingdoms period
삼월	N. March
3층 (삼층)	N. third floor
삼키다	V. to swallow
삽시다. (사다)	V. Let's buy. (to buy)
상자	N. box
상쾌하다	D.V. to be refreshing
상항	N. San Francisco
새	N. bird
새로운 (새롭다)	ADJ. new (to be new)
새싹	N. new bud, sprout
새우	N. shrimp
샌프란시스코	N. San Francisco
생각	N. thought, idea
생각하다	V. to think, to consider
생기다	V. occur, to happen
생선	N. fish
생선장수	N. fish merchant
생활	N. everyday life, living
서대문	N. the Great West Gate
서양 음식	N. Western dish
서울	N. Seoul
서점	N. bookstore
석-	ADJ. three (used with some noun counters), e.g., 석달, 석장, 석잔
선물	N. gift, present

선물용	N. to be used as a gift
선생	N. Mr., Mrs., Miss, Ms.; teacher
선수	N. athlete, player
설사	N. diarrhea
설탕	N. sugar
성함	N. name (hon. word)
세계적	ADJ. international, worldwide
세	ADJ. three
세살	N. three years old
세우다	V. to establish, to erect
세종대왕	N. the great King Sejong
셋	N. three
셔츠	N. shirt
소	N. ox, cow
소금	N. salt
소련	N. Soviet Union
소매	N. sleeve
소식	N. news
소아과	N. pediatric medicine
소주	N. hard distilled liquor
소풍	N. picnic
속	N. inside, interior; stomach
속담	N. proverb, common saying
손	N. hand
손기정	N. Sohn Ki-jung, marathon champion in 1936 Olympics
손님	N. guest
솟아나다	V. to spring up, to rise
쇠	ADJ. cow's, of a cow
소고기	N. beef
수구	N. water polo
수박	N. watermelon
수영	N. swimming
수영하다	V. to swim

수요일	N. Wednesday
수학	N. mathematics
숙제	N. homework
순수한 (순수하다)	ADJ. pure (to be pure)
술	N. liquor, wine
숨	N. breath
숨을 쉬다	V. to breathe
쉬다	V. to rest
쉬워요. (쉽다)	D.V. (It) is easy. (to be easy)
스무 살	N. twenty years old
스미스	N. Smith
슬프다	D.V. to be sad
-시	N. hour; o'clock
시간	N. time, period, hour; class
시계	N. watch, clock
시계탑	N. clock tower
시다	D.V. to be sour
시설	N. facility
시외	N. suburb
시원하다	D.V. to be cool, refreshing
시월	N. October
시작하다	V. to start, to begin
시작되다	V. to be started
시장	N. market; mayor
시합	N. contest
시험	N. test, exam
식다	V. to get cold, to cool off, to cool
식당	N. restaurant, cafeteria
식사	N. meal
식사(를) 하다	V. to have a meal
식은 (식다)	ADJ. cold, cooled off
식품	N. groceries, food
식후	N. after a meal

신라	N. Shilla (dynasty)
신문	N. newspaper
신문 기자	N. news reporter
실례	N. discourtesy
실례이지만	CONJ. I'm sorry but . . ., Excuse me . . .
싫다	D.V. to dislike
싫어하다	V. to dislike
십이월	N. December
십일월	N. November
싱겁다	D.V. to be bland
싱싱하다	D.V. to be fresh
싸다	D.V. to be inexpensive, cheap
싸움	N. fight
쌍둥이	N. twins
썰다	V. to cut, to slice
쓰고 (쓰다)	CONJ. write and, writing (to write)
쓰다	D.V. to be bitter; V. to write; to use
-씨	N. Mr., Mrs., Miss, Ms.
씨름	N. wrestling
아니요. (아니다)	ADV. no (not to be)
아닙니다. (아니다)	D.V. (It) is not.
아래	N. below, underneath
아름답다	D.V. to be beautiful
아무리	ADV. no matter how
아버님	N. father (hon.)
아세아/아시아	N. Asia
아저씨	N. uncle
아주	ADV. very, extremely
아주머니	N. aunt
아침	N. morning
아침거리	N. things for breakfast

아파서 (아프다)	CONJ. because (I am) sick (to be sick)
아흐레	N. nine days
안-	ADV. not
안	N. inside
안 걸리다	V. does not go through (telephone)
안경	N. eye glasses
안과	N. ophthalmology
안녕하십니까? (안녕하다)	V. How are you? (to be well)
안녕히 (안녕하다)	ADV. well, carefully
알다	V. to know
알리다	V. to let someone know, to announce
알려지다	V. to be known
알맞다	V. to be suitable, appropriate
알약	N. tablet, pill
앞	N. front
야구	N. baseball
야채장수	N. vegetable merchant
약	N. medicine
약	ADJ. approximate, about
약방	N. pharmacy
약속	N. promise, appointment
약제사	N. pharmacist
얇다	D.V. to be thin (flat object)
양념	N. spices
양복점	N. tailor shop
어구	N. phrase
어깨	N. shoulder
어느	PRON. which
어둡다	D.V. to be dark
어디	PRON. where
어떠세요?	How is it?
어떤	PRON. what kind of, a certain

어떻게 (어떻다)	ADV. how
어떻다	D.V. to be in a certain manner
어려워요. (어렵다)	D.V. (It) is difficult. (to be difficult)
어렵습니다. (어렵다)	D.V. (It) is difficult. (to be difficult)
어머님	N. mother (hon.)
어서	ADV. please (as an urging adverb)
어지럽다	D.V. to be dizzy
언어	N. language
언제	PRON. when
얼굴	N. face
얼마(나)	ADV. how much, how long
없어요. (없다)	V. (There) is not. (to have not)
-에게서	POST. from (for personal nouns)
-에 대해서/대하여	POST. concerning, about
-에 따라	POST. according to, following
에레베타	N. elevator
-여	POST. about, -odd
여관	N. inn
여기다	V. to consider, to regard
여드레	N. eight days
여든	N. eighty
여러	ADJ. many, various, several
여름	N. summer
여보세요	N. Hello! (on the phone)
여쭈다	V. to tell, to ask (to hon. person)
여행을 가다	V. to go on a trip
여행하다	V. to travel
역사	N. history
연기	N. smoke; postpone
연락하다	V. to get in touch, to communicate
연필	N. pencil

열	N. fever, temperature; ten
열두 시	N. twelve o'clock
열리다	V. to be opened, to be held
열흘	N. ten days
염불	N. Buddhist prayer
엿새	N. six days
영국	N. England
영문학	N. English literature
영식	N. Young-shik (male name)
영어	N. English
영화	N. movie, film
영화관	N. movie theater
영희	N. Young-hie (female name)
옆	N. side
예	N. example; yes
예를 들다	V. to show as an example
예술	N. art
옛	ADJ. old, ancient
옛날	N. old days
오는 길에	ADV. on the way (coming) to/from
오늘	N. today
오른쪽	N. right side
오셨습니까? (오다)	V. Did (you) come? (to come)
오월	N. May
온	ADJ. entire
온도	N. temperature
온면	N. a hot noodle soup
옷	N. clothes
왔습니다. (오다)	V. (I) came. (to come)
왕	N. king
왕국	N. kingdom
왜	ADV. why
외과	N. surgical medicine

외교관	N. diplomat
외국어	N. foreign language
외양간	N. stable
요일	N. days of the week
요즈음/요즘	N., ADV. these days, lately
우물	N. a well
우산	N. umbrella
우체국	N. post office
우표	N. stamp
운동	N. sports, exercise
울다	V. to cry
울리다	V. to ring; to cause someone to cry
원가	N. orginal price
-월	N. month of, month
월요일	N. Monday
위	N. top, above
위스키	N. whiskey
위하다	V. to support
위하여/위해/위해서	ADV. for the sake of
유럽	N. Europe
유명	N. fame
유명하다	D.V. to be famous
유월	N. June
육상	N. track and field
은행	N. bank
음식	N. food
음악	N. music
의사	N. medical doctor
의자	N. chair
의하다 (의하여)	V. to be based on(according to)
이/리	N. Lee (surname)
이	N. tooth
이-	PRON. this

이것	N. this, this thing
이기다	V. to win
이레	N. seven days
이름	N. name
이미	ADV. already
이발소	N. barbershop
이분	N. this person (polite)
이비인후과	N. otorhinolaryngology (ear, nose, and throat)
이에요. (이다)	V. It is. (to be)
이웃	N. neighbor
이월	N. February
이제	ADV. now
이틀	N. two days
인기	N. popularity
인기가 있다	V. to be popular
인류	N. humankind, human being
인사	N. greeting
인삼	N. ginseng
-일	N. date, day
일본	N. Japan
일부분	N. a part
일요일	N. Sunday
일월	N. January
일을 하다	V. to work, to do work
1층 (일층)	N. first floor, ground floor
읽었습니까? (읽다)	V. Did (you) read? (to read)
읽으십시오. (읽다)	V. Please read. (to read)
잃다	V. to lose
임무	N. duty
입	N. mouth
입니까? (이다)	V. Is (it)? (to be)
입니다. (이다)	V. (It) is. (to be)
입다	V. to wear, to put on clothing

있어요. (있다)	V. There are. I have. (to exist)
있습니까? (있다)	V. Is (there)? (to exist, to have)
있습니다.	V. There is.
잊다	V. to forget
-자	N. character, letter, e.g., 한자, 세자
자	ADV. well, then
자그마하다	D.V. to be smallish
자동차	N. automobile
자랑	N. pride
자랑스럽다	D.V. to be proud, to be boastful
자주	ADV. often
작년	N. last year
작다	D.V. to be small
잔	N. cup
잔뜩	ADV. much, a lot, fully
잘	ADV. well
잘다	D.V. to be small
잠깐	N. a short while, a moment
잡아오다	V. to catch and bring
-장	N. piece (of paper, or flat item)
장/시장	N. market
장래	N. future
장마철	N. monsoon season
장을 보다	V. to go grocery shopping
재	N. Buddhist offering
재미	N. interest, fun
재미있습니까? (재미있다)	D.V. Is (it) interesting? (to be interesting)
재질	N. talent, potential
재채기	N. sneeze
잿밥	N. food served at a Buddhist ceremony
쟁반	N. tray

저	PRON. I (humble)
저것	N. that over there, that thing
저녁	N. evening; evening meal
저분	N. that person (polite)
적당하다	D.V. to be appropriate, to be suitable
적히다	V. to be written (passive form of 적다)
전	N. before
전공하다	V. to major in
전부	N., ADV. all, total
전시회	N. exhibition
전하겠어요. (전하다)	V. (I) will deliver (it). (to relay)
전해 주시겠어요? (전해 주다)	Would (you) relay (it for me)? (to relay for someone)
전화	N. telephone
전화를 걸다	V. to telephone
점심	N. noon; lunch
점심 때	N. lunchtime
점원	N. sales clerk, salesperson
정구	N. tennis
정구장	N. tennis court
정부	N. government
정식	N. a formal dinner, a regular meal
정신	N. spirit, mind, mentality
정종	N. rice wine, sake
정치학	N. political science
정형외과	N. orthopedics
제	PRON. I (humble, used with -가)
제 (저의)	PRON. my (humble); one's own
제이차 세계대전	N. Second World War

제일	N., ADV. number one; the first, the most
제 일과	N. chapter one, lesson one
제일차 세계대전	N. First World War
제주도	N. Che-joo Island (southernmost island of Korea)
조상	N. ancestor
조선 왕조	N. Chosŏn dynasty
조선 인민 공화국	N. Democratic People's Republic of Korea
조금/좀	ADJ. a little, some
좀	ADV. please
종로	N. Chong-ro (a street name in Seoul)
종로 일가	N. First Street of Chong-ro
종류	N. kind, type, sort
종업원	N. employee
좋다	D.V. to be good; to like
좋겠어요. (좋다)	D.V. (It) would be good.
좋습니다. (좋다)	D.V. It's fine/good. (to be good)
좋아하다	V. to like
죤	N. John
주다	V. to give
주말	N. weekend
주무시다	V. to sleep (hon.)
주문하다	V. to order
(어/아) 주세요. (주다)	V. (AUX.) to do as a favor for someone (to give)
주소	N. address
주식	N. main food, staple
주일/주	N. week
주중	N. weekdays; during the week
주차장	N. parking lot
준비	N. preparation
준비되다	V. to be prepared, to be ready

준비하다	v. to get ready
중국	N. China
중국어	N. Chinese language
중요하다	D.V. to be important
중학교	N. middle school
쥐	N. mouse, rat
즐겁게 (즐겁다)	ADV. happily (to be enjoyable, to be fun)
지금	ADV. now
지내십니까? (지내다)	v. (How do you) pass the time? (to pass the time)
지냅니다. (지내다)	v. (Someone) passes the time. (to pass the time)
지다	v. to lose
지도	N. map
지방	N. local area, country
지어 드리다	v. to make (for someone)
지우개	N. eraser
지하철	N. subway
지혜	N. wisdom
직업	N. occupation, job
진리	N. truth
질문	N. question
집	N. house, home
집사람	N. wife (when referring to one's own wife)
지으셨다 (짓다)	v. (hon.) made (to build, to create)
짜다	D.V. to be salty
짧다	D.V. to be short
-쯤	POST. about
찌개	N. stew soup
찌다	v. to steam, to stew
찜	N. stew, steamed food

차	N. car, automobile; tea
차다	D.V. to be cold
찬	ADJ. cold, chilled
참	ADV. very, real
참기름	N. sesame oil
창문	N. window
창호	N. Chang-ho (male name)
채소	N. vegetables
책	N. book
책방	N. bookstore
책상	N. desk
처음	N. the first time, beginning
천	N. one thousand
천만	N. ten million
천만에요.	V. You're welcome. Don't mention it.
철	N. season
철수	N. Chul-soo (male name)
체조	N. gymnastics
체조하다	V. to exercise
초가을	N. early fall
축구	N. soccer
출석	N. attendance
춥다	D.V. to be cold (weather)
치고 (치다)	V. to play (tennis, etc.) (literally, to hit)
치과	N. dentistry
친구	N. friend
칠월	N. July
칠판	N. blackboard
칼	N. knife
캐나다	N. Canada
캐다	V. to dig up
캐어오다	V. to dig up and bring
컴퓨터	N. computer

코	N. nose
코오피 숍	N. coffee shop
콜라	N. cola
콩기름	N. soybean oil
크게 (크다)	ADV. loudly (to be loud/big)
크리스마스	N. Christmas
타다	V. to get on (a car), to ride
타이프/타자기	N. typewriter
타자치다	V. to type
탁구	N. table tennis, ping-pong
탓	N. blame, fault
태권도	N. tae-kwon-do
태풍	N. typhoon
택하다	V. to take (a course), to choose
터지다	V. to be broken, to be torn, to burst
토요일	N. Saturday
토하다	V. to vomit
통일	N. unification
통하다	V. to pass through (through)
통화	N. phone call, getting through
통화중이다	V. phone is busy
튀기다	V. to deep fry
튀김	N. deep-fried food
특별한 (특별하다)	ADJ. special (to be special)
특성	N. special characteristics
틈	N. crack, in between, among
파란색 (파랑)	N. blue color (blue)
파운드	N. pound
팔	N. arm
팔다	V. to sell
팔월	N. August

패스	N. pass
펜	N. pen
편리	N. convenience, comfort
편지	N. letter
편찮다	D.V. to be sick/ill (hon.)
포도	N. grape
포도주	N. wine
표현하다	V. to express
푸르다	D.V. to be green/blue
푹	ADV. fully, completely
풍속	N. custom
피	N. blood
피곤하다	D.V. to be tired
피아노	N. piano
피자집	N. pizza house
필요하다	D.V. to be necessary, to be needed
하늘	N. sky
하다	V. to do
하루	N. one day
하세요. (하다)	V. Please do. (to do)
하품	N. yawning
학교	N. school
학생	N. student
학자	N. scholar
한-	ADJ. about (estimate); one
한국	N. Korea
한국어	N. Korean language
한글	N. Korean writing system
한 번	ADV. once, one time
한 시	N. one o'clock
한 시간	N. one hour
한자	N. Chinese characters

할 (하다)	V. MOD. to be done (in the future) (to do)
할머니	N. grandmother
할아버지	N. grandfather
핥다	V. to lick
합기도	N. hap-ki-do, a martial art
합하다	V. to add, to put together, to combine
해	N. sun; year
행사	N. event, happening
허리	N. waist, the middle of the body
헤엄치다	V. to swim
현대 미술관	N. Museum of Modern Art (modern art gallery)
형 (님)	N. older brother (to a male) (hon.)
혜경	N. Hye-kyung (female name)
호랑이	N. tiger
호텔	N. hotel
혹시	ADV. if, by any chance
혼동	N. confusion
화병/꽃병	N. vase
화요일	N. Tuesday
회답	N. response, reply
후 (-후에)	N. after (after doing...)
후추 (가루)	N. pepper (powder)
훈련	N. training, discipline
흔히	ADV. frequently, commonly
흘리다	V. to shed
흥정을 하다	V. to bargain
희망	N. hope
희망하다	V. to hope, to wish
흰색/하양	N. white color, white

English–Korean Grammar and Notes Index

Korean–English
Grammar and Notes Index

-에 의하여	"in accordance with," "by," "from," L26
오는 길에	"on the way (coming)," L17
-와/-과	"and," L3
-와/과 같이	"(together) with," L9
왜	"why," L8
위하다	"for," "for the sake of," L22
-(으)나	concessive connective, "although," L19
-(으)니까	causal, "because," "as," "since," L24
-(으)랴!	rhetorical statement/question, L26
-(으)러	"in order to," "for," "for the sake of," L10
-(으)려고 하다	"plan to," "intend to," "is about to," L17
-(으)로	direction marker, "to," "through," L12
-(으)로	"as," "in the role of," L7
-(으)로	"by/in" (as in "divided by/in"), L19
-(으)며	"and on the other hand," "while at the same time," L14
-(으)면	conditional, "if," "when," L12
-(으)면 안되다	"must not," L21
-(으)면 좋겠다	"it would be nice," "I wish," L20
-(으)시	honorific marker for verbs, L1
-(으)십시요, -(으)세요	polite command, L8
-은/-는	topic marker, L2
-은데/는데/ㄴ데	consequence, "but," "for," "and," "so," "while," "since," "when," "as," L15
-은/ㄴ/는데요	unfinished ending, L20
-은/ㄴ/듯하다	"as if," L23
-은/ㄴ후에	"after doing," L11
-을/ㄹ	verbal modifier (future), L15
-을/를	direct object marker, "to," L4
-을/를 같이 하다	"to share," L19
-을/ㄹ까(요)	"will it?" "I wonder if," L23
-을/ㄹ께(요)	"will do," L25

Designer: Sandy Drooker
Compositor: Pacific Demand, Inc.
Text: 10/13 Bookman & 신명조
Display: Bookman & 신명조
Printer: Maple-Vail Book Mfg. Group
Binder: Maple-Vail Book Mfg. Group